THE BUSH PRESIDENCY

SOUTHAMPTON STUDIES IN INTERNATIONAL POLICY
Published by Macmillan in association with the Mountbatten Centre for International Studies, University of Southampton

General Editor: Dilys M. Hill

Other academic members of the editorial board: Martin Alexander, Ralph Beddard, Stevan K. Pavlowitch, John Simpson

This series was established in 1986 to encourage the publication of multidisciplinary studies of those public policies with significant international components or implications. Areas of special interest include arms control and defence policies, environmental policies, human rights, maritime and space issues, Third World development questions and the EU.

Published titles

Ralph Beddard and Dilys M. Hill (*editors*): ECONOMIC, SOCIAL AND CULTURAL RIGHTS: Progress and Achievement

Ian Forbes and Mark Hoffman (*editors*): INTERNATIONAL RELATIONS, POLITICAL THEORY AND THE ETHICS OF INTERVENTION

Dilys M. Hill (*editor*): HUMAN RIGHTS AND FOREIGN POLICY: Principles and Practice

Dilys M. Hill, Raymond A. Moore and Phil Williams (*editors*): THE REAGAN PRESIDENCY: An Incomplete Revolution?

Darryl A. Howlett: EURATOM AND NUCLEAR SAFEGUARDS

Mark F. Imber: THE USA, ILO, UNESCO AND IAEA: Politicization and Withdrawal in the Specialized Agencies

Caroline Thomas and Paikiasothy Saravanamuttu (*editors*): THE STATE AND INSTABILITY IN THE SOUTH

The Bush Presidency

Triumphs and Adversities

Edited by

Dilys M. Hill
Reader in Politics
University of Southampton

Phil Williams
Professor in International Security and
Director, the Matthew B. Ridgway Center
University of Pittsburgh

 in association with the
MOUNTBATTEN CENTRE FOR INTERNATIONAL
STUDIES
UNIVERSITY OF SOUTHAMPTON

First published 1994 by
THE MACMILLAN PRESS LTD
Houndmills, Basingstoke, Hampshire RG21 2XS
and London
Companies and representatives
throughout the world

ISBN 0–333–59442–8

A catalogue record for this book is available
from the British Library.

Printed in Great Britain by
Mackays of Chatham PLC
Chatham, Kent

Contents

Acknowledgement

The editors are indebted to Mrs Sandra Wilkins, Department of Politics, University of Southampton, for making the preparation of this volume possible.

THE MOUNTBATTEN CENTRE FOR INTERNATIONAL STUDIES

The Mountbatten Centre for International Studies (MCIS), located in the Department of Politics at the University of Southampton, conducts many cooperative and individual research programmes and activities. Current areas of research include nuclear non-proliferation, human rights, international environmental issues, naval peacekeeping, European and Asian security, civil–military relations and police studies.

MCIS activities include residential seminars by its Defence Studies Unit as well as a programme of seminars and public lectures. The Centre is interdisciplinary, relying for its resource base on many departments within the University including History, Law, Education, and Aeronautics and Astronautics.

Links have been established with the Centre d'Histoire Militaire of the University of Montpellier, the Fondation pour les Etudes de Défense Nationale, Paris, and the Faculté des Affaires Internationales, Université du Havre. The Centre also participates in the work of the team on Political Culture in Eastern Europe at the Ecole des Hauts Etudes en Sciences Sociales, Paris. Members of the Centre have participated in the work of the European Science Foundation and the International Congress of Historical Sciences.

Publications of the Centre include the Southampton Studies in International Policy book series, in association with Macmillan, and a monograph and newsletter series produced by the programme on nuclear non-proliferation. MCIS was established in 1990 in succession to the Centre for International Policy Studies (founded in 1983). The Mountbatten Centre bears the name of the Earl Mountbatten of Burma (1900–1979) whose papers are housed at the University of Southampton.

Notes on the Contributors

Michael Foley is Professor, Department of International Politics, University College of Wales, Aberystwyth. He is a leading expert on American politics, particularly on the United States Congress, and is the author of *Laws, Men and Machines: Modern American Government and the Appeal of Newtonian Mechanics* (London, 1990), and *American Political Ideas: Traditions and Usages* (Manchester, 1991).

Steve Garber is a Presidential Management Intern at the National Aeronautics and Space Administration, NASA.

Dilys M. Hill is Reader in Politics in the Department of Politics, University of Southampton. She has written extensively on urban and domestic policy in Britain and the United States and is co-editor (with M. Glenn Abernathy and Phil Williams) of *The Carter Years: The President and Policy Making* (London and New York, 1984), and with Raymond A. Moore and Phil Williams of *The Reagan Presidency: An Incomplete Revolution?* (London and New York, 1990).

Raymond A. Moore is Distinguished Professor Emeritus, Department of Government and International Studies, University of South Carolina, Columbia, South Carolina. He has held Ford Foundation and other fellowships at institutions in America and in Australia, Pakistan and South Korea. He is the author, with Marcia Lynn Whicker, of *When Presidents are Great* (Englewood Cliffs, NJ, 1988), and contributor, and co-editor with Marcia Lynn Whicker and James P. Pfiffner, of *The Presidency and the Persian Gulf War* (New York, 1993), and contributor and co-editor of *The Reagan Presidency: An Incomplete Revolution?* (London and New York, 1990).

Gillian Peele is Fellow and Tutor in Politics, Lady Margaret Hall, University of Oxford, and has published widely on American and British politics and government. She is the author of *Revival and Reaction: The Right in Contemporary America* (Oxford, 1984), contributor, and co-editor with C.J. Bailey and

Bruce Cain, of *Developments in American Politics 2* (London, forthcoming 1994), and contributor to *The Reagan Presidency: An Incomplete Revolution?* (London and New York, 1990).

Marcia Lynn Whicker is Professor, Department of Public Administration at Rutgers University, Newark, New Jersey, and has written extensively in the field of presidential studies and international affairs. She is the author of *Controversial Issues in Economic Regulatory Policy* (Berkeley, 1993) and is a contributor, and co-editor with Raymond A. Moore and James P. Pfiffner, of *The Presidency and the Persian Gulf War* (New York, 1993).

Phil Williams is Professor of International Security, University of Pittsburgh, and Director of the Matthew B. Ridgway Center. He is the author of a large body of work on defence policy and international affairs. His works include *Crisis Management* (London, 1986), *The Senate and US Troops in Europe* (London, 1986) and *Superpower Detente: A Reappraisal*, with Mike Bowker (London, 1988).

Stephen Woolcock is Senior Research Fellow, European Programme, Royal Institute of International Affairs, Chatham House, London. He has written widely on trade and industrial issues in Europe and the world economy. His recent publications include *Market Access Issues in EC–US Relations: Trading Partners or Trading Blows?* (London, 1992); and with Michael Smith, *US–EC Relations in a Transformed World* (London, 1993). He was a contributor to *The Carter Years: The President and Policy Making* (London and New York, 1984).

Tinsley E. Yarbrough is Professor in the Department of Political Science, East Carolina University, Greenville, North Carolina, and a leading expert on the judiciary and on civil rights. He is the author of *John Marshall Harlan: Great Dissenter of the Warren Court* (New York, 1992), *Mr. Justice Black and his Critics* (Durham, NC, 1988), and was a contributor to *The Reagan Presidency: An Incomplete Revolution?* (London and New York, 1990).

1 Introduction: The Bush Administration – An Overview

Dilys M. Hill and Phil Williams

THE PUZZLE

The presidency of George Bush is something of an enigma in contemporary American politics. Unlike the Carter administration, which is the only other real single-term presidency of the second half of the twentieth century, the Bush administration appeared highly competent, and the President himself obtained far higher ratings in opinion polls than Jimmy Carter ever did. Moreover, unlike Carter who was reluctant to use military force, George Bush was a highly successful war president and Commander in Chief. At the end of the war in the Gulf Bush had an approval rating of over 80 per cent and appeared politically unassailable. Yet he ended up as a one-term president who ran an extremely lack-lustre political campaign and lost to a Democratic candidate who only months earlier had been on the verge of pulling out of the presidential race.

Although President Bush failed to imprint himself on the American consciousness in the same way as his predecessor, Ronald Reagan, he not only presided over a period of historic change in international politics but did so in a way which added a degree of predictability and stability in a world characterized by enormous upheaval. This was not surprising. Bush came to office as probably the most experienced president since Richard Nixon. Not only had Bush served as Reagan's Vice President for eight years but he was also former CIA Director and had been Ambassador to China and to the United Nations. The sense of continuity and experience were reflected in a very professional if sometimes highly negative presidential campaign in 1988 in which Bush captured 53.4 per cent of the vote, carried 40 states, and won 426 of the 538 electoral college votes. Although the turnout in 1988 was 50.1 per cent – the lowest since 1924 – Bush appeared to be the natural successor to a popular president, and one who guaranteed continuity and stability, not only in terms of supply-side economics and a focus on moral values but also in the emphasis on foreign policy and security.

Yet when examined more closely the victory of 1988 was less impressive than it first appeared. Even with the Democratic Party in disarray and a particularly colourless opponent, Bush had been forced into very negative campaigning, mounting harsh attacks on what was presented as the dangerous liberalism of Dukakis. Part of the reason for this was that the Republicans seemed to lack an agenda beyond 'more of the same'. Although he won an easy victory in the presidential race, therefore, Bush did not have coat-tails. On the contrary, in the congressional elections the Democrats gained three seats in the House and one in the Senate, leaving Bush with less partisan support in Congress than any newly elected or re-elected president in recent history.

The Reagan legacy was also rather mixed. The budget deficit had grown enormously throughout the Reagan years and there was considerable concern that the United States had become a great power in decline.[1] Japan and Western Europe were challenging the United States economically and there was growing, if grudging, acknowledgement that the United States economy and society suffered from serious structural defects which would prove very difficult to repair. If the political context was not entirely favourable and the economic challenges formidable, however, the Bush administration was reasonably well placed to deal with them. There were high expectations that Bush would be both more pragmatic and more competent than Reagan, that he would bring to the presidency experience, wisdom and political intuition of a high order. The extent to which these expectations were met, in various policy areas, is one of the major concerns of this book – and is a theme that is dealt with more fully in the conclusion. At the outset, however, it is necessary to look at the personality, the leadership style and the key personnel choices of George Bush.

PERSONALITY AND LEADERSHIP STYLE

Although personality is not all that matters in the modern presidency, it remains a good starting point for understanding the strengths and weaknesses, the achievements and limitations of particular presidents and their administrations.[2] In the case of the Bush administration, some of the inconsistencies and apparent paradoxes can be traced back to the rather enigmatic personality of George Bush who exhibited traits which in many respects appeared contradictory. As one analyst put it: 'Bush is a host of contradictions: ... economic conservatism and *noblesse oblige*, upper-class social habits and a liking for country music and horseshoes; competitive drive and a conciliatory mien; verbal clumsiness and athletic grace. Politically, this confusion has served Bush well over the years but has left nebulous the nature of his Oval Office ambitions.'[3]

This argument could well be extended. Bush was the ultimate pragmatist, yet one who engaged in extreme ideological attacks when these became necessary for political survival or electoral success. His sense of reserve and gentleness seemed to go hand in hand with a desire to prove that he was tough, a desire exacerbated by political criticisms that he was weak. Indeed, it is arguable that Bush triumphed in the 1988 election partly because he was able to lay to rest – at least temporarily – the so-called wimp factor: the suspicion that he was too weak and vacillating to be a successful president.[4] Yet, if the attacks on the liberalism of Dukakis revealed an unexpected ruthlessness in the Bush political campaign, when the election was over the theme Bush chose to emphasize was reconciliation. Although this seemed surprising it was not really out of character; as several commentators noted, one of the few consistencies about George Bush was inconsistency.

Moreover, although George Bush clearly had long-held aspirations for the presidency, this desire was not rooted in a political or ideological programme. On the contrary, he was the ultimate pragmatist, rejecting what he dismissed as the 'vision thing' in favour of an approach which treated issues on their merits and regarded political compromise as the norm. In many respects this made him the perfect Vice President: in spite of his disdain for 'voodoo economics' Bush served Reagan loyally for eight years, recognizing that this was part of his own apprenticeship for the presidency. The problem, though, was that when the apprenticeship was over and he had obtained the presidency, he did not know what to do with it. As Kerry Mullins and Aaron Wildavsky noted in 1992: 'What is one to think of a president who, after some thirty-odd years in politics, has few apparent policy preferences? ... who regards "the vision thing" – charting a path and then moving people in that direction, as his predecessor had done – as if it were a disease?'[5]

Part of the reason for this rejection of ideological programmes and grand schemes may have been the recognition by Bush that many of Reagan's problems and weaknesses had come from an overly doctrinaire approach to policy issues. Like other incoming presidents before him, the new incumbent regarded his predecessor as providing a series of lessons about what to avoid. The problem for George Bush, however, was that having rejected much conservative Republican ideology he had nothing to put in its place: he was a president without a cause. Bush, for example, could never have accepted, introduced and committed himself to the Strategic Defense Initiative in the visionary, if misguided, way that Ronald Reagan did. This is not to imply that he lacked principles; simply to argue that the reverse side of his pragmatism was a lack of commitment to a definite and clear political programme. As Anna Quindlen put it, the emperor has clothes but there is nothing inside: there is no 'there' there.[6]

Inevitably, this lack of commitment to political ideas or programmes precipitated a renewal of the allegations that Bush was weak and vacillating. This was almost certainly something that Bush greatly resented – both personally and politically. Yet, if he was concerned with dispelling this image, especially in foreign policy, he was certainly not unique. For most American presidents throughout the Cold War an image of strength has been regarded as indispensable. It has even been argued that there were occasions when presidents defined situations as crises not so much because they threatened national security but because they challenged presidential images of strength, resolve and determination.[7]

Although it is easy to exaggerate this point, it may have had particular saliency for Bush. His willingness to use force not only reflected calculations of American self-interest but also his desire to counter criticisms of personal weakness. As a result, in the crises in both Panama and the Gulf, the issues were reduced partly to personalities. Bush wanted Noriega out of power in Panama, while in the Gulf the confrontation became a very personal test of will and strength between himself and Saddam Hussein. Although much of the rhetoric about Saddam was designed to mobilize support for United States actions in the Gulf, it also had an intense personal quality. There was a real sense of anger and of moral self-righteousness in the President's condemnation of Iraq's invasion and subsequent annexation of Kuwait.

If Bush was often rather hazy about what he stood for, he was very clear about what he was against. One result of the strong rhetoric, though, as Bob Woodward has noted, is that 'the president was left painted into a corner by his own repeated declarations. His obvious emotional attachment to them was converting presidential remarks into hard policy. The goal now, more than ever, was the liberation of Kuwait at almost any cost.'[8] Yet Bush rose to the challenge, providing immensely skilful leadership in mobilizing and maintaining a multinational coalition against Iraq and eventually achieving his objective of expelling Iraqi forces from Kuwait. The gulf Crisis perhaps more than any other single event revealed that although Bush was neither a man nor a president with a strong sense of vision, he did not lack a strong sense of values or strong conviction. Amongst the things he seems to have cherished most were order and stability. In fact Mullins and Wildavsky argue that Bush operated within a cultural context of inclusive hierarchy which aimed to integrate all elements of the American polity (classes, races, interests) into a cohesive whole in which leaders serve followers and followers grant them the authority due to their position. Bush's urge was to pull everybody into one cooperative whole.[9] The starting point for this was a belief in the central role of the family which was not only crucial in maintaining stability but was also the most basic hierarchy on which all others depended.[10]

The centrality to Bush of a sense of cooperative order was also reflected in the presidential style he adopted. Although Bush presented himself as the rightful heir to Ronald Reagan and promised to govern with 'more of the same' he was also concerned with softening the impact of government policies and creating what he termed a 'kinder, gentler America'. Indeed, this theme of 'kinder and gentler' was enunciated in him nomination acceptance speech, echoed in his Inaugural Address, and endlessly repeated. On winning, Bush became the kindly grandfather stressing the need for harmony and the theme of reconciliation.[11] The emphasis he placed on these and his other values was also evident in his management style.

There were several ways in which the management style Bush adopted as president reflected his strong personal values – especially family, hierarchy and order. Bush brought into his administration people from nearly every phase of his career, surrounding himself with what was in effect an extended professional family. At least ten people in his sixteen-member cabinet had known him for ten years or more. The Bush administration, more than any other in recent memory, was a gathering of friends. The President appointed people from his campaign, his circle of friends, and from people he had served with under Reagan, Ford and Nixon. Most were pragmatists who also happened to be conservative – rather like the President himself. Bush relied heavily on his senior advisers and almost always followed their consensus. Indeed, his approach to his top officials was characterized by 'an emphasis on cooperation and a strong desire to maintain close relations'.[12]

Bush had particularly good relations with his key advisers in the national security field – National Security Adviser, Brent Scowcroft, Secretary of State James Baker and Secretary of Defense, Richard (Dick) Cheney – which was also the area where his own interest and expertise made him the most comfortable. This led to a relaxed informal style of decision-making that had both strengths and weaknesses. The strength was that by creating a very relaxed atmosphere and an emphasis on group cohesion, the Bush administration was able to avoid some of the clashes amongst top officials – Vance versus Brzezinski, Shultz versus Weinberger – that had proved politically debilitating for the two previous administrations. The shortcomings were that the informality sometimes degenerated into a free-wheeling approach that discouraged a systematic consideration and careful scrutiny of options and that glossed over differences amongst the advisers. There are at least hints of some of these problems in Bob Woodward's description of decision-making in the Gulf Crisis: 'When the principals met, Bush liked to keep everyone around the table smiling – jokes, camaraderie, the conviviality of old friends. Positions and alternatives were not completely discussed. Interruptions were common. Clear decision rarely emerged.'[13]

If Woodward's description reflects the close personal relationship that Bush had with many members of his inner circle, this was closely linked to a second element in the Bush presidential style – a preference for agreement and accommodation. This stemmed partly from the President's guiding conception of what might be termed a cooperative hierarchy. The President was generally conciliatory, willing to bring people in, and engage in full consultation, qualities that accorded with his fundamental pragmatism. This wide consultative process also served as 'a substitute for strong ideological commitment and a vision for how these problems might be solved'.[14] In one sense Bush stood for the system or the process: for the President political cooperation and coalition-building were the preferred method of resolving problems.

Another element of the President's leadership style, and one which seemed to contradict the consultative elements, was a tendency by Bush to assert his leadership and remind people who was in charge. This was sometimes manifested in secretive working patterns and an insular management style that did not extend far beyond the executive suite. Secrecy for President Bush resulted not from a phobia about leaks but from his thinking on how to get things done. Although this contradicted the image of Bush as open, warm and inclusive, Mullins and Wildavsky suggested that the key to this apparent paradox was that at heart Bush emphasized hierarchy: although he wished to bring people into the system, he had strong feelings about their roles within that system.[15] The system was particularly closed during crises. In the Gulf Crisis, in particular, there was little evidence of consultation with experts on the region from either the State Department or elsewhere.

A fourth element in the President's style stemmed from his essential pragmatism: unlike Reagan and his deep-seated if simplistic adherence to a radical ideological stance, President Bush was a hands-on pragmatist with a preference for competence over ideology. Partly a function of the absence of commitment by Bush to visionary ideals or programmes, this approach was also a result of his working experience over a long period in a variety of executive positions in government. It was manifested in a problem-by-problem approach, a pass-over-the-desk style which dealt with issues and then passed on. This had both positive and negative consequences. A more hands-on approach meant that Bush was more in control of his staff and his advisers. What was accomplished was his, and opportunity for subordinate freelancing of the kind that had led to the Iran-Contra affair were strictly limited. On the negative side, the hands-on approach led to accusations that the President was essentially reactive, that he lacked not only a strategy and the kind of long-term leadership stamina to sustain proposals in the domestic arena but also a real sense of where he wanted the United States to go in foreign policy.

Nor was this the only negative consequence. Another result of the President's style was a lack of consistency in approach, albeit in response to changing political circumstances and needs. In the first year of the administration, for example, Bush sought to be consensual rather than polarizing in his approach to Congress and the public.[16] This was evident in his Inaugural Address in which he stated that this was 'the age of the offered hand' to Congress, and in the initial emphasis on consultation, conciliation and bipartisanship. Indeed, during his first year the President moved to the centre on environmental issues and on federal support for child care and generally 'overcame Democratic opposition in Congress more by clever positioning that by political pressure'.[17] Yet by 1992 Bush was running for president against Congress, drawing parallels between his problems on Capitol Hill and those faced by Harry Truman in the late 1940s. By the fourth year of the administration, the conciliatory pragmatism of the President's first year had been transformed into a confrontational approach based partly upon frustration with Congressional obstructionism and partly upon the belief that there were real political gains to be made through such a stance. One problem with the pragmatism of President Bush was that it seemed at times to degenerate into little more than political opportunism.

The other problem resulting from the President's political style was that 'strong presidential leadership was limited to the international arena' and even here was largely confined to responding to crises.[18] Even in foreign policy there was little effort by the administration to be proactive. Domestic policy initiatives were even fewer and more modest and there were complaints that the administration lacked an overall design or as Bush himself put it, 'the vision thing'. Only Bush's oft-repeated vow to oppose tax increases continued to structure the congressional agenda. For all this, as Thomas Mann has suggested, the Bush presidency – at least initially – appeared well suited to the political context of a relatively quiescent public opinion within which it had to operate, and was consistent with the interpretation of the 1988 presidential election as a referendum on the Reagan presidency and its management of the economy.[19] Given the radical thrust of the Reagan years, the constraints of federal deficits and Democratic control on Congress, the main requirement seemed to be for a consolidating administration. Not only did the Bush administration appear to meet this need, but, at the outset, Bush and his team were masterful in mounting the spectacle of an unspectacular president.[20] This is not to imply that there were no controversies. Some of these came in the choice of key personnel and it is to this aspect of the administration that attention must now be given.

CHOICE OF PERSONNEL

If President Bush set out to conciliate rather than antagonize, his nominations for key positions were not always well received. In 1989 his nomination of former Senator John Tower for Secretary of Defense was defeated, while his 1991 nomination of Judge Clarence Thomas for the Supreme Court proved even more controversial – even though it was eventually upheld. In the case of Tower, the opposition was unexpected, but once the decision had been made, Bush remained loyal even though this appeared to jeopardize his relationship with Congress. Yet the President also moved quickly to fill the position after Tower's defeat. His second choice, Dick Cheney, was more flexible than Tower and proved to be good at the dual task of defending military budgets and programmes to Congress while encouraging flexibility and change within the Department of Defense itself.

If the opposition of the Tower nomination was unexpected, the choice of Thomas, which came at a very different point in the presidency, seemed to display a blatant disregard for congressional and public sensitivities: 'In the face of a Senate controlled by the opposite party, the president nevertheless nominated an individual of dubious judicial experience with an ultraconservative track record in an open effort to strengthen the conservative majority on the Court.'[21] The ultimate effect, however, may have been to alienate many professional women, who were offended by the Republican assault on the integrity of Anita Hill and who subsequently voted against Bush in 1992.

Other choices were less controversial and reflected the President's natural desire to surround himself with people he knew and trusted. Not surprisingly, there were some holdovers from the Reagan administration. James Baker, Reagan's Chief of Staff and later Secretary of the Treasury, had been Bush's campaign manager. He was made Secretary of State. Clayton K. Yeutter, US trade representative under Reagan, became Secretary of Agriculture and was later brought back into the White House as Domestic Policy Assistant. Bush asked long-term confidant Nicholas F. Brady to stay on at Treasury. Reagan had named Brady to the post in August 1988 when Baker left to run the Bush election campaign and he was to be the chief architect of the Savings and Loan bailout plan. Other holdovers were Lauro F. Cavazos, who had been appointed as Secretary of Education in August 1988, and Attorney General Richard Thornburgh. Not since Hoover took over from Coolidge in 1929 had three Cabinet members been retained.

Other appointments included Elizabeth H. Dole as Secretary of Labor. Dole was replaced by Lynn Martin (also a woman) when she resigned to become head of the American Red Cross. Manuel Lujan, at Interior, like the President was a nonconfrontational pragmatist and was approved by the business community. Richard A. Mosbacher, who was appointed to head the Commerce Department, had been chief fundraiser for Bush's 1988 campaign and would leave in January 1992 to chair Bush's re-election campaign. Louis W. Sullivan, president and founder of Morehouse School of Medicine in Atlanta, was Secretary of Health and Human Services (HHS) and was the only African-American in the Cabinet. More surprising was the choice of Jack Kemp who was appointed to Housing and Urban Development (HUD). Although Kemp had the support of Vice

President Quayle, both his temperament and ideological convictions meant that he was not trusted as a team player – at least
until after the Los Angeles riots – and he was rather isolated.
Apart from Kemp the Cabinet was drawn mainly from the ranks
of pragmatic conservatives with Washington experience.

For management of the decision-making process, Bush let
himself in for trouble by making a strange choice of principal
manager in the form John Sununu who had been a key figure
in the New Hampshire campaign – and allowing Sununu to
hire a relatively inexperienced White House staff.[22] In the first
months of the administration this led to a series of tactical
errors, including the messy rejection of Tower. Most of the
management difficulties were subsequently ironed out, partly
because Sununu began to rely on Richard Darman, the
Director of the Office of Management and Budget and a sophisticated holdover from the Reagan administration.[23] For all his
shortcomings, however, Sununu found his influence as Bush's
chief political adviser greatly strengthened when Lee Atwater
(Bush's campaign manager and then Chairman of the Republican National Committee) succumbed to a fatal illness.

Darman too became increasingly important partly because of
his close relationship with Bush but also because budgetary
issues were so important. The 1990 budget deal with Congress
strengthened the position of OMB because it had the final say
in projecting the costs of new federal programmes. Indeed,
Darman was reputed to have something of a veto power over
domestic policy proposals and also clashed with Cheney over
the extent of cuts to be made in the military budget.[24] Although
an effective manager and facilitator Darman became the target
of the Republican right for encouraging the President to seek
bipartisan compromises.

Overall though there was a belief that Bush had assembled a
professional team and that the administration was not obsessed
with narrow definitions of loyalty or White House control of all
appointments as had been the case in the Reagan administration.[25] Moreover, in both foreign and domestic matters, Bush
chose to rely for substantive advice on his moderate and experienced Cabinet, and, initially, at least, limited the White House
staff to a coordinating role.[26] The President required advocates
of contending views to debate the issues in his presence and
when making domestic policy decisions he relied on a process of

'multiple advocacy' in which a range of options were presented, refined, criticized and assessed around the table.[27] On occasion the President would also go outside the formal channels for advice, using his large network of Washington contacts.[28]

The President continued the Reagan second term Cabinet Council system of Economic Policy, chaired by Nicholas Brady, Domestic Policy, chaired by Richard Thornburgh, and National Security, chaired by Brent Scowcroft. Each Council developed a system of working groups which enabled them to handle a high proportion of policy matters. The most important and volatile issues though were rarely entrusted to Cabinet Councils but were dealt with instead by a coterie of senior advisers.[29] Five staff members exercised the bulk of power: the big three – Sununu, Darman and Scowcroft – together with Roger B. Porter and Michael J. Boskin. After Sununu and Darman settled the broad lines of policy and legislative strategy, Domestic Policy Advisor Porter looked after the details.

The biggest potential problem in all this was John Sununu, who was short of both tact and experience in Washington. Sununu brought to the White House strong conservative credentials and was seen by anti-abortion activists as their main ally in converting Bush's pro-life rhetoric into policy. He also supported business against environmentalists, and successfully opposed several Energy Department proposals considered too expensive or interventionist. Sununu like to compare himself with Sherman Adams, another former Governor of New Hampshire, who had become chief of staff for Eisenhower. When he came to Washington he even went so far as to obtain Adams' old licence plate number for his personal use. Sununu had a good relationship with Bush and for a while he acted as Bush's top legislative strategist, political adviser and domestic policy-maker.[30] As things started to go awry, however, he increasingly became a magnet for criticism. Castigated for his travel at government expense, Sununu became a symbol of Bush's larger problems and went from lightning rod to convenient scapegoat when Bush's standing in the polls fell.

Sununu was replaced by Samuel K. Skinner in early December 1991. Skinner had become Bush's Transportation Secretary in 1989 and had managed successive crises – the Eastern Airline strike, the *Exxon Valdez* oil spillage in Alaska, and California's earthquake disaster in 1990 – in ways which suggested he was an accomplished troubleshooter. He also knew how to deal with Congress and had successfully orchestrated the passage of two major bills – highways and aviation – while at Transportation. There was still a feeling though that his management style was more akin to IBM than Washington and after a short honeymoon he was subject to fierce criticism from Republicans who said he was not up to the job.

Yet the problems facing Skinner should not be ignored. By the time he replaced Sununu they were already formidable: Bush had lost 40 points in the polls, there was an approaching State of the Union message, and Pat Buchanan was entering the primaries. Skinner's response was to initiate a comprehensive review of White House staff operations – a corporate, structural approach to a problem that simply added another layer of management, when the real problem was one of substance. The ultimate weakness was not that Skinner, or his predecessor, failed to manage the policy-making process but that the President failed to set a direction for addressing substantive problems.[31] Ultimately structures and staffs are secondary to the president – and the central problem in the Bush administration was the lack of guidance and impetus from the top, at least on domestic policy.

THE BUSH ADMINISTRATION: AN OVERVIEW

The Bush administration went through three phases: a period of domestic consolidation and foreign policy review, a major foreign policy crisis which dominated the period from August 1990 to March 1991, and a subsequent period of malaise which emerged gradually in the last half of 1991 and developed into a full-blown crisis of leadership during the 1992 election year.

The first year was a relatively successful one for the President. Apart from the Tower nomination most other issues seemed to go smoothly. Although the administration was criticized for its passivity in foreign policy, the conventional arms control proposal announced by the President at NATO's Fortieth Anniversary Summit in May 1989 successfully addressed major splits within the Western Alliance and responded to the new opportunities in dealing with Moscow. And even in domestic policy, the meagre legislative output of Bush's first year did not harm his standing. Creative accounting meant that Gramm-Rudman-Hollings deficit reduction requirements were technically met while the President's 'tactical positioning on domestic issues' kept Democrats 'off balance and unable to advance a compelling agenda of their own.'[32] Most important pieces of legislation, such as the bailout of Savings and Loan, were not campaign issues but bipartisan responses to perceived crises.[33] If the administration did not push a domestic agenda, however, its foreign policy initiatives had a positive spillover onto the domestic side, undercutting early criticisms that the President was timid and lacking imagination.[34]

At this point Bush appeared to be the Great Incumbent, with an agenda which, for the most part, was as low key and soothing as his character. The President's performance had displayed his familiarity with public policy and his command of the issues and seemed to auger well for continued competence.[35] Although he was a status quo president who did not articulate a vision for change, the administration argued that not every incumbent ought to have a grand vision or lead a new crusade.[36]

Ironically, in the summer of 1990 the Bush administration did embark on a crusade – against Saddam Hussein. The invasion of Kuwait provoked a major diplomatic and military campaign in which the administration succeeded in creating and maintaining a large multinational coalition, deployed massive forces to the Gulf and fought a very successful air and ground war which succeeded in ejecting Iraqi forces. The confrontation in the Gulf was presented by the administration as the defining moment in the Bush presidency and certainly 'illustrated what presidents look best at doing: successfully commanding the armed forces in a crisis and engaging in high-level diplomacy.'[37]

Yet by the end of a year which had witnessed perhaps the most impressive performance of American arms since 1945, President Bush had gone from victory in the Gulf to malaise at home. The third and final phase of the Bush presidency was one in which the President was embattled. What had appeared in 1989 as a slow start or an emphasis on consolidation, in late 1991 and 1992 became a crisis of leadership. The administration not only appeared to lack imagination in responding to domestic problems but seemed to be insensitive to domestic needs. Initially the Bush administration had 'crafted a strategy for governance' that made 'a virtue of the constraints on its leadership.'[38] While this could work in the honeymoon period it was wholly inadequate in response to domestic economic and social woes – and from being an asset early on it became a serious liability, contributing significantly to the unravelling of the Bush administration in 1992.

Although the President tried to blame the Democrats in Congress for the failure to deal with domestic economic problems, in the final analysis he could not escape the responsibility for what by November 1992 had become a profound sense of crisis. This was based partly on the feeling that, for the first time in American history, the next generation might not be better off than the current one and partly on the sense of real disappointment with an administration which had initially seemed so competent. The irony in all this was that Bush had 'built an advisory and management apparatus' that would have responded marvellously to the leadership that he simply failed to provide.[39]

NOTES

1. This became a popular theme largely as a result of the work of Paul Kennedy, *The Rise and Fall of the Great Powers* (New York: Random House, 1987).
2. For a fuller discussion of the importance of personality see James David Barber, *The Presidential Character: Predicting Performance in the White House* (Englewood Cliffs, NJ: Prentice-Hall, 1972); James David Barber, *The Pulse of the Politics: Electing Presidents in the Media Age* (New York: W.W. Norton, 1980). See also Michael Nelson, 'The Psychological Presidency', in Michael Nelson (ed.), *The Presidency And The Political System*, 3rd edn. (Washington DC: Congressional Quarterly Press, 1990), pp. 189–212, especially p. 200.
3. 'George Bush', *National Journal*, 10 June 1989, p. 1405.
4. See Nelson, op. cit., p. 208.
5. Kerry Mullins and Aaron Wildavsky, 'The Procedural Presidency of George Bush', *Political Science Quarterly*, Vol. 107, No. 1, Spring 1992, pp. 31–62 at p. 31.
6. Anna Quindlen, 'No There There', *New York Times*, 6 May 1992, A29.
7. Thomas Halpern, *Foreign Policy Crises: Appearance and Reality in Decision-Making* (Columbus, Ohio: Bobbs-Merrill, 1971).
8. Bob Woodward, *The Commanders* (New York: Simon & Schuster, 1991), p. 302.
9. Ibid. p. 38.

10. Ibid.
11. 'Taking Charge of Divided Government', *President Bush: The Challenge Ahead* (Washington DC: Congressional Quarterly Inc., 1989), p. 4.
12. Mullins and Wildavsky, op. cit., p. 40.
13. Woodward, op. cit., p. 302.
14. Mullins and Wildavsky, op. cit., p. 42
15. Ibid. p. 45.
16. See Thomas Mann, 'Breaking the Political Impasse', in Henry J. Aaron (ed.), *Setting National Priorities* (Washington DC: The Brookings Institution, 1990), p. 295.
17. Ibid.
18. Ibid., p. 296.
19. Ibid.
20. Bruce Miroff, 'The Presidency And The Public: Leadership As Spectacle', in Nelson (ed.), op. cit., p. 307.
21. Jack W. Germond and Jules Witcover, 'The Political Price of Thomas's Win', *National Journal*, Vol. 23, No. 42, 19 October 1991, p. 2565.
22. Paul J. Quirk, 'Presidential Competence', in Nelson (ed.) op. cit., p. 182.
23. Ibid.
24. Burt Solomon, 'Darman Sheathes His Stiletto In New White House Power Equation', *National Journal*, Vol. 24, No. 1, 4 January 1992, p. 34.
25. James P. Pfiffner, 'Establishing the Bush Presidency', *Public Administration Review*, Vol. 50, No. 1, January/February 1990, p. 68.
26. Quirk, op. cit., p. 182.
27. The idea of multiple advocacy was developed by Alexander George. See his *Presidential Decision Making in Foreign Policy: The Effective Use of Information and Advice* (Boulder, Colo.: Westview Press, 1980). For the Bush use of multiple advocacy see John P. Burke, 'The Institutional Presidency', in Nelson (ed.), op. cit., p. 403.
28. Quirk, op. cit., p. 182.
29. Burt Solomon, 'In Bush's Image', *National Journal*, Vol. 22, No. 27, 7 July 1990, p. 1642.
30. Burt Solomon, 'Sam Skinner's Managerial Skills Won't Assure A New Bush Message', *National Journal*, Vol. 23, No. 50, 14 December 1991, p. 3038.
31. Ibid., p. 3039.
32. Mann, op. cit., p. 294.
33. Thomas Weko and John H. Aldrich, 'The Presidency And The Election Campaign: Framing the Choice in 1988', in Nelson (ed.), op. cit., p. 280.
34. Mann, op. cit., p. 295.
35. Quirk, op. cit., p. 181.
36. Pfiffner, op. cit., p. 66.
37. Bert Rockman, 'How Is The President Doing?', *Brookings Review*, Vol. 9, No. 3, Summer 1991, p. 56.
38. Mann, op. cit., p. 296.
39. Mullins and Wildavsky, op. cit., p. 53.

2 Managing the Bush White House
Marcia Lynn Whicker

When George Bush was elected president in November 1988, the United States confronted many complex and difficult tasks. Among the challenges on the national agenda were:[1]

- to revise the educational system;
- successfully to integrate diverse ethnic and religious minorities and immigrants, tapping the creative energies of each;
- to integrate the US economy into the global economy;
- to address the increasing disparity between the rich and the poor;
- to develop a viable health delivery system at a reasonable cost in terms of share of GNP;
- to restore the technological edge of the United States in manufacturing;
- to return the US to the cutting edge in new technologies;
- to increase exports and address the balance of trade;
- to contain if not lower the federal deficit and national debt;
- to develop long-term capital and human investments to assure future economic growth;
- to facilitate and structure a budding New World Order in international affairs.

As twilight set on the twentieth century, the Bush White House was ill-structured to manage these complex tasks. Sorting out the reasons is like opening a series of doors. Behind the door of policy mismanagement was an ineffectively organized White House. And behind the door of ineffective White House structure lay the mal-leadership of George Bush. We will start here at the primary source of policy failures: Bush's mal-leadership style, and examine the implications for White House organization. White House organization, in turn will be linked to policy outcomes – including some successes, but also many fizzles and

17

failures, especially on the homefront. In 1988 when Bush assumed office, politics was characterized by decentralized insti- tutions, federalism, separation of powers, divided government and partisan gridlock. In such an environment, complicated, challenging and difficult domestic agendas required leadership of an activist and visionary presidency. Bush failed to exhibit this required leadership and vision in domestic policy. Even his actions in foreign policy were reactive rather than proactive.

MAL-LEADERSHIP AND THE PRESIDENCY

Leadership scholars typically focus upon the desirable qualities and styles that lead to high organizational and institutional performance.[2] An emphasis upon leadership effectiveness and techniques, however, does not promote distinctions between good leadership and bad leadership, both of which in the short run might be equally effective. For lack of a better term, here we call such socially desirable leadership that promotes goals beneficial to society *moral leadership*. Some – but less – attention has been devoted to leaders who undermine social goals and the well-being of the people who follow them.[3] We call this negative (but nonetheless sometimes skilled in the short run) leadership *mal-leadership*.

Mal-leader is the term used here to connote the maladjusted manager. It may be applied to mid-level managers in the bureaucracy all the way up to the president. A mal-leader is defined using two key criteria from leadership research: task competence and human relations skills.[4] In the case of the mal- leader, these positive skills are conspicuous by their absence. Mal-leaders employ destructive or inept interpersonal rela- tions, and counterproductive task skills. But it is not only the deficiencies in human relations and task skills that define the mal-leader. As Burns defined transformational leaders in terms of their positive effect on followers,[5] mal-leaders also transform their followers in terms of negative effects. Mal-leaders attempt to displace task accomplishment with maneuvering in pursuit of non-task related ends. They replace cordial, supportive human relations activities with unpleasant, self-protecting per- sonal interactions. Mal-leaders may differ from each other stylistically but in general they lack task and human relations skill, pursue goals other than those sanctioned by the organization, and on occasion display a malicious streak that sometimes brings out the worst in subordinates.

Just like mal-leaders, moral leaders come in different varieties. There is no single 'moral leader' mold from which all who might be classified as such emerge. Yet despite their diversity, moral leaders do share certain basic common characteristics. Among them are knowledge of themselves, knowledge of the external world, self-motivation and drive, the ability to motivate others, and integrity. Moral leaders are able to formulate persuasive, uplifting messages for followers, cultivate the talent of others, and have what George Bush called 'the vision thing'. Presidents, in particular, shape our visions of the possible and direct our energies towards it. When our visions are elevated toward higher achievements, and our efforts encouraged to be disciplined yet creative and innovative, much is accomplished. Moral leaders provide us with this vision and direction. When our visions are reduced to viewing fellow citizens as our greatest threats and our energies directed toward defeating each other, much is lost. Mal-leaders encourage these base instincts to the loss of productivity and individual self-esteem.

Mal-leaders are the antithesis of moral leaders. Mal-leaders may be technically skilled and quite manipulative. They may have a strong sense of how to fight organizational battles. But the basic motive of mal-leaders is the opposite of that of moral leaders. Moral leaders uplift; mal-leaders tear down. Moral leaders promote progress; mal-leaders result in regress. Moral leaders generate confidence; mal-leaders generate fear.

There are seven types of mal-leaders: the absentee leader, the controller, the busybody and the hedonist are more benign types of mal-leader. The enforcer, the street fighter and the bully are more malicious forms. All presidents exhibit, on occasion, some characteristics of one or another mal-leader style. In the case of Bush, and his predecessor Reagan, these mal-leader tendencies were sufficient to have a major impact upon White House management and organization. Our goal here is to identify Bush as a 'busybody' mal-leader, and to contrast that with Ronald Reagan's 'absentee leader' type. We will examine the organizational and policy implications of Bush's mal-leadership style.

Bush frequently exhibited the characteristics of a busybody mal-leader. The busybody is an indecisive, ineffective mal-leader who craves affection, is fearful of alienating others, and specializes in rumor-mongering. This mal-leader sets himself up as the center of a communications network so that others must constantly turn to him to 'tattle' on others. By failing to make decisions to resolve conflicts among subordinates, this mal-leader assures that the flow of complaints and information about conflicts and therefore the attention he receives will be continuous.

By contrast, Bush's predecessor, Reagan, more commonly exhibited the characteristics of an absentee leader style. The absentee leader is a disengaged, remote mal-leader who is tangentially involved in organizational decisions, manipulates symbols more than substance, and does not mind the organizational store. This mal-leader is more mindless than malicious, but eventually creates chaos and malaise from the turmoil and infighting that is perpetrated by underlings who are malevolent and who sense a leadership vacuum.

Consider the case of Reagan as an absentee leader. Reagan rarely seemed interested in policy details, repeating to the public familiar stories of individual histories rather than conveying information about programs and policies. He implicitly and explicitly delegated major decision-making authority to others. He seemed ignorant of major operations underway in his own White House, including and especially the Iran-Contra affair.[6] He took lengthy and frequent vacations. He started work late and left early most days.

Reagan's fate rose and fell with the skills of those under him. Under the short-lived but effective troika of Jim Baker, Ed Meese and Michael Deaver during his first administration, the Reagan administration achieved major successes.[7] In the case of the troika, the communal or commission leadership structure provided for checks on the weaknesses and excesses of any one of the three who were operating jointly as second in command for the president. In addition, David Stockman kept a firm grip on budget policy as director of the Office of Management and Budget, while innovative structures such as the Cabinet Council system were employed. As a result, policy directions were clear.

By Reagan's second term, the irascible and autocratic Donald Regan had replaced the troika as Chief of Staff. Decision-making veered into ethically shaky and even illegal ground. In addition to the Iran-Contra affair, the administration confronted failures at the Reykjavik conference, in the Bork and Ginsburg Supreme Court nominee rejections, and the Defense Department scandal. This rise and fall of President Reagan's fate was driven by the capabilities of his subordinates, rather than his own. His absentee leadership style allowed his subordinates rather than himself to set the tone of his administration.

BUSH AND MAL-LEADERSHIP

President Bush, by contrast to Ronald Reagan, emerges as a busybody mal-leader. The classification of Bush as a mal-leader is marked by five key characteristics. These key characteristics are: excessive nervous energy and motion; indecision and haphazard decision-making; craving attention; rumor-mongering; and 'hail-fellow-well-met'. Each of these characteristics is considered in turn.

Excessive nervous energy and motion

One characteristic of busybodies is immense but unfocused energy. In today's era of psychological labeling whereby every behavior pattern which is more than one standard deviation from normality is suspect, busybodies would be labeled borderline hyperactive with an attention deficit disorder. Busybodies jump from one topic to another with an abundance of energy, sometimes leaving their subordinates fatigued and even bewildered.

Bush exhibited the characteristics of high energy levels and a lack of focus. At times, he seemed to have a personal perpetual motion machine driving him. His schedule was hectic and even frantic, but the lack of a specific agenda that had been a hallmark of the White House during the Reagan years made much of Bush's motion appear almost random, Bush traveled frequently abroad. By the end of 1990, half way through his first and only term, Bush had visited twenty-nine countries, as many as Reagan visited during his two terms in office.[8] Berman and Jentleson describe Bush's style as one of 'sheer personal energy...'.[9] Only the Gulf War in 1991 curbed his travels abroad. Bush entertained frequently at both the White House and Camp David, giving the appearance of abhorring solitude.

Nor did Bush's characteristic of energetic motion diminish with his election defeat in 1992. During his lame duck period, Bush seemed to pick up the pace of actions in his favored sphere of foreign policy. He resumed bombing of Saddam Hussein. Even so, his advisers worried about his mental health and his seeming depression. They encouraged Bush to consider humanitarian intervention in Somalia, in part to give Bush something to do. In the waning weeks of his presidency, Bush followed their advice, committing US troops to Somalia to restore sufficient order to allow food and non-military supplies to be delivered to a starving, war-torn population. American help was welcome to the starving Somalians, dying daily by the thousands. A major factor contributing to Bush's actions, however, was his nervous energy and his advisers' concern for dispelling his post-election depression by renewed action.

Throughout his administration, Bush's informal speaking style was uneven and irregular, indicating a difficulty in focusing on a linear thought pattern from beginning to end. News magazines and papers regularly published 'Bushisms' and 'Bush-speak', examples of staggered, choppy sentences when Bush spoke off the cuff.[10] Yet Bush spoke to the press more often than other modern presidents.[11] In shaping his leadership to the demands of television and an electorate shaped by public opinion polls, Stuckey and Antczak found him 'subject to the variety of whims, inconsistencies, and short attention spans that increasingly characterizes the viewing audience, and thus the voting public.'[12] During the second 1992 presidential debate in Richmond before an audience of ordinary citizens when Bush was in the heat of the struggle of his political life, he could be seen glancing repeatedly and impatiently at his watch, anxious for the debate to end, rather than concentrating on strategies to respond to questions. These characteristics are compatible with those of a busybody mal-leader.

Indecision and haphazard decision-making

The second characteristic of busybody mal-leaders is indecision. Busybodies recognize how decisions based on good intentions and made by reasonable criteria with all available information at the time can be distorted in the retelling and made to seem unreasonable. Indeed, busybodies readily recognize this distortion, precisely because they themselves become very good at it. Busybodies try to avoid becoming the object of such distortion by avoiding making decisions, but are only partially successful. Eventually, their own indecisiveness becomes the basis for rumors among subordinates and peers. When forced to make decisions, their judgments appear haphazard, with options inadequately analyzed prior to reaching a conclusion. After the decision, then, great effort is required to justify the option selected.

Four examples illustrate Bush's indecisiveness and tendency to make decisions in a haphazard fashion. The first example was his selection of J. Danforth Quayle as a vice presidential running mate in 1988. Bush consulted none of his senior advisers in making his final choice and appeared to make the decision on the basis of minimal analysis. Goldman and Matthews later described Bush's haphazard decision process as 'a hell of a way to pick a prospective president'.[13] When Bush selected his Vice President, he had never sat down with Quayle for an in-depth discussion, had never asked him a single question about his beliefs, and had never ascertained Quayle's understanding of public policy issues. Subsequently, Quayle's selection was explained as an attempt to balance the ticket ideologically and placate the increasingly militant and vocal right wing of the Republican party. It was also explained as an attempt to appeal to younger voters of baby boom age and below, and that his 'Ken doll' good looks would appeal to women.

Later, Bush was heard to blame others for his poor decision, claiming he had been sold a 'bill of goods' about Quayle, and that people had overstated Quayle's standing in Capitol Hill, his campaign skills and his prospect for producing a big gain in the polls.[14] Despite Quayle's credible performance in the 1992 vice presidential debate, throughout most of Bush's term in office Quayle proved to be a negative rather than a positive asset. His public mistakes in speaking and lightweight image contributed little to the difficult task of governing and did little to improve Bush's image. Having made one bad decision in 1988, Bush was confronted with another decision in 1992: whether to dump Quayle from the ticket as some were urging or to keep him as the vice presidential running mate. Bush's action to keep Quayle may be charitably interpreted as personal loyalty; a less charitable interpretation is that it is yet another example of his indecisiveness in a difficult situation. When confronted with a hard choice, Bush chose the path of least resistance.

A second example of Bush's indecisiveness followed by haphazard decision-making was his decision to enter the Persian Gulf War. Subsequently, evidence was revealed that the Bush administration continued the policies of the Reagan White House of providing technologies to Saddam Hussein that could be used in building sophisticated weapons, including nuclear weapons. Reagan capitulated to US businesses that benefited from trade with a known dictator who had killed and abused competitors in his own country. Bush perpetuated the policy of providing Saddam's regime with US aid and trade, despite evidence that Saddam was increasingly dangerous. When presented with intelligence reports that Saddam intended to invade Kuwait, Bush did nothing before the event.

After Saddam Hussein's invasion of Kuwait, Bush appeared to set US goals in the Middle East in an haphazard manner. Bush's public statement that he intended to reverse the occupation of Kuwait was made after a series of hasty meetings in a crisis atmosphere, rather than after systematic consultation with his military advisers.[15] General Colin Powell, in Europe at the time, was surprised by the announcement, and General Norman Schwarzkopf had to brief the Saudis before he had been fully apprised of the decision himself.[16] Bush's decision in November 1990 to escalate the number of troops in Saudi Arabia from 200,000 to 500,000 was tantamount to a decision to go to war, but without any formal underpinning justification. Only after these de facto decisions to combat Saddam militarily did Bush put together a supporting coalition at the United Nations and secure a resolution from Congress condoning support for the anti-Saddam United Nations resolution. Nor did Bush decisively end the threat Saddam posed to US interests, but, critics contended, ended the war prematurely, leaving Saddam in power, still a source of instability to the region and still a potential nuclear threat.

A third example of Bush's indecisiveness concerned urban policy and how to deal with decaying city infrastructure, increasing crime and deteriorating social fabric. Bush, for whom urban policy was never a high priority, failed to develop a coherent strategy toward the cities and their deep-seated troubles. Bush's 'weed and seed' plan for urban renewal proved little more than symbolism. Even the Los Angeles riots failed to force the development of a coherent policy. Jack Kemp, former Republican Congressman and Secretary for Housing and Urban Development, was the highest ranking official in the administration who advocated an activist platform to deal with the problems of the poor. Yet Kemp's proposals received little attention and were mostly ignored.[17] Especially in dealing with the poor and the cities, the Bush administration showed indecisiveness and drift.

Budget policy constitutes a fourth area of indecision and haphazard decision-making. The massive hemorrhaging of federal budget deficits that began in the Reagan administration with its adoption of supply-side economics continued through the Bush years. Despite the sharp and incisive intellectual skills of Richard Darman, Director of the Office of Management and Budget, Bush proved unable to put forth a plan for dealing with deficits and the growing national debt. During the budget summit in the fall of 1990, Bush retracted, under pressure from Congress, his famous campaign promise of 'Read my lips: No new taxes', and agreed to a tax increase. Even that proved insufficient to achieve the goal of significantly reducing federal deficits. By 1992 at the end of Bush's term in office, the deficit was almost $300 billion. Bush publicly recanted his 1990 agreement to raise taxes during the 1992 campaign, blaming Congress and bad advice for his ill-fated decision to reverse policy in this area.

Craving attention

The third characteristic of busibodies is their craving for attention. They structure events and people to flow through them, placing themselves in the center or 'thick of things'. Their communication patterns resemble the hub–spoke flight patterns common among air carriers in the US market. Busybodies have set themselves up to be the hub or center of the communications network. Their subordinates and co-workers form the spokes. In any event, given their formal leadership position, considerable communication would flow through the offices and across the desks of busybodies. But busybodies, by dint of their personality and style, manage to create much more than the normal level of communication, and to force it under their control, even when doing so is clearly not efficient nor in the best interest of the organization.

Repeatedly, Bush refused to share the presidential limelight with strong subordinates. Bush's selection of Quayle showed he was unwilling to have a strong second-in-command who would be a heartbeat away from the presidency. The sole advantage of Quayle's selection, critics contended, was Quayle would not overshadow Bush. Indeed, Bush appears to have selected as vice president someone as malleable, loyal and invisible as he himself had been to Reagan.[18]

Bush's exile of the charismatic and populist Kemp to HUD also revealed his unwillingness to share the limelight. Kemp had been a potential presidential rival in 1988, and could have become one again in 1992. Unlike the more patrician and upper-crust Bush, Kemp appealed to the blue-collar and working-class constituencies. Kemp's appearances with the President were carefully controlled so that Kemp did not upstage Bush. Kemp had infrequent access to the Oval Office and was not in Bush's inner circle of advisers. Apparently, Bush's fears of being upstaged by Kemp were well founded. In his one major public appearance with Bush after the Los Angeles riots, Kemp managed to do precisely that.[19] While a stronger president would have used Kemp's popularity to advance administration policies, Bush continued to view Kemp as a rival and sought to curb his influence.

Those strong personalities that Bush did tolerate in close proximity were either flawed or bland. Either way, they did not detract from Bush's pre-eminence and popularity. Bush's first Chief of Staff, John Sununu, former Republican governor of New Hampshire, proved vocal and visible but flawed. Known for his incredibly high IQ and quick mind, Sununu was also known for his quick temper, acerbic nature, arrogance and impatience. None of these characteristics endeared him either to the press or the public, thus making Sununu no threat to Bush. Ultimately, Sununu's arrogance over the use of government perks and abuse of travel privileges forced him to resign.

Richard Darman, director of OMB and a former official in the Reagan administration, was also known for his bright mind and quick response, and for his arrogance and impatience at times with others, including Congressmen. Darman lacked the public appeal enjoyed by Kemp, and was described as the consummate bureaucrat, always prepared with facts and figures. He posed little or no threat to Bush's political popularity.

Despite helping Bush to win the presidency in 1988 and having worked in the Reagan White House, Jim Baker, Bush's long-time friend, was appointed Secretary of State rather than serving directly in the White House. Throughout his career, Baker appeared willing to be the person behind the scenes, bolstering the careers of others. Throughout his long-time friendship with Bush, Baker showed his willingness to serve as a court adviser with few pretensions to the 'throne' of independent power. When he received his own bailiwick as Secretary of State, Baker continued his tradition of not upstaging or overshadowing his boss. When Bush's 1992 campaign continued to flounder, Bush recalled his old time friend from the lofty affairs at the State Department to the bowels of partisan campaigning. Informal reports revealed Baker's reluctance to give up governance to captain a sinking electoral ship. Even so, Baker, the loyalist, did shift, as Bush wanted to head up the 1992 campaign.

Bush like most chief executive busybodies, favored a centralized organizational structure in order to enhance the communications and attention flowing to the mal-leader. Unlike Presidents Kennedy, Carter, Johnson and Reagan who were 'backdoored' into eventually appointing a centralizing Chief of Staff, Bush adopted this organizational structure for his White House as soon as he assumed office. When Sununu was forced to resign as Chief of Staff, he was immediately replaced with the then Secretary of Transportation, Samuel K. Skinner, Bush's former campaign director in Illinois. Although described by some as flamboyant, Skinner was much less ideological than Sununu. Skinner's experience, however, both in the Cabinet where he was in charge of the clean-up of the *Exxon Valdez* oil spill in Alaska and previously as chairman of the Regional Transportation Authority of Northeastern Illinois, was in domestic policy, which was low priority for the Bush administration.[20] Skinner presented no threat to Bush in his primary focus of foreign policy. The events that dominated the Bush presidency after Skinner became chief of staff were the Gulf

War, the collapse of the Soviet Union, and the end of the Cold War – areas in which Skinner had little expertise.

Bush at times created councils and task forces to deal with specific issues. Quayle was appointed to head up the Council on Competitiveness. Kemp was appointed to lead a task force on economic empowerment to coordinate the administration's anti-poverty programs. While the Council on Competitiveness did successfully eliminate some government regulations, by and large these councils remained outside the mainstream of decision-making in the Bush White House. William Bennett, appointed to head up the administration's anti-drug effort, was outspoken and threatened to issue report cards on the anti-drug efforts of state and local officials, but ultimately fell short of expectations.[21] Similarly, the White House Domestic Policy staff spent months analyzing proposals on welfare reform but ultimately did not make any recommendations for presidential initiatives, nor were any attempted.

Unlike Reagan, who enjoyed a Republican dominated Senate for six of his eight years in office, Bush faced Democratic majorities in both houses throughout his entire term, contributing to Bush's difficulty in passing a domestic policy. But even allowing for these problems with Congress, Bush's centralized administration and appointment of specific task forces proved inadequate to compensate for his lack of concern and attention to domestic policy. Most of the communication flows ultimately pursued through the Bush White House were not necessarily used to provide policy development or coherence, but rather to place Bush at the center of the hub–spoke communications pattern that busybodies favor. Indeed, some critics contended that Bush was more interested in being president for its own sake than for the power it presented to shape policy outcomes.

Rumor-mongering

The fourth characteristic of Bush as a mal-leader was the manipulation of rumor or gossip in his administration. If actors are the intellectual cousins of absentee leaders who 'play' at being leader without becoming emotionally involved, and perfectionists are the intellectual cousins of controllers, then gossips are the cousins of busybodies. Gossips collect information about the affairs of others, both public and private, and transmit that information to interested parties. So do busybodies. At times, busybodies seem to be predominantly megaphones, rebroadcasting and amplifying for a bigger audience titillating and often inflammatory information they have just received about others. Thus, gossips and busybodies are similar in their focus upon information transmission.

Yet unless gossips are newspaper columnists or television reporters, they have no motive beyond achieving a sense of identity with others by vicariously sharing in their experiences. Busybodies not only transmit information, but sometimes repackage that information to their own benefit, selectively omitting key information to shape subordinate opinions, affect decisions and implement preferred positions. At times busybodies exaggerate other information for the same ends.

If there is no legitimate information, less benign busybodies will at times manufacture some, by passing forward information flimsily based on fact, and at times, unfounded rumors. Busybodies are skilled at innuendo, developing impressions among others as much as from what is implied but left unspoken in an emotionally charged environment as from what is said. Invariably, these rumors work on the surface to the benefit of maintaining the busybody's authority and power, and to implement preferred positions. Once an unfounded rumor is loose, then various subordinates react differently. Their reactions to the rumor or rumors then become the basis for more information that the busybody can package, repackage and manipulate to advantage. Frequently, the rumors circulated by busybodies have one group pitted against another; being relatively weak, busybodies retain control by a 'divide and conquer' strategy.

The leadership effectiveness of busybodies is further undermined by the fact that all their information packaging and repackaging and outright rumor-mongering takes considerable time and energy. Busybodies may meet frequently with subordinates to create, quell, dispel and disavow rumors circulating through the organization. Since much of this information manipulation has no organizational purpose beyond the perpetration of busybody power, productivity begins to suffer. In later stages of organizational decline, productivity is greatly handicapped, since rumor manipulation requires written memos as well as much time spent in meetings and in massaging others.

The confirmation of Clarence Thomas, an African-American and former head of the Equal Employment Opportunity Commission in the Reagan and Bush administrations, to the US Supreme Court shocked the nation with its gossipy nature and low level of discourse. During the confirmation hearings, Anita Hill, an African-American female law professor from the University of Oklahoma, made public charges of sexual harassment against Thomas. While the attacks on Hill's credibility were led by Republicans in the Senate, particularly Arlen Specter from Pennsylvania and Orrin Hatch from Utah, the Bush administration provided support for, and made substantial contributions to keep its nomination from being rejected.

Bush's presentation of the threat of Saddam Hussein posed to the United States prior to US entry in the Gulf War was a masterful repackaging of information. Saddam was initially presented to the American public as a viable counter-threat to the villain and US enemy Ayatollah Khomeini from Iran. As such, Saddam Hussein was deserving of US aid and technology. In the repackaging, however, Saddam became a dangerous dictator as evil as Hitler.[22] The cruelty and depravity of Saddam had not changed, since he had gassed Kurds and capriciously killed competitors while he was still 'the enemy of our enemy' to the US. Furthermore, Saddam's invasion of Kuwait differed from his earlier attacks on Iran primarily in its success rather than its intent. Rather, the presentation of Saddam to the American public changed. Bush skillfully manipulated the image of Saddam in the American public to enhance his policy goals. When a poll in November 1990 showed that the public was most fearful of Saddam Hussein's nuclear capacity, the administration shifted its public discussion of the threat of Saddam to emphasize that danger. Thus, Saddam, always a sadistic dictator, was skillfully repackaged from his initial presentation as an anti-Iranian US ally to that of a madman run berserk.

Further evidence of Bush's skill at manipulating and squelching unfavorable rumors may be found in his handling of the investigation of the Iran-Contra affair. Despite being present at meetings which took crucial decisions to involve the highest levels of the US government in an illegal 'arms for hostages' deal, Bush repeatedly claimed to have been 'out of the loop' and uninvolved in these decisions. The extent of his actual involvement remains unknown. Yet toward the end of his presidential term key subordinates, including former Secretary of Defense Caspar Weinberger, were indicted on charges relating to the case.

Recognizing the negative public reaction that might result from his personal intervention, Bush refused to contemplate action in the Iran-Contra case until after the 1992 election. Only after the election did Bush decide to pardon six people charged or convicted in the case, presenting his motives as humanitarian ones. Bush argued that the pardoned people in the Iran-Contra affair had suffered enough. With the pardon, however, Bush wiped out years of investigation by special prosecutor and nemesis Lawrence Walsh. In addition to Weinberger, others pardoned included Duane Clarridge, former head of CIA covert operations in Latin America; Clair George, a former CIA official; Robert McFarlane, Reagan's former National Security Adviser; Elliot Abrams, a former Assistant Secretary of State; and Alan Fiers Jr, head of the CIA's Central American task force. Conveniently, Bush also wiped out any potential for public hearings on whether his contention of non-involvement was false, effectively smashing rumors that he had been more actively involved in Iran-Contra than he acknowledged.[23]

Bush election campaigns, both in 1988 and 1992, also illustrate the rumor-mongering and 'divide and conquer' facet of Bush's character. Both campaigns sunk to new lows in attacking politics and negative advertising. In the 1988 campaign, Bush vigorously attacked his Democratic opponent, Massachusetts Governor Michael Dukakis, on the Massachusetts' furlough program. The facts were rather more complex. The furlough program had been instituted when Frances Sargent, a Republican, was governor, and continued during the leadership of conservative Democrat Edward King who had defeated Dukakis after his first term. Nevertheless, it was Dukakis who was singled out by Bush for giving 'a generous vacation' to 59 criminals convicted of violent crime.[24] When a Bush campaign focus group found that crime was a sensitive issue with the public, Bush accused Dukakis of being soft on crime. The campaign put forth the Willie Horton television advertisement which played on popular fear of crime in a racist manner. The television message emphasized that at least one person on a furlough during Dukakis's governorship had committed additional crimes.

Bush derided Dukakis as a technocrat who knew how to run the trains on time but didn't know where they were going. No environmentalist himself as the administration's subsequent stand against a biodiversity treaty at the Rio conference proved, Bush attacked Dukakis's record in that area with a television advertisement highlighting pollution problems in the Boston Harbor. The Bush campaign also succeeded in inflaming two non-issues into attacks on Dukakis. The first was Governor Dukakis's veto of a bill requiring all public school teachers in Massachusetts to start the school day by leading their classes with the Pledge of Allegiance. Bush used this example of gubernatorial veto to attack Dukakis's patriotism. The second was Dukakis's membership in the American Civil Liberties Union, which Bush used to paint Dukakis as a McGovern-type 'card-carrying liberal' outside of the mainstream of American politics.

In 1992, Bush was deprived of his 1988 mastermind of negative campaigning and attacking advertisements, Lee Atwater. Atwater, who had developed a brain tumor, died in 1991, expressing regret before his death for his electoral tactics. The Bush campaign attempted negative attacks again in 1992, but less successfully. The entry, then exit, then re-entry of Ross Perot as a privately funded independent candidate brought confusion. Both major party nominees angled to attract Perot voters, and were reluctant to attack Perot directly. Bush, however, did attack Democratic nominee Bill Clinton with vigor. Bush was aided in his efforts early in 1992 by a public declaration from Genifer Flowers that she had been Clinton's lover. Clinton recovered politically from that setback, however, with a nationally televised response on the show *Sixty Minutes*. Bush then began to attack Clinton's patriotism on the grounds that Clinton had avoided military service during the Vietnam war. Pressure was also placed on Clinton to confess that he had used marijuana. Clinton, however, withstood these attacks and his popularity continued to rise in the polls.

In 1992 the Democratic Party Convention in New York in July, with its emphasis on unity and reform policies, provided a stark contrast to the Republican Party Convention in Houston in August. The theme of the Republican Convention was divisive – emphasizing traditional family values, criticisms of alternative lifestyles, and attacks on Clinton and the Democrats, while de-emphasizing policy proposals, especially on the economy. The presidential debates also presented to the public a contrast between Clinton discussing policy and Bush attacking Clinton on character and leadership. Ultimately, Bush's 'divide and conquer' strategy failed to restore his popularity that had been at an all-time high for modern presidents immediately after the Gulf War. Bush's negative and disorderly campaign attempts to use rumor and innuendo to derail Clinton ultimately failed, and Bush lost the White House after one term.

Hail fellow well met

The fifth and final characteristic of the busybody mal-leader is that of affability. Unlike other mal-leaders who appear to be sullen and angry most of the time, or who are unavailable and unapproachable, busybodies are both accessible and approachable. Busybodies are relatively charming and affable on the surface, and appear to be good listeners. They must have these characteristics in order to make interactions with them a pleasant experience. And interactions must be pleasant so that people will interact, providing the attention and gossipy information that busybodies crave. Busybodies usually have their door open. When even lowly subordinates call to get appointments with comparatively high-level busybodies, they are able to do so with relative ease, since busybodies are afraid to deny an audience to any supplicant. They never know, by such denial, what key information they will miss, who is fighting with whom, and indeed, whether or not malicious rumors are circulating about themselves. Bush's free and frequent interaction with White House press corps, and his high number of press conferences illustrate his 'open door' policy.

Bush also exuded the affable sociability that busybodies frequently exhibit. Unlike earlier presidents, especially Nixon and Carter who appeared aloof and detached, Bush was warm and friendly. Nor did Bush generate the personal animosity of these former presidents. His nickname of 'Poppy' conveyed an avuncular figure. His popular image was one of someone who liked people. He conveyed the chumminess of someone who wanted a 'kinder, gentler America', brought about by 'a thousand points of light' from simultaneously spontaneous acts of private volunteerism. Duffy and Goodgame describe Bush as exceptionally well mannered, generous and considerate of others.[25] At both the White House and Camp David Bush frequently surrounded himself with people in a gregarious manner.

Bush's affable and open nature was further demonstrated in the manner by which he dealt with the increasingly vocal and strident right wing of his own party. Bush chose a strategy of appeasement through appointment rather than open combat and confrontation.[26] The right wing of the Republican Party with which Bush had to deal had three identifiable factions: the 'Old Right' associated with William F. Buckley concerned with law and order issues and composed predominantly of upper-middle-class people dissatisfied with US institutions; the 'New Right' associated with Richard Viguerie and others, financed by direct mail campaigns, and supportive of supply-side economics and traditional morality; and the 'Christian Right' or 'Religious Right' linked to the Reverend Jerry Falwell and Pat Robertson eager to insert religious values into public life.

Bush sought to appease these factions by placing members of the right wing in highly visible positions. Among highly placed conservatives were Dan Quayle as Vice President and John Sununu as White House Chief of Staff. The attempt to appoint John Tower, a former Republican senator from Texas with Old Right links, as Secretary of Defense ran foul of personal scandal linked to Tower in the Senate confirmation process. Dick Cheney, the replacement nominee, also had solid conservative credentials. Other leading appointments of right-wing Republicans included Dick Thornburgh as Attorney General, Richard Darman as Director of the Office of Management and Budget, and William Bennett as anti-drug crusader. Jack Kemp as Secretary of HUD was initially claimed by the right wing but later was rejected from the fold when he dismissed as failures the conservative remedies for urban problems.

Nor did Bush ignore moderates in his appeasement-through-appointment strategy. Appointments from the moderate Republican faction included Louis Sullivan as Secretary of Health and Human Services, Jim Baker as Secretary of State, Nicholas Brady as Secretary of Treasury, and Robert Mosbacher as Secretary of Commerce. Some appointments below the Secretary level even came from the almost defunct liberal wing of the

Republican party, including Bryce Harlow at Treasury and Bruce Glebe as Director of the US Information Agency.[27]

THE IMPACT OF BUSH'S BUSYBODY STYLE ON WHITE HOUSE MANAGEMENT

Bush's 'busybody' leadership style had an important, and ultimately debilitating, effect on the operation of the White House. Five aspects of this impact stand out.

Policy drift and indecisiveness

The first impact of the busybody style is policy drift. Busybodies think they make tough decisions, but in fact rarely buck majority opinion within their organizations, for to do so might jeopardize the very group membership they so crave and need. Thus busybodies are almost never willing to use the full powers of their office to implement a controversial decision.

Bush similarly failed to use the powers of the presidency to set a new direction for US policy. Bush failed to provide decisive leadership on key issues confronting the US – including dealing with the deficit, rebuilding the cities, acknowledging the growing disparity of income and wealth between rich and poor, confronting the growing educational deficit between the US and other countries, reinvesting in American infrastructure to halt declines in productivity, and reshaping the economy to improve export capacity. Rather, Bush continued the growing drift associated with the supply-side policies of the Reagan administration. By the 1992 presidential campaign, Bush's failure to establish a social and economic agenda became apparent. He argued that he would develop a plan during his second administration, but a disillusioned American public, eager for change, did not give him that chance.

Growing isolation from public concerns

The second impact of the busybody style is disillusioned isolation. Despite all their apparent openness, busybodies do not develop a 'walk around' style of management where they walk around their organizations and constituencies unannounced, to give shy, busy or otherwise involved employees and constituents a chance to reach them, and to observe first hand what is going on. What is going on in the organization in terms of actual work is more boring to the busybody than the information, gossip about personal peccadilloes and worse, and rumors and reports on sometimes raging factional battles that naturally stream through his door if he just stays in his office and encourages such flows. Thus, busybodies may lose touch with what is actually going on the organization.

Despite his extensive foreign travels, Bush did not venture into the federal bureaucracy to determine what was going on, or to various constituencies among citizens to keep his finger on the public pulse. Never in touch with the poor and underclasses, Bush, under urging from Kemp, agreed to give a speech advocating some of Kemp's anti-poverty ideas in February of 1991. Yet Bush rebuffed Kemp's idea that he give the speech to an audience of poor people, and Bush delivered the address instead to a group of well-paid lobbyists in a Washington hotel ballroom, with a response of stony silence.[28]

Unlike his successor, Bill Clinton, Bush did not embrace town meetings or other forums that would bring him in contact with average people. On one occasion, he indicated ignorance of how grocery store supermarket check-outs work, a slip widely reported in the press. By 1992, the Clinton campaign was skillfully exploiting popular culture outlets such as MTV and various talk shows. The Bush campaign, by contrast, after the loss of Atwater, had no well placed aides who knew popular television shows and music. Bush's many and frequent interactions with peer world leaders did not compensate for his loss of touch with his own constituencies at home. Nor did his frenetic schedule result in a walk-around management style where he could observe ordinary people living ordinary lives confronting real problems.

Nor did Bush seem to have a firm grasp on the full cost of the Savings and Loan crisis and develop strategies for dealing with it. He backed away from an earlier proposal to make beneficiaries of Savings and Loans companies pay for the bailout through a fee on deposits. Instead, in 1989, he signed into law a comprehensive plan to use tax dollars to pay over $150 billion for the bailout. By 1990, the General Accounting Office was estimating the cost of the bailout would be over

$500 billion. Coupled with the involvement of Bush's son in one failed S & L, the administration's response contributed to the image of a president willing to take from average citizens to finance buyouts and bailouts for more affluent investors.

A deficit in specific policy expertise

The third impact of the busybody style is lack of policy expertise. Most busybodies have never been interested enough in the substance of the work of their organizations to acquire essential skills. Later their own schedules of holding court over complaining employees prevents them from having the time to keep up with professional developments in the field to the same extent that other leaders would. Busybodies consequently lack the technical skills to evaluate new product proposals and other proposed innovations fully, as well as the emotional fortitude to risk embracing new ideas even if the outcomes of such evaluations were favorable.

Despite his many jobs in the government and politics, Bush developed few domestic policy skills. Some of his jobs were partisan, such as Republican Party Chair from 1973 to 1974, and contributed to his busybody tendencies of communication. With the exception of his election to Congress between 1967 and 1971, most of Bush's other major jobs were appointed and in the area of international affairs. He served as chief US liaison to China between 1974 and 1975, as Director of the Central Intelligence Agency between 1976 and 1977, and as Reagan's Vice President from 1981 to 1989. Yet despite his background in international affairs and his willingness to take credit for the collapse of communism, Bush presented few ideas for how to deal with it, or the subsequent ethnic conflict and cleansing that the end of the Cold War unleashed. Unlike Carter who fostered ground-breaking peace talks in the Middle East, Bush put forth no vision or strategy for how to increase stability in the region, other than going to war with Saddam Hussein. Nor did Bush have a plan for how to deal with the disintegration of the Soviet Union, the shift to market economies in eastern Europe, and the warfare in Yugoslavia. Bush talked about a New World Order but did not present the United States with a vision of what it would or should entail or what should be the role of the US within it.

**Misuse of information channels and loss of public
confidence**

The fourth impact of the busybody style is in the area of public
confidence. Busybody-led organizations are often colorful
places where everyone seems *busy* feeding communication
channels, but the information flowing through the channels
may not contribute to productivity, may be irrelevant to organizational problems, and worse, may even be destructive. The
use of State Department files during the 1992 campaign to
check on Clinton's travels to the Soviet Union while a Rhodes
Scholar shows the extent to which formal information channels could be abused in the Bush administration.

By 1992, public confidence in government had plummeted.
A Time/CNN poll found that 63 per cent of the American
public had little or no confidence that government officials
talk straight, and 75 per cent felt there was less honesty in government than there had been a decade ago. The public was
generally cynical about politicians, however, with 40 per cent
of respondents saying that George Bush did not usually tell the
truth, compared to 36 per cent who said the same thing about
Clinton.[29] Seventy-one per cent believed Bush's 'no new taxes'
pledge in 1988 was a conscious lie rather than a required
reversal in policy. Sixty-three per cent thought Bush was lying
about his claims to be 'out of the loop' when the Reagan
administration decided to sell arms for hostages. Thirty per
cent believed that his denial of an affair with a staff member
was a lie.

Abortion and the Clarence Thomas appointment were two
other areas where Bush was viewed as fudging the truth. Bush
had regularly declared that 'my position on abortion hasn't
changed.'[30] Yet Bush backed the 1973 *Roe* v. *Wade* decision
when he ran for president in 1980. He moved to the right as
Vice President under Reagan during the 1980s, and in order to
curry favor with GOP conservatives, eventually opposed abortion and *Roe* v. *Wade*. In nominating Thomas to the Supreme
Court in 1991, Bush insisted that Thomas was 'the best man'
for the job. But Bush's own aides admitted that Thomas's qualifications were modest and he would not have been considered
for the nomination had he not been a conservative black
Republican.

Intra-party and organizational conflict

The fifth and final impact of the busybody style is on organizational relations. As time passes and the malcontents figure out how pliant and indecisive a busybody truly is, factional infighting and conflict increases. Factions know the busybody will not punish other competing factions for misbehavior or inflicted injustices, but similarly they also know that the busybody will not punish them. In fact, unlike street fighters, busybodies do not traffic in rewards and punishments, but rather are prone to treat everyone, regardless of merit or damage, gingerly and equally. Eventually, organizations headed by busybodies become a free-for-all. Like absentee leaders, busybodies create a power vacuum that allows malcontents to perform as they like, and eventually attracts them. The power vacuum created by the absentee leader arises from detachment and distance. The power vacuum created by the busybody arises from indecisiveness. Nobody benefits from the conflict in the long run, for it rapidly becomes destructive, with no strong leadership to counter personally aggrandizing employees and interest groups. Productivity plummets. Despite the atmosphere of constant busyness, the activities of subordinates are increasingly devoted to covering and 'kicking asses', and everyone loses.

Within the Bush administration, tensions erupted that frustrated coherent policy development. A primary tension emerged between Darman and Kemp that stymied the development of urban policy. Darman also battled with Nicholas Brady at Treasury for the heart and soul of Bush's budget policy. Sununu clashed with Darman and others. Sam Skinner, Sununu's replacement as Chief of Staff had but a brief honeymoon in this job before conflict erupted under him as well.[31] President Bush, when appointing Skinner, simultaneously asked Gene Croisant, then an executive vice president at RJR Nabisco and a long-time friend of Skinner's, to do a comprehensive review of White House operations. After eight weeks, Skinner finally had to ask his old friend, who seemed more interested in developing the ideal management structure than examining the daily tasks involved in running the White House, to leave. Skinner stated his intentions to replace some of the weak links in the White House staff, but eventually ended up adding on another layer of management, including Domestic Policy Counselor Clayton Yeutter, Deputy Chief of Staff W. Henson Moore, and public relations liaison Sherrie Rollins. Furthermore, he chose to leave disgruntled incumbents in place rather than remove them and streamline a chaotic management structure.

Because Skinner was more inclusive than Sununu, more people seemed to be issuing orders, yet few people seemed to be carrying them out, and little follow-through occurred. Skinner seemed overwhelmed by the sheer volume of problems he confronted as the focal point of Bush's centrally organized White House, which led to procedural errors. One example was that of Skinner taking four days to return a telephone call to New Mexico Republican Senator Pete Domenici, one of the President's most important allies in Congress. Criticism of Skinner grew and conflict developed over how he was handling the job. Critics contended that Skinner viewed himself as a corporate salesman selling a valued product – President George Bush – while market research (political polls) showed otherwise: that the public was disappointed with Bush and his policy drift. Critics contended that Bush needed more handling, packaging and marketing. Yet Bush himself vacillated on how much handling he wanted, promoting it one day and rejecting it the next, contributing to the growing conflict over mismanagement in the White House and in his 1992 campaign.

The conflict within the White House over how to handle Bush paled, however, before the conflict that erupted within the Republican Party in the primaries. First, Bush fended off an overstated threat from the right wing Neo-Nazi David Duke in Louisiana, whose presidential and senatorial candidacies fizzled. Yet Duke was just a forerunner for the most formidable candidacy of right winger Pat Buchanan. Conflict within the party and the challenge to a sitting president weakened Bush, just as Edward Kennedy's challenge to Jimmy Carter in 1980 weakened Carter in his race against Ronald Reagan. Although Buchanan did not win any primaries, his dogged determination in attacking and denigrating Bush's policies contributed to public dissatisfaction with administration performance.

CONCLUSION

The description of George Bush as a busybody mal-leader is not a perfect fit. Supporters of Bush may argue that his success in the Gulf War and advances in international affairs were impressive. Further, Bush seemed to be serving on the 'presidential watch' when the bill for Reagan's failed supply-side policies was coming due in the form of deteriorated productivity, growing deficits, foreign-financed national debt, increasing unemployment, and declining living standards for the poor and middle class. Bush was dealt a rough hand in the economy. Yet his busybody tendencies contributed to administrative drift and policy inaction in crucial areas confronting the public. Ultimately the voters agreed with administration critics, since pundits viewed Clinton's election as more of a rejection of Bush than a positive embrace of Clinton. In the final poll that all presidents care about – that on election day – Bush lost his bid for a second term. Ultimately, for George Bush, being a well-traveled affable hail-fellow-well-met was not enough.

NOTES

1. Robert B. Reich, *The Work of Nations: Preparing Ourselves for Twenty-first Century Capitalism* (New York: Alfred A. Knopf, 1991); Paul Kennedy, *The Rise and Fall of Great Powers* (New York: Random House, 1987); Marcia Lynn Whicker and Raymond A. Moore, *Making America Competitive* (New York: Praeger, 1988); Kevin Phillips, *The Politics of Rich and Poor: Wealth and the American Electorate in the Reagan Aftermath* (New York: Random House, 1990).
2. Elliot Jaques and Stephen D. Clement, *Executive Leadership: A Practical Guide to Managing Complexity* (Cambridge, Mass.: Basil Blackwell, 1991); Philip B. Crosby, *Leading: The Art of Becoming an Executive* (New York: McGraw-Hill, 1990); James L. Lundy, *Lead, Follow, or Get Out of the Way* (San Diego, Calif.: Avant Books, 1986); Peter Koestenbaum, *Leadership: The Inner Side of Greatness* (San Francisco: Jossey-Bass, 1991); Joe D. Batten, *Tough-Minded Leadership* (New York: AMACON, 1989); Michael Maccoby, *Why Work: Motivating and Leading the New Generation* (New York: Simon & Schuster, Touchstone Books, 1988).
3. Warren Bennis, *Why Leaders Can't Lead: The Unconscious Conspiracy Continues* (San Francisco: Jossey-Bass, 1989); Manfred F.R. Kets de Vries, *The Irrational Executive: Psychoanalytic Explorations in Management*

(New York: International Universities Press, 1984); M.F.R. Kets de Vries and D. Miller, *Unstable At The Top* (New York: Mentor, 1987); Alistair Mant, *Leaders We Deserve* (Oxford: Martin Robertson, 1983); Leonard W. Doob, *Personality, Power and Authority* (Westport, Conn.: Greenwood Press, 1983).

4. P. Hershey and K.H. Blanchard, *The Management of Organizational Behavior*, 4th edn. (Englewood Cliffs, NJ: Prentice-Hall, 1984); R.R. Blake and J.S. Mouton, *The Managerial Grid* (Houston, Tex.: Gulf, 1964); R. Likert, *The Human Organization: Its Management and Value* (New York: McGraw-Hill, 1967); J. Misume, *The Behavioral Science of Leadership: An Interdisciplinary Japanese Research Program* (Ann Arbor, Mich.: University of Michigan, 1985); E.A. Fleishman and E.F. Harris, 'Patterns of Behavior Related to Employee Grievances and Turnover', *Personnel Psychology*, Vol. 15, 1962, pp. 43–56.

5. James MacGregor Burns, *Leadership* (New York: Harper & Row, 1978); see also B.M. Bass, *Leadership and Performance Beyond Expectations* (New York: Free Press, 1985).

6. Haynes Johnson, *Sleepwalking through History: America in the Reagan Years* (New York: W.W. Norton, 1991); Ann Wroe, *Lives, Lies and the Iran-Contra Affair* (London: I.B. Tauris, 1991).

7. Marcia Lynn Whicker, 'Managing and Organizing the Reagan White House', in Dilys M. Hill, Raymond A. Moore and Phil Williams (eds), *The Reagan Presidency: An Incomplete Revolution?* (London: Macmillan, 1990).

8. Larry Berman and Bruce W. Jentleson, 'Bush and the Post-Cold-War World: New Challenges for American Leadership', in Colin Campbell SJ and Bert A. Rockman (eds), *The Bush Presidency: First Appraisals*, (Chatham, NJ: Chatham House, 1991), pp. 93–128.

9. Ibid., p. 99

10. Michael R. Beshchloss and Strobe Talbott, *At The Highest Levels: The Inside Story of the End of the Cold War* (Boston: Little, Brown, 1993), p. 260.

11. Mary E. Stuckey and Frederick J. Antczak, 'Governance as Political Theater: George Bush and the MTV Presidency', in Ryan J. Barilleaux and Mary E. Stuckey (eds), *Leadership and the Bush Presidency: Prudence or Drift in an Era of Change?* (Westport, Conn.: Praeger, 1992), pp. 24–36.

12. Stuckey and Antczak, op. cit., p. 25.

13. Peter Goldman and Tom Matthews, *The Quest for the Presidency 1988* (New York: Simon & Schuster/Touchstone, 1989), pp. 315–330.

14. Ibid., p. 315.

15. James P. Pfiffner, 'Presidential Policy Making and the Gulf War', in Marcia Lynn Whicker, James P. Pfiffner, and Raymond A. Moore (eds), *The Presidency and the Persian Gulf War* (Westport, Conn.: Praeger, 1993), pp. 3–24.

16. Bob Woodward, *The Commanders* (New York: Simon & Schuster, 1991), pp. 311–313.

17. Jason De Parle, 'How Jack Kemp Lost the War on Poverty', *The New York Times Magazine*, 28 February 1993, pp. 26 ff.

18. Goldman and Matthews, op. cit., p. 315.

19. De Parle, op. cit., p. 58.
20. William A. Degregorio, *The Complete Book of U.S. Presidents*, 3rd edn. (New York: Barricade Books, 1991), pp. 686–687.
21. Paul J. Quirk, 'Domestic Policy: Divided Government and Cooperative Presidential Leadership', in Colin Campbell SJ and Bert A. Rockman (eds), op. cit., pp. 69–92.
22. Marcia Lynn Whicker, 'The Case Against the War', in Whicker, Pfiffner and Moore (eds), op. cit., pp. 111–129.
23. Evan Thomas with Bob Cohn and Ann McDonald, 'Pardon Me', *Newsweek*, 4 January 1993, pp. 14–18.
24. Elizabeth Drew, *Election Journal* (New York: William Morrow, 1989), pp. 304–305.
25. Michael Duffy and Dan Goodgame, *Marching in Place: The Status Quo Presidency of George Bush* (New York: Simon & Schuster, 1992).
26. Matthew C. Moen and Kenneth T. Palmer, '"Poppy" and His Conservative Passengers', in Barilleaux and Stuckey (eds), op. cit., pp. 133–146.
27. Ibid., pp. 137–138.
28. De Parle, op. cit., p. 47.
29. Paul Gray, 'Lies, Lies, Lies', *Time*, 5 October 1992, pp. 32 ff.
30. Ibid., p. 34.
31. Majorie Williams, 'An Eagle Scout Gets His Wings Clipped: The Unhappy Brief Tale of Sam Skinner as White House Chief of Staff', *Washington Post National Weekly Edition*, 15–21 June 1992, pp. 6–9.

3 The President and Congress
Michael Foley

When Bush entered the White House, it was quite evident that he wished to assume the traditional role of the contemporary presidency. By background and temperament he was a man of government. 'I don't hate government', he said in his acceptance speech to the 1988 Republican party convention. 'I believe public service is honorable.'[1] He was convinced that he possessed the necessary credentials for his conception of the trusteeship presidency. He was a consummate Washington insider, with extensive experience in government and an impressive network of allies and colleagues. After eight years of conspicuously loyal service as vice president, he now wished to ameliorate the strident zeal of Reaganism in favour of a 'kinder and gentler nation'.[2] His moderate Republicanism prompted him to mix consensus and consolidation with mild initiatives in areas like education, child day-care and environmental protection. But the chances of such patrician obligations being fulfilled were heavily circumscribed by three specific constraints – all of which were felt most strongly in his relationships with Congress and all of which would have a direct bearing on Bush's professional and public reputation as president.

First, Congress remained dominated by the Democratic Party which had just been stung by its third presidential election defeat in a row. The party was particularly aggrieved by the manner of its defeat. Its nominee Michael Dukakis had not only lost an opinion poll lead of 18 points, but was widely thought to have done so by Bush's negative campaigning techniques, in which the Vice President had smeared the Democrats as being soft on crime and weak on patriotism. Reagan's victory in 1980 could be attributed to a general movement of opinion in response to the stagflation of the late 1970s. But Bush's win, to the Democrats, was more attributable to an overly aggressive

44

and even dirty campaign in which the opposition party had been plastered with the odium of 'government'. In their critique of Bush's legitimacy, the Democrats could point to the huge scale of ticket-splitting which had reproduced another Democratic Congress. Bush even had to suffer the minor disgrace of being an incoming president who not only failed to bring at least one chamber under the control of his own party, but who entered the White House with a net loss of Republican seats in both the House (–3) and the Senate (–1).

Directly after his election, Bush sought to reassure the legislature that he would not be in a 'Congress-bashing mode'.[3] He had very little alternative. For the next four years he would be dependent upon the Democratic Party in the matter of both legislation and public reputation. The President's plea for bipartisanship was clearly evident in his inaugural address:

> To my friends – and yes, I do mean friends – in the loyal opposition – and yes, I mean loyal: I put out my hand. I am putting out my hand to you, Mr Speaker. I am putting out my hand to you, Mr Majority Leader. For this is the thing: This is the age of the offered hand ... The American people await action. They didn't send us here to bicker. They ask us to rise above the merely partisan. 'In crucial things, unity' – and this, my friends, is crucial.[4]

Bush's desperation for a rapprochement was not only born out of the disparity in party seats but out of a change of attitudes. During the Reagan years, the Congressional Democrats had become accustomed to a form of guerrilla warfare with the White House that had given them the experience of, and the appetite for, challenging the presidency on a range of issues. As a consequence, following the high-water mark of 1982, Reagan's success in Congress had plummeted from an 82.4 per cent level down to 65.8 per cent in 1984 and to 47.4 per cent in 1988.[5]

To make matters worse for Bush, the Congressional Democrats were becoming a far more cohesive entity. This was partly because of a growing convergence in Southern and Northern Democratic constituencies and partly because of a deliberate effort by an increasingly resourceful leadership to close ranks during the years of Reagan's declining influence. In 1987–88 (i.e. 100th Congress), the Democratic leaders in the House, for example, exploited its revamped whip system and the chamber's improved technical facilities not merely to draw up its own set of policies, but to 'enact into law the entire agenda, often over the president's objections and sometimes over his veto.'[6] This solidarity in the Democratic ranks, alongside the concomitant decline in the conservative coalition of Republicans and conservative Democrats, meant that Bush would be required to rely upon genuine and wide-ranging bipartisanship for his objectives, rather than on splinter groups of dissident Democrats Unfortunately for Bush, he would experience the full force of the paradox of required bipartisanship – namely that at the very time when a president's resources are low enough for him to need bipartisan support, they are also sufficiently depleted to make a genuine condition of bipartisanship very unlikely.

The second restraint was the federal deficit. By accident or design, the financial indiscipline of the 1980s had generated the ultimate financial discipline of debt. Despite protestations to the contrary, Reagan had always been quite amenable to the existence of the deficit. This was because, in the absence of new revenues, the deficit prevented the onset of major new programmes into a zero-sum game of financial allocation. As the traditional spending party, the Democrats were confronted with the prospect of a Reaganite veto on expenditure long after Reagan's departure from the White House. The only practical alternative was to have a president who would not veto revenue increases and would share responsibility for higher taxes. In the 1988 election campaign, however, Bush had tied himself unequivocally to 'no new taxes' – thereby tying his hands and foreclosing expenditure options. By the same token, Bush was aware that the deficit was a standing indictment of Washington government and that as a new president he could suffer political damage if he were not seen to be actively involved in trying to reduce it. Apart from the fact that Bush had modest spending plans of his own, and that the existence of the Gramm-Rudman-Hollings Act threatened arbitrary and politically dangerous reductions, the President knew that the public issue of the budget was dominated by the shadow of the deficit and the need to address it. Bush, therefore, was doubly limited by the deficit. He was inhibited by its magnitude. But he was also prompted by a sense of presidential responsibility to react to the evident need to bring the deficit under control.

Bearing in mind his weak party base and the necessity of negotiating closely with Democratic leaders on the deficit, Bush was aware of a third constraint in his relationship with Congress. This was the 'no surrender' spirit of the Republican right wing which was strongly resistant to any retreat from the Reaganite orthodoxy and was intent upon a far more partisan posture against the Democrats in Congress. The right wing not only prided itself on being the conscience of the party but also its energy source in the shape of party activism and fund-raising. Savouring its identity as a group outside the modern mainstream yet wholly dedicated to American values, it had always distrusted Bush as an Ivy League 'insider' prone to compromise and, therefore, to appeasement. While Bush was intent upon coming out from Reagan's shadow and establishing his own presidency in the name of pragmatic rather than conviction politics, he was also aware that he was being eyed suspiciously by the right wing. If he had any doubts about the limitations of his own mandate, they were swiftly dispelled in March 1989 with the election of Newt Gingrich (R – Georgia) as Republican chief whip in the House of Representatives. A strident conservative with a reputation for being a backbench 'bomb-thrower', Gingrich won the post by promising an altogether more activist and robust form of legislative leadership that would convey the frustrations of the minority party both to the Democrats and to the White House.

Congress, for its part, was also conscious of the need to protect itself from unfavourable publicity. Given its multiple composition and its argumentative spirit, Congress tended to suffer from adverse public reaction whenever Washington government was perceived to be in a state of indecision. The Congressional Democrats, therefore, were keen to maintain their initiative in shaping the public agenda and in forming major policy, but not to the extent of issuing a broad and direct challenge to President Bush. It wanted to avoid being held responsible for any breakdown in government. This was partly born out of a conventional impulse to afford a honeymoon period of settling in for a new president, but it was also derived from a keen appreciation of the Congressional Democrats' own very public weaknesses.

Since the mid-1980s, Congressional Democrats had become increasingly associated with large and powerful economic interests. If the 1970s had been marked by strong Congressional action on price controls, pollution regulation, consumer safety and occupational health, the early 1980s witnessed a reactive rise in organized conservative resistance to federal regulation. Corporations and trade associations began a highly effective campaign to reverse their eroded structural advantages in public policy-making by an insurgency movement of grass-roots lobbying organized by newly formed political action committees (PACs). Many corporations switched tactics away from giving blanket support to incumbents and changed to investing in an aggressive drive to defeat the Democrats. The Democrats' response was to try and reverse this trend towards a business-regenerated Republican party by using their access in Washington to bring back business support. As PAC money began to flow back to the incumbents, the Congressional Democrats became much more closely enmeshed with special interests and with the ethical ambiguities of campaign finance and influence trading in what was becoming an increasingly deregulated market-place of business activity.

By 1988, Democratic incumbents in the House had come to rely on PAC contributions for over half of their campaign finance. The dependency relationship of Democrats with special interests had 'produced a political and ethical crisis in the Democrat party'.[7] It was a crisis which opened the party to Republican charges that it was an electoral organization geared less to achieving a public mandate and more to being a 'vehicle of groups seeking special breaks'.[8] At the end of the 1980s, polls showed that the Democrats had all but lost their traditional leads on questions such as which party better represented the working people of America and which party could be trusted most with education and the problems of unemployment. The electoral invulnerability of individual Democratic incumbents, therefore, was matched by the vulnerability of their public reputation as a collective entity in Congress. Despite being the 'out' party at the presidential-national level, its symbiotic relationship with Washington and its sub-governments and clienteles meant that it was permanently in danger of being characterized not merely as an 'in' party, but *the* party of government privilege.[9] Its potential for precisely this form of public disparagement was realized at the very outset of the new Bush administration. Investigations into the mammoth Savings and Loan scandal brought to light direct evidence of complicity amongst Democratic members of Congress in the governmental laxity that had led to the mismanagement of over $250 billion of investors' funds. The stock of the Congressional Democrats declined even further with the leadership's public recognition of the need to tighten the membership's rules of ethical conduct; with the announcement that speaker Jim Wright would himself be investigated by the House Ethics Committee; and by the membership's intention to accept a 51 per cent Congressional pay increase without a public vote. However much Democrat partisans may have wanted Congress to enhance its political integrity, such an objective had to be persistently conditioned by a realistic acknowledgement that its public reputation would often be at the mercy of charges of individual irresponsibility and collective misconduct.

Both Bush and Congress, therefore, proceeded with great caution. Each knew that their electoral mandates were of a very marginal nature and that they would have to cooperate with one another to achieve anything of substance. The Congressional Democrats were keen to hold Bush to the social agenda that he advanced in the presidential campaign. They often sought to push him to accept much stronger legislation and/or higher expenditures than he had envisaged. This left the President with the decision to compromise under duress, or to opt for a politically embarrassing veto, or to accept the contested legislation and undermine both his own position on taxes and his relationship with his party's vociferous right wing. On the other hand the Democrats had to be careful over provoking a veto and being held publicly responsible for losing legislation by a president with ready access to the national media. Likewise, they had to guard against prevailing over a president who might effectively dissociate himself from the offending legislation and leave Congress with the responsibility for breaking the budget and increasing the deficit.

On the other side, George Bush had to provide the impression of purposeful presidential government at work within the inhibiting framework of dual party control. He had to work with the knowledge that attempts to placate the Democratic leadership might militate against his own party base – even to the extent of rupturing the Republican Congressional forces and of making him even more dependent upon Democratic goodwill. Despite such problems, President Bush had to resort to sustained negotiations with Congress, in order to strengthen his claims to responsible executive leadership. He had very little choice in the circumstances. Not to have done so would have ceded the policy initiative to Congress and would have wholly subverted his chosen role of providing responsible government.

The net effect of this mutual circumspection was a condition that might best be termed the 'active engagement of thin ends'. Ronald Reagan used to lead with the broad end of his ideological wedges. His budgets were normally declared to be 'dead on arrival' in Congress and he effectively dissociated himself from the subsequent negotiated settlements. Bush, by contrast, was a professional pragmatic Washingtonian who preferred open channels to confrontation. As a consequence, he committed himself to the cause of bipartisanship with energy and apparent conviction. He busied himself in breaking down the barriers between the White House and the Congress. He played sports with members, attended their fund-raisers, supported their campaigns and made trips to the Capitol building – even going so far on one occasion as appearing unannounced on the floor of the Senate. He seemed intent on compensating for a weak party position by developing new sources of political obligation and by exploiting every contact he had built up in his professional life as a Washingtonian.[10]

The chief problem of Bush's dedication to open channels was that it came to be seen as less of a strategy and more of an objective in its own right. Even the limited agenda that Bush set for himself, and that arguably was the only sustainable agenda in a coalition of minimal bipartisanship, was so thin in substance that it led to speculation as to whether Bush had any serious agenda at all. The situation was exacerbated by his frequent shifts of position, the mixed signals coming from the White House, and the administration's ambiguity over priorities. So variable was the president's sense of direction that at the beginning of 1992 Kerry Mullins and Aaron Wildavsky were prompted to draw the following conclusion: 'It is easy to lose track of the numerous times President Bush has changed his mind on public policy and/or the reasons for it ... The number of policy reversals is much greater than commonly recognized.'[11] Once again, it is possible to argue that flexibility is a requisite feature of bargaining with such limited resources. Nonetheless, Bush's 'flip-flops' on policy led increasingly to the conclusion that the President was not so much pursuing a course of flexible response as betraying an absence of genuine convictions. While he built up a reputation for knowing how to press the right buttons in Washington to evoke a response, he did not appear to know what he wanted to achieve with this political facility. One Congressman likened the President 'to the little dog who chased the bus: once he caught it, he didn't know what to do with it.'[12]

As the early bipartisanship reverted into more direct confrontation, a less generous construction of Bush's behaviour laid emphasis on the achievement of malaise by design. It was strongly suspected that Bush's commitment to his social agenda was only skin deep and that its real function was to outflank the Democrats with a minimum of resources. Although the President was intent upon associating himself with grand initiatives in an area like education, his pledge of 'no new taxes' effectively meant that very little money would be available to back up any new programmes. As one White House official explained in 1991:

> The key around here has always been stopping the Democrats. If we couldn't stop them, we tried the next best thing: turning the Democratic drive for reforms into Republican alternatives. We wanted to try to turn an apparent political liability into something we could claim credit for.[13]

Bush's ambiguity, therefore, was not tactical in nature so much as strategic in its design to produce a way of simultaneously refuting and affirming the Reaganite legacy.

Congress too was actively engaged in limited ends and for similar reasons. Like the President, members of Congress also experienced a lack of mandate for change. They found Bush's energetic vacuousness difficult to contend with because it would often have the effect of devolving responsibility for substance into Congress. Congress not only found it difficult to lead, it had a strong self-interest in not even attempting to lead. It was intent upon keeping the President tightly engaged in the policy process, in order to ensure a greater distribution of political responsibility for any action. Against a background of a steady stream of ethics scandals, and with polls always showing a tendency for the public to regard Congress as more blameworthy for government deadlock than the presidency,[14] members of Congress had to remain cautious. It was prudent for them to adhere to the same dimensions of limited and negotiable ends as that of a Republican president with a self-evidently modest agenda and with a political advantage in minimal governmental action.

The net effect of these mutual strategies of limited culpability was a four-year period of very limited achievement. The pattern was set in the first year of his administration. Normally, incoming presidents can expect to receive a generally favourable response from Congress in the year following a presidential election. According to the figures published by *Congressional Quarterly* since 1952, the average level of Congressional approval given to those measures supported by a president in his first year was 78.3 per cent. If Gerald Ford – whose first year was wholly exceptional in that he succeeded Richard Nixon in the wake of the Watergate scandal – is eliminated from the figures, the average stands at 81.6 per cent. President Bush's rating by the *Congressional Quarterly* was a mere 62.6 per cent – i.e. 'the worst legislative performance by an elected post war president in his inaugural year.'[15] The same pattern was repeated in each of the next three years. In 1990, the level of Congressional support for Bush was 46.8 per cent. In 1991, it was 54.2 per cent and in 1992 it reached 43 per cent. Again, these levels compared unfavourably with his predecessors, as demonstrated in Figure 3.1. The differential between the support for Bush and the average support given to each of his seven predecessors in the corresponding years of their presidencies was –15.7 per cent in 1989, –31.8 per cent in 1990, –19.2 per cent in 1991, and –28.2 per cent in 1992.

The figures reflect not only Bush's impoverished political position but also the changes in Washington politics. In a Congressional context of rising party unity, vigorous party leadership, especially by the Democrats, increased Republican frustration in the House of Representatives, and a slump in the old conservative coalition, Bush's modest agenda – modestly put – was largely lost from view. 'Presidential positions' were

Congressional support Eisenhower to Reagan compared to Congressional support for President Bush

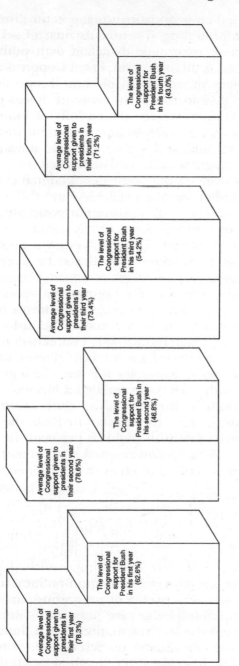

Figure 3.1 Comparison between the average levels of Congressional support given to seven postwar presidents (from Eisenhower to Reagan), and the level of support given to President Bush. (Figures derived from the *Congressional Quarterly*'s 'presidential-support' indices.)

*Note that as no 'presidential-support' scores were possible either for President Kennedy's fourth year or for President Ford's fourth year, the average level of Congressional support given to postwar presidents in their fourth year is based upon five rather than seven presidents.

Average level of Congressional support given to presidents in their first year (78.3%)

The level of Congressional support for President Bush in his first year (62.6%)

Average level of Congressional support given to presidents in their second year (78.6%)

The level of Congressional support for President Bush in his second year (46.8%)

Average level of Congressional support given to presidents in their third year (73.4%)

The level of Congressional support for President Bush in his third year (54.2%)

Average level of Congressional support given to presidents in their fourth year (71.2%)

The level of Congressional support for President Bush in his fourth year (43.0%)

often nothing more than negotiating stances in the continuous attrition of coalition building. These constructs of accommodation were far more susceptible to defeat than other presidential proposals had been in the past. Previous presidents had often attached their name, their political status and the authority of their position to a number of selected high-priority measures. Support would then be collected for them if for no other reason than to save the integrity of the presidency. Bush demurred from such forceful direction. In his inaugural address, Bush had sought to differentiate himself from his predecessor's style of leadership. 'Some see leadership as high drama and the sound of trumpets calling.' Bush did not share this vision: 'A president is neither prince nor pope, and I don't seek "a window on men's souls".'[16]

Nevertheless, the President did need Congress to move in response to his limited measures. His efforts at compensating for his political constraints by relying upon the force of cordiality, and what he hoped would be a beguiling absence of confrontation, were largely fruitless. In a study of Bush's relations with Congress, Richard Fleischer and Jon R. Bond found the President received a considerably lower level of support than was anticipated by their regression model of Congressional allegiance to previous administrations.[17] What was particularly significant in this study was that it isolated and measured the support given to Bush by the President's closest friends and associates in Congress, i.e. those to whom he had been most cordial and therefore those who could be expected to be most responsive to the President's 'outstretched hand'. But Fleischer and Bond found the reverse to be true:

> It was not just that support from Bush's friends failed significantly to exceed predicted levels. Instead, these members tended to provide considerably less support than predicted. Indeed, the group identified as having the closest political and personal ties to Bush was the most undersupportive.[18]

The conclusion reached by Fleischer and Bond was that, notwithstanding the pleas of a president in urgent need of help from his friends on Capitol Hill, it was party and ideology that invariably determined the level of support. For a president to succeed in Congress, there was no alternative other than paying in 'the coin of the realm – policy substance'.[19]

Given the context of the 'active engagement of thin ends' between the presidency and Congress, Bush's numerous defeats were not perhaps as damaging as they might have been to other presidents. In risking little, he was often thought to have lost little, compared to many of his predecessors who opted for the strategy of staking presidential reputation upon achieving Congressional compliance. By the same token, Bush's 'victories' afforded little credit and were in many cases negative in character and politically damaging in their effects.

For example, in 1991 Bush signed a new Civil Rights Act into law. The legislation was designed to counteract a series of Supreme Court decisions that had made it more difficult for aggrieved workers to bring discrimination lawsuits to court. Bush claimed that he had successfully eliminated those elements of the original proposal which, the Republicans had alleged, would have led to employers having to hire quotas of minorities and women to avoid anti-discrimination lawsuits. Notwithstanding the extent to which the quota threat had been a bogus pretext to block the measure, Bush's declared success in achieving a compromise was acquired at great cost. The background to this action is instructive. In 1990, Bush became only the third president in American history to veto a civil rights bill. As the veto failed to be overridden by only one vote in the Senate, Bush became personally responsible for the first defeat of a major piece of civil rights legislation for a quarter of a century. The veto compromised the Republican Party's campaign to recruit more African-American and Hispanic members and to increase its ethnic minority support in general. Virtually the same bill was presented to Bush in 1991. This time he approved it. In doing so, he compounded his earlier 'principled' stand against quotas with what appeared to be an unprincipled readjustment in response to purely political considerations. His *volte face* was widely interpreted as having far less to do with any victory over quota threat and far more to do with the President's desire to distance himself from the vociferous racism of figures like David Duke on the far right of the party; to reinstate himself with the minority constituencies and woman voters in preparation for the 1992 presidential election; and to avoid a probable veto override in the Senate, where the conservative coalition could no longer be relied upon even to appear, let alone to prevail, in a civil rights vote.[20]

Bush's earlier veto had antagonized minorities and subverted his long-established personal pledge to the principle of
'affirmative action'. His later recantation only served to blur
the reasons for his original opposition, and to lose him the
respect he sought on the Republican right, and to cast doubt
on both the President's principles and on his allegiance to
them. To make matters even worse, he used the signing ceremony to give a minimalist construction of the measure which
was quite contrary to the spirit of the legislation as it had been
understood by the Congressional negotiators who had produced it. Bush's actions, therefore, had managed to antagonize the left, the right and even the centre ground.

Another example of this form of qualified victory was provided by the Clean Air Act of 1990. A package of proposals was
passed, but only because the Senate went to enormous lengths
to protect what was a compromise measure. It had been negotiated by the Bush administration to weaken a bill which had
already been presented to the Senate by its Environmental and
Public Works Committee. Given that the choice was between
half a loaf or no loaf at all, Senate leaders George Mitchell and
Robert Dole wanted to defeat such 'deal-breaking' proposals as
the Wilson-Wirth Amendment and the Kerry Amendment.
These measures would have restored the tough controls on
motor vehicle emissions and urban smog that the Senate negotiators had dropped in their deal with the White House. In
securing the passage of the bill, Bush claimed credit for initiat-
ing and supporting a process that had led to the first landmark
legislation in the field since 1977. At the same time, the background of White House opposition to the Senate's original bill
left the public with the impression that the Clean Air Act was
weaker than it needed to be to achieve its objectives.

Many of Bush's other victories in Congress could only be
characterized as cases of negative achievement. These would
include his 46 vetoes. All but one of them were sustained
largely owing to the efforts made by the beleaguered Republican minorities in the House and especially in the Senate. But
probably more effective than actual vetoes in contributing to
Bush's sphere of negative achievement were his threats to veto
prospective legislation. These warnings were numerous and
sweeping in scale. They were also effective because of Bush's
noted success in defeating attempts at veto overrides. The

chief White House lobbyist in the Senate said in 1990: 'We
have a lot of veto threats out there, but we don't take any of
them lightly ... They are all there for a reason.'[21] As a consequence, they were taken seriously by Congress. 'His threats
have credibility',[22] affirmed Senator Richard Lugar. For example, in 1991, the prospect of a presidential veto effectively
demolished the negotiations between the House and the
Senate on what would have been a major piece of legislation
on crime control. Bush insisted that the proposal did not go
far enough in restricting the channels of appeal for convicted
criminals, or in relaxing the rules on evidence which had not
been acquired through the proper procedures. Even though
the President himself had originally proposed the Crime Act to
Congress, it was his veto threat that eliminated its chances of
being passed into law.

Another area which was particularly susceptible to veto
threats was the abortion issue. Bush persistently warned that he
would veto any legislation designed to loosen or overturn
federal restrictions on a whole range of areas related to abortion. The tactic was so successful that it led to bitter accusations
that the Bush administration was defying majority support in
both houses of Congress and relying instead on a rump of a
third of either one chamber or another to impose its views on
the rest of the membership.

Lastly, some of Bush's victories in Congress were so qualified
by the costs of achieving them that they amounted to being
practically pyrrhic in nature. These do not refer to the President's effectiveness in preventing Congressional action. They
refer rather to his success in achieving positive objectives, but
in inflicting so much collateral damage in doing so that they
raised doubts about the President's political conduct and
judgement in pursuing them. The nomination of Clarence
Thomas to the Supreme Court provides a case in point.

The President asserted that Thomas was simply the best man
for the job. This was clearly not the case. It was evident that
Bush had selected an African-American conservative judge to
replace an African-American liberal judge. He calculated that
many Southern Democrats would not vote against Thomas for
fear of antagonizing their black supporters, and that because
of this he would acquire, with as little controversy as possible, a
staunchly conservative judge. The reverse proved to be the

case. As Bush's disingenuous claims to meritocratic selection
were dramatically eroded, and as Thomas's character suffered
from the Judiciary Committee's examination of his personal
background and sexual behaviour, Bush had to devote more
and more political capital to preserving the momentum of the
nomination. In the end, Bush prevailed but not without great
cost to both himself and his nominee. A much damaged
Clarence Thomas was approved in the Senate by 52 to 48 – the
narrowest margin for any nominee to the Supreme Court this
century.

But Bush's most notable pyrrhic victory came in the budget
agreement of October 1990. Against a background of increasing public dismay over the inability of the President and Congress to fashion a budget that would seriously address the
problem of the deficit, Bush was ultimately forced into a position where he had to disavow his election pledge not to raise
taxes. Bush's previous strategy had been to rebut tax increases,
to evade difficult choices and to place Congress in the position
of either finding expenditure cuts or of publicly advocating
revenue rises. The Democrats' refusal to be entrapped into
taking the initiative on politically unpopular decisions on taxes
and/or social spending cuts led in October 1990 to the sort of
deadlock that closed government offices and turned visitors
away from museums and art galleries.

As public concern turned to resentment, Bush felt compelled
to try and preserve his public reputation by a display of presidential leadership. He agreed to the responsible option of a
revenue increase. The President took pride from a budget settlement that was projected to cut the deficit by $500 billion in
five years. Bush himself 'privately regarded the budget pact as
his greatest domestic achievement'.[23] But what may have been a
success in financial management for Bush was at the same time
something of a political disaster for the President. The result of
the budget accord was to 'lessen fear of the deficit, to remove
the issue from party debate, and to free the Democrats to talk
about fairness while hindering the Republicans from attacking
high taxes'.[24] He had been wholly outmanoeuvred by the Congressional Democrats. They provoked him into a full-scale
public attack on their proposal for a 10 per cent income tax sur-
charge upon millionaires; they highlighted his long-standing
allegiance to cutting the level of capital gains tax; and they

forced him to capitulate on the central theme of his presidential victory in 1988. Far from showing presidential leadership, Bush reversed himself twice during the negotiations, established the tax fairness issue firmly in the Democratic party and in one stroke abandoned the one principle that had given his administration some semblance of a political identity.

Bush may have thought that he was securing his position for the 1992 presidential election. But in doing so, he utterly compromised the many Republican candidates in the 1990 midterm elections, whose programmes were based on supporting the President's stance against taxation. In the subsequent disarray, the President's approval ratings slumped by over 20 points. Barring a major scandal, it was the most dramatic decline in popularity recorded by any twentieth century president. To make matters worse, in the mid-term Congressional elections that followed the budget deal the President's party failed in its drive to reverse the loss of seats that it suffered in 1986 and 1988. Instead, it suffered even further losses in both the Senate (–1) and in the House (–8) to produce an alignment on Capitol Hill that would extend the contentiousness of 'divided government' into the second half of Bush's term.

By 1992 the political gamesmanship between the presidency and the Congress had reached such a level that they effectively dragged each other down in the public estimation. Bush took pride in the fact that only one of his vetoes had been overridden. He also took comfort in his successful defence of presidential prerogatives in the field of foreign policy and national security.[25] But his actual achievements in securing economic and social policy from Congress were minimal. This was due mostly to his tentativeness with anything that might risk the enlargement of government, rather than to any chronic obstruction of a presidential agenda. Nevertheless, he felt justified in making the Democratic 'do-nothing' Congress a major campaign issue in his drive for re-election. He attempted to offload responsibility for his own timidity in domestic policy onto what he described as a 'very recalcitrant Congress' that habitually rejected his calls for cooperation. 'I think the people know that I've held out my hand to Congress and its been a frustrating experience.'[26] Even after the triumph of Desert Storm in which Iraqi resistance had been crushed in just one hundred hours, Congress had failed to move on Bush's request that action be taken on two of his domestic bills within one hundred days. 'I thought a hundred days was fairly reasonable,' he said. 'I was not asking the Congress to deliver hot pizza in less than 30 minutes. That would be revolutionary for the Congress.'[27]

The Congress, for its part, drew attention to the President's preoccupation with foreign affairs, to his inconsistencies and lack of resolve in domestic policy and to the enervating effects of a president content with minimal governmental action during an economic recession. Bush's hapless attempts to deal with the truculent sectors of both the Democratic party and his own Republican party in Congress increasingly made him appear to be complacent and even indifferent towards an array of pressing economic and social problems. Just as Bush became ever more a captive of Washington's interior priorities, so Congress also succumbed to public indictments of detachment and unresponsiveness. Indeed, more blame was attached to Congress than to the presidency for the condition of 'gridlock' which was widely assumed to be the malicious barrier to every available antidote to every known social and economic problem. The outrage at such perceived irresponsibility was further compounded by a series of exposés of the personal privileges and money-making opportunities enjoyed, and abused, by members of Congress. These revelations further undermined public confidence in Congress and allowed President Bush to adopt a position of righteous indignation against the 'hopelessly tangled Congressional web of PACs, privileges, partisanship and paralysis'[28] of the membership. The increasing levels of public frustration and cynicism shown towards Washington prompted a swathe of Congressional resignation announcements (61) during the 102nd Congress. Together with those who were defeated in primaries (20) and those who were running for other posts (13), the forthcoming 103rd Congress was assured of an exceptionally large turnover in membership.[29] President Bush looked forward to the 'new Congress':

> I want it to be a newer than new Congress ... We want to move this country forward to solve the problems of education, solve the problems of crime in the neighbourhoods. And the way to do it is to give me a new Congress with which I can work.[30]

Unfortunately for Bush, he would not be in a position to enjoy the opportunities afforded by any 'new Congress'. His tenure in the White House was ended by the Republican party's defeat in the 1992 presidential election. The 'old Congress' had done too much to implicate the President in the sense of domestic stagnation that had prompted such a large-scale change of personnel at both ends of Pennsylvania Avenue.

NOTES

1. Quoted in President Bush's acceptance speech to the Republican party Convention 18 August 1988. Congressional Quarterly, *Congressional Quarterly Almanac, 100th Congress, 2nd Session, 1988.* Vol. XLIV (Washington DC: *Congressional Quarterly* Inc., 1989), pp. 42a–43a.
2. *Congressional Quarterly Almanac, 100th Congress, 2nd Session, 1988*, p. 43a.
3. Quoted in Michael Binyon, 'Democrats vow rough ride in Congress', *The Times,* 10 November 1988.
4. Quoted in President Bush's Inaugural Address on 20 January 1989. *Congressional Quarterly Weekly Report,* 21 January 1989, p. 143.
5. These figures are drawn from the *Congressional Quarterly*'s 'Presidential support' ratings. These assess, on a yearly basis, the level of support given by Congress to those measures upon which the president has taken a position.
6. Barbara Sinclair, 'Governing Unheroically (and Sometimes Unappetizingly): Bush and the 101st Congress', in Colin Campbell SJ and Bert A. Rockman (eds), *The Bush Presidency: First Appraisals* (Chatham, NJ: Chatham House Press, 1991) p. 159.
7. Thomas B. Edsall, 'Democrats on the Take', *New York Review of Books,* 20 July 1989.
8. Ibid.
9. Brooks Jackson, *Honest Graft: Big Money and the American Political Process* (New York: Alfred A. Knopf, 1989).
10. Fred Barnes, 'Playing Ball', *New Republic,* 9 April 1990.
11. Kerry Mullins and Aaron Wildavsky, 'The Procedural Presidency of George Bush', *Political Science Quarterly,* Vol. 107, No. 1, Spring 1992, p. 58.
12. Quoted in 'Mixed Signals, "Agenda Gap" Plague Bush's First Year', Congressional Quarterly, *Current American Government,* Spring 1990, p. 98.
13. Quoted in Michael Duffy, 'A Case of Doing Nothing', *Time,* 7 January 1991.
14. During the budget crisis of September–November 1990, it was clear that when the public was asked to allocate responsibility for the gridlock in Washington, primary blame was assigned to Congress. In

one poll, the public was asked: 'Who is more to blame for the difficulty in reaching an agreement?' While 29 per cent mentioned Bush, 42 per cent believed it to be the Congress (*Time*, 24 September 1990). After a further month of deadlock, public impatience had shifted significantly towards Congress with 23 per cent believing the President to be more responsible for the problem, compared to 61 per cent who thought that Congress was to blame (*Time*, 22 October 1990).

15. 'Mixed Signals, "Agenda Gap" Plague Bush's First Year', op. cit., p. 98.
16. Quoted in President Bush's Inaugural Address, op. cit., p. 143.
17. Richard Fleischer and Jon R. Bond, 'Assessing Presidential Support in the House II: Lessons from George Bush', *American Journal of Political Science*, Vol. 36, No. 2, May 1992, pp. 525–541.
18. Ibid., p. 536.
19. Ibid., p. 540.
20. For the decline of the 'conservative coalition', see 'Congressional Coalition on the Wane', Congressional Quarterly, *Congressional Quarterly Almanac, 102nd Congress, 1st Session, 1991*, Vol. XLVII (Washington DC: Congressional Quarterly Inc., 1992), pp. 22B–24B.
21. Quoted in 'Bush: Mixed Results but Veto-Proof', Congressional Quarterly, *Congressional Quarterly Almanac, 101st Congress, 2nd Session, 1990*, Vol. XLVI (Washington DC: Congresstional Quarterly Inc., 1991), p. 16.
22. Ibid.
23. Duffy, op. cit.,
24. Harvey Mansfied, 'The Vision Thing', *Times Literary Supplement*, 7 February 1992.
25. 'Bush Crusades on Many Fronts to Retake President's Turf', Congressional Quarterly, *Current American Government*, Fall 1990, pp. 59–63.
26. Quoted in Michael Kramer and Henry Muller's interview with President Bush, 'Bush on Record', *Time*, 24 August 1992.
27. Quoted in a speech given by President Bush on 12 June 1991. *Congressional Quarterly, Congressional Quarterly Almanac, 102nd Congress, 1st Session, 1991*, Vol. XLVII, p. 15E.
28. Quoted in a speech given by President Bush on 20 March 1992. *Congressional Quarterly Weekly Report*, 28 March 1992, p. 831.
29. 'Record Rate of Retirements Suggests Major Shake-up', *Congressional Weekly Report*, 4 April 1992.
30. Quoted in Kramer and Muller's interview with President Bush, op. cit.

4 American Political Parties and the Bush Presidency
Gillian Peele

The 1992 American elections which dramatically ended the presidency of George Bush and elected to the White House Governor Bill Clinton also constituted a remarkable reversal in the fortunes of America's two major parties. The Republican Party which had held the presidency since 1980 was demoralized after a campaign which was generally agreed to have been inept and ill-coordinated. Apart from the loss of the presidency the Republicans had to acknowledge further failure in the outcome of the Congressional elections where the anticipated gains in House seats in the wake of redistricting did not materialize. Above all, the intellectual climate appeared to be shifting and the ascendancy of free-market and neo-liberal ideas which had been the hallmark of the Reagan era seemed to be giving way to ideas which stressed a more positive role for government.

Inevitably perhaps much of the blame for the Republicans' misfortunes was attributed to President Bush personally. Certainly this was the natural explanation of the Republican right which had never viewed Bush as one of its own. Although by 1992 the conservative movement was itself divided over ideology and tactics, conservative columnist Pat Buchanan's challenge to George Bush in the 1992 Republican primaries underlined the extent to which the incumbent President was at odds with his party.

It was not, however, only the right of the Republican Party which saw George Bush as the cause of Republican weakness in 1992. Many other Republicans noted the failure of Bush to engage in the kind of party-building activities which his predecessor Ronald Reagan had done. Most significantly, there was harsh criticism of Bush's failure to articulate any overall vision of what his presidency was supposed to achieve. This policy vacuum was most apparent in domestic politics which became crucial to the survival of the Bush administration once the threat of communism had receded and the voters had ceased to be impressed with Bush's foreign policy success in the Persian Gulf. By contrast with long-term aspirations of many of those around President Reagan, the Bush administration seemed devoid of philosophy and strategy to an extent which made the 1992 election campaign difficult to manage successfully.[1]

There were, however, a number of other elements which contributed to the electoral outcomes of 1992, not least the factionalism which been apparent in Republican ranks virtually from the start of the Bush presidency. Internal divisions in a political party are not necessarily fatal to electoral success, but the effect of the bitter internal disputes on the Republican Party throughout the years 1988–92 was to demoralize the party.

Republican factionalism manifested itself in a number of different ways. There were incessant wranglings between the President and the congressional Republican Party over budgetary policy, especially after Bush in 1990 retreated from his 1988 campaign commitment that he would not introduce new taxes. There was the raucous primary challenge of Pat Buchanan on a populist platform of 'America First'. And there was the crusade of those who wanted the Republicans to emphasize social issues more extensively. The last group included both the secular gurus of the conservative movement such as Paul Weyrich of the Free Congress Foundation and the religious right which was restructured during the Bush presidency.

One effect of the renewed strength of the religious right was further factionalism within state parties as adherents of Pat Robertson's Christian Coalition (which was formed in 1989) attempted to capture the Republican Party from within. Robertson's constituency was slightly different from that of the Reverend Jerry Falwell's Moral Majority. It appealed especially to charismatic Christians as opposed to evangelicals – a theological division which made it unlikely that Robertson would be able to unite the whole Christian right behind him.[2] Nevertheless, Robertson's Christian Coalition had by 1992 achieved a substantial membership and a visible presence in the Republican Party. As a result of a determined drive to influence the delegate selection process at the 1992 Republican National Convention, Robertson's Christian Coalition was able to exert pressure over the platform writing process, excluding for example any softening of the party's stance on abortion. The

image of the Republican Party as relayed from its 1992 Convention at Houston in Texas to millions of television viewers
reflected these strands in the Republican Party and especially
its religious right. The style of the religious right was dramatically brought home to voters as indeed was the power base
which the religious right had acquired within the GOP. Just
how damaging that Convention was remains to be seen, but
there is little doubt that when the Republican Party most
needed to demonstrate unity, it found its processes hijacked by
forces which had frequently been underestimated.[3]

The Bush defeat in the 1992 election cannot, of course, be
entirely attributed to Republican failures. The resurgence of
Democratic Party organization and fund-raising capacity over
the period 1988–92 was itself a major development in the
American political struggle. And the contest between the parties in the years of the Bush presidency took place against the
background of an anti-government mood evidenced *inter alia*
by the appeal of term limitation initiatives and the popular
strength of Ross Perot's 1992 presidential bid.

It has yet to be determined how far Perot's 1992 candidacy
affected the outcome of the presidential race or whether there
is sufficient commonality of outlook among Perot voters to
provide the base for a new political movement in the United
States. What the Perot candidacy did do, however, was to
remind observers of the fragility of the major parties' hold on
the electorate and of the continuing debate about the future
of parties in the American system.[4] Although it would be
impossible to examine all of these themes in depth in the
space of a short essay such as this, by focusing on some of the
main trends in the life of the parties during the four years of
the Bush presidency it is possible at least to shed some light on
the changing structure of American party organization and
ideology. Before taking up some of these more general themes,
however, it is necessary first to provide a brief overview of the
key changes in the two parties during the Bush years.

REPUBLICAN ORGANIZATION 1988–92

The Republican Party's organization in the Bush presidency
cannot be understood without an awareness of the enormous

revitalization brought about during the period of Bill Brock's chairmanship of the Republican National Committee. From 1977 to 1980 Brock strengthened the national party organization by building up its fund-raising capacity (principally through the application of new computer technology for direct mail), by helping state and local organizations with services to candidates, and by developing a coherent theme for the party as a whole.[5] The organizational reforms complemented other changes in the political environment – most notably the growth of a powerful conservative movement – which formed the backdrop for Ronald Reagan's 1980 electoral victory.[6]

After Brock's resignation in 1981, however, the chairmanship of the party became a somewhat difficult position as it frequently does when there is an incumbent president of the party. Indeed, after the short tenure of Richard Richards as chairman, the post was redefined to allow for a general party chairman (Paul Laxalt) and a chairman in charge of day-to-day operations (Frank Fahrenkopf).

In 1988, after a campaign which opponents labelled as dirty and negative, Bush moved swiftly to place his own choice of chairman at the head of the party.[7] The nominee was Lee Atwater, Bush's feisty campaign manager who was seen as largely responsible for the hard-hitting style of the campaign.[8] (Roger Ailes, Bush's campaign consultant, and James Baker were the other key figures credited with the style of the 1988 campaign.) Atwater was young and, unusually for a RNC chairman, had come directly from the hands-on management of a campaign. He was also the first RNC chairman to come from the Deep South and he was sure that his native region was the key to continuing Republican control of the presidency – largely because of its susceptibility to Republican appeals on such issues as affirmative action. The Atwater appointment was interpreted as a shrewd move by Bush to fend off any attacks from the right and to provide a better party base for his reelection prospects in 1992. It was also assumed that Atwater had the campaigning expertise to build Republican strength in the congressional and gubernatorial elections.

The legacy of Atwater's campaign tactics (especially the infamous Willie Horton television advertisement) in many ways harmed the Bush presidency as a whole. In addition Atwater's reputation for mean and aggressive political manipulation led him into difficulty in the early months of his chairmanship. In June 1989, amid the controversy over Speaker Wright's forced resignation, there was leaked a memo which attacked the newly elected House Speaker Thomas Foley's character and appeared to accuse him of homosexuality. The memo – which led to the resignation of Republican Party Communications Director Mark Goodin – was ultimately repudiated by Atwater who was able to secure a vote of confidence from the Republican National Committee.[9] Indeed many Republicans liked the aggressive tactics favoured by Atwater and the whole affair brought out something of a division between Congressional leaders like Senator Robert Dole and Robert Michel – who viewed the memo with distaste and like Bush repudiated it – and the RNC who supported their chairman's willingness to play 'hardball' electoral politics.

Atwater's tenure of the Republican chairmanship was cut short by a fatal brain tumour which was first discovered in March 1990. The illness of Atwater left a real gap in RNC organization which proved damaging at the 1990 mid-term elections. Although other senior party figures such as Robert Mosbacher and Samuel Skinner had been tipped for the post, Bush turned to former Education Secretary and drugs 'czar' William Bennett at the end of 1990 to take up the job. Bennett was to be given responsibility for the day-to-day management of the party, although he left the ailing Atwater a role as general chairman.

At first Bennett seemed an inspired choice since, like Jack Kemp, he had ideas about how the Republicans could build a distinctive domestic agenda. Many of these ideas – which became known as the 'new paradigm' – involved strengthening individual choice in such areas as educational choice through vouchers, the encouragement of tenant ownership of public housing and tax cuts. The 'new paradigm' (which owed much to the ideas of James Pinkerton) was thus inherently opposed to bureaucracy and regulation and much more systematically anti-government and libertarian than the Bush administration as a whole. Bennett already had strong credentials with the Republican right and initially he looked set to reinvigorate the party around a new policy agenda.[10] However, after a brief period of activity he was forced to withdraw from the job because of the restrictions which it placed on his ability to receive honoraria.

The search for a new RNC chairman proved embarrassing. It was reported that a number of individuals including Craig Fuller, James McClure and Mitchell Daniels had been approached but had refused the job. There was speculation about the cause of their refusal but two major factors were the restrictions which the post placed on outside earnings and the fact that in the run-up to the 1992 presidential election the party chairman would be overshadowed by the campaign team put in place by the President himself.

A successor to Atwater was eventually found in January 1991 when Clayton Yeutter, Bush's Secretary for Agriculture, agreed to take the post. Although Yeutter, in marked contrast to Atwater, had no direct campaign experience, he had a good deal of administrative expertise. Conservatives such as Paul Weyrich called the choice 'cautious', while other Republicans saw the appointment as one designed to heal the factionalism in the party.[11]

FACTIONALISM IN THE GOP

The fact that the Republicans had won the presidency in 1988 did not prevent factionalism and divisions from manifesting themselves at the federal level and within the various state parties. It must of course be borne in mind that American political parties are much less cohesive than British ones and that different states exhibit different patterns of party politics.[12] Nevertheless the extent of Republican factionalism at the state level had risen during the 1980s and was much publicized in the Bush years. In Arizona, for example, the Republican Party was severely weakened by the activities of a faction based on two conservative groupings – the backers of former Governor Evan Mecham and the religious charismatic groups that had organized around the 1988 Robertson presidential bid.[13] Something of the flavour of Arizona's Republican politics is captured by the resolution pushed through by the Christian right at the 1989 state Convention. This resolution affirmed that America was a 'Christian nation ... a republic based on the absolute laws of the Bible, not a democracy.'[14]

In Lousiana, it was reckoned in 1992 that more than half of the state party's central committee was Christian Coalition supporters.[15] And in Virginia, which in 1991 registered substantial Republican gains from the Democrats at the state legislative level, much of the new Republican activism was attributed to Robertson's 'generic party building activity' – the mobilisation of the religious right at the grass roots.[16]

The generalized hostility between right-wing factions in the Republican ranks may have impaired the effectiveness of the Bush administration from the beginning. Observers noted the way in which sub-cabinet appointments were influenced by right-wing pressure sometimes to the extent of forcing the withdrawal of highly qualified candidates. In this process Bush's own non-involvement was compounded by the right-wing preferences of John Sununu, the man appointed Chief of Staff.[17] Sununu, a former Governor of New Hampshire of Lebanese descent, owed his appointment in large part to the help which he had given to Bush in the 1988 New Hampshire primary after Bush had run third to Senator Dole and to Pat Robertson in the Iowa caucuses. Sununu exacerbated tensions between the Republicans in Congress and the White House by his abrasive style, and he impeded the smooth coordination of domestic policy because of his determination to counter the policy initiatives of those he saw as ideological enemies, notably William Reilly at the Environmental Protection Agency.[18]

Certainly there were tensions between the administration and the Republican forces in Congress from an early point in the Bush administration. But these tensions turned into a massive breach in 1990 when Bush, in order to secure a budget deal with the Democrats, abandoned his 1988 campaign commitment not to increase taxes. Few Republicans supported the President's package which was constructed on the basis of Democratic Party support. Ed Rollins had in fact written a memo to Republicans in Congress arguing that they could regard themselves as free to support or not the Bush package. Newt Gingrich was furious with the President and the episode was in many ways a defining moment both for presidential–legislative relations and for relations between the right of the party and the Bush administration. Sununu exacerbated these tensions by threatening that in the mid-term elections Bush might campaign against those Republicans who had opposed the budget deal – a threat which many Republicans regarded as hollow given their wish to distance themselves from the Bush administration.

The visible internal divisions in Republican ranks and the about-turn on taxes inevitably weakened Republicans in the November 1990 mid-term elections. Republicans blamed Bush for their poor showing. With the loss of nine seats, Republicans in the House were reduced to their lowest number for a decade, thereby strengthening Democratic control even further. In the Senate one seat changed hands. The interpretation put on these results was that the tax issue was crucial. There was a strong correlation between Republicans who had run well and opposition to the 1990 tax rise. By contrast Republicans and Democrats who had supported the budget package appeared to have fared badly.

Following those 1990 mid-term elections there were hotly contested leadership elections in the Congressional Republican Party in both houses of Congress. In the House of Representatives, the more aggressive, younger conservative elements sought to change the character of the leadership to reflect their views. Although House minority leader, Robert Michel, was reelected without opposition, the insurgents sought to displace the incumbent chairman of the House Republican Conference (the third highest leadership post) – Jerry Lewis (R – California) – with Carl Pursell (R – Michigan) and to displace Guy Vander Jagt. Lewis, who was also the ranking minority member on the House Appropriations Committee, had been the only member of the House Republican leadership (apart from Michel) who had backed Bush's budget package of tax increases and spending cuts, a position which reflected a long career of legislative bargaining and compromise with the Democratic majority. While the bargaining style adopted by Lewis could be justified in terms of opportunities to shape legislation, it did not suit the preferred style of the Republican right which wanted to take a much more oppositional stance.[19] Although Lewis survived the challenge, he was angry with Newt Gingrich who had backed his opponent on ideological grounds rather than following the customary norm of supporting a fellow member of the party leadership.[20]

Conservative insurgency in the House was paralleled in the Senate where the Republicans voted 22–21 to oust Senator

John Chafee (R – Rhode Island) as Chairman of the Republican Conference and to replace him by Senator Thad Cochran of Mississippi. Cochran was generally more conservative than Chafee but it was also crucial that Chafee had split with the White House over the civil rights bill.[21]

In fact the 1990 mid-term elections indicated the depth of the difficulties confronting both Bush and the Republican Party. Republicans saw their distinctive issues being eroded. In part they could rejoice that one of their principle concerns – the communist threat – had receded because of the collapse of the Soviet empire. But they were angry about their distinctive stance on taxes being undermined by their own president.

Another key element of the Republican issue agenda became problematic at this time. Abortion had been the most significant of the 'social issues' which many Republicans saw as crucial to winning the votes of morally conservative Democrats. However, by 1990 the political impact of the abortion issue was by no means clearly favourable to the Republicans. In a sense, as David Broder pointed out, the Reagan administration was able to have 'the best of both worlds' on abortion because it could present itself as solidly anti-abortion and thereby attract the votes of those who felt similarly that abortion was immoral. On the other hand those who supported free choice could still vote Republican knowing that the Supreme Court was unlikely to overturn its 1973 *Roe* v. *Wade* decision.[22]

The Bush administration did not, however, have the luxury on the issue that the Reagan administration had enjoyed. The Supreme Court in 1989 handed down its *Webster* decision which gave much more discretion to the states on the issue.[23] Restrictions on abortion became much more of a real threat as states became the battleground for nearly 600 anti-abortion bills. However, public opinion was clearly shifting and the prominence of the abortion measures in the 1990 mid-term elections worked to the Republicans' disadvantage. The poor Republican showing in 1990 was followed in 1991 by a Senate race in which the pro-choice Democrat Harris Wofford defeated the anti-abortion candidate, Richard Thornburgh, who had been Bush's (and Reagan's) Attorney General. The potential damage which the abortion issue could do to Republican unity was highlighted in 1991 by the Republican Governors' Association where moderate Governors Tom Kean and Jim Thompson urged their fellow governors to change the policy. However, in many states this was virtually impossible as anti-abortionists were well entrenched.

The Republicans thus found themselves after the 1990 mid-term elections with substantial doubts about their policy image especially on the domestic policy front. The factionalism within the Republican ranks had also been exacerbated by the elections themselves and the sense of betrayal over taxation. One point of interest for students of the relative strength of the various factions within the Republican Party was the extent to which the moderate wing of the GOP – for long eclipsed by the right – was slightly strengthened as a result of the 1990 mid-term elections.[24] In part this reflected a geographical shift in Republican strength away from its sunbelt base; in part it reflected the election of moderate Republicans especially at the gubernatorial level.

Bush's political position was – temporarily as it turned out – transformed by the progress of the crisis in the Persian Gulf. Bush's strong stand against Iraq and the Democrats' disarray over the conflict reinforced Bush's standing with the right of his own party. (The Democrats voted against the resolution authorizing President Bush to initiate hostilities in Iraq.)

The transformation of the President to a commander-in-chief role inevitably strengthened his electoral support and the ultimate victory boosted the President's popularity ratings. Even the conservatives who had criticized Bush in the latter part of 1990 and were still mistrustful of him because of his tax apostasy found reason to applaud his 1991 State of the Union address.[25] In addition to its determined position *vis-à-vis* Iraq, the President began to use language which signalled support for a new domestic policy agenda along the lines advocated by Kemp and Bennett. Although the speech did not actually use the word 'empowerment', it did emphasize the need to provide more opportunities for individuals especially through new educational policies.

Voters' memories are, however, short. Whatever triumph Bush acquired from his foreign policy achievements was rapidly overtaken by the onset of recession. By the end of 1991 Bush's poll ratings had slipped considerably so that in December 1991 the proportion of the American electorate

who approved of his handling of the economy stood at just
24 per cent. In December 1991 Bush's overall approval rating
was 47 per cent. In these circumstances it was hardly surprising
that Bush should have anticipated that what had been earlier
dismissed as a 'no-go' year for Democrats should have been
transformed into a much tougher competition. At the same
time there were challenges for the Bush candidacy from the
right. One of them from David Duke, an ex-Ku-Klux-Klan
member who had earlier failed in a gubernatorial bid in
Lousiana, was more an irritant than a real threat and the GOP
organization was quite effective in keeping him off the ballot.
However, a challenge from Pat Buchanan, Reagan's former
Communications Director, was less easy to dismiss.

Buchanan's major message was geared to appeal to those who
were economically threatened. He wanted the United States to
adopt a much more protectionist policy towards America's trade
competitors, especially Japan and the European Community.
And he was critical of American support for countries whose
trade policies damaged the United States. Buchanan's philosophy had strong roots in the isolationist traditions of the right. It
was, however, at odds both with the libertarian, market-oriented
thrust of groups like the Cato Institute and with the neo-
conservatives who had joined the Reagan coalition in the late
1970s and 1980s on the basis primarily of the need for a global
fight against communism. Indeed, Buchanan drew a sharp dis-
tinction between himself and the latecomers to conservatism –
neo-conservatives. He called himself a 'paleo-conservative' and
enunciated his distinctive right-wing views in his book *Right from
the Beginning* and in his other writings and speeches.[26] His was a
visceral conservatism that contrasted markedly with the more
intellectual offerings of figures such as Irving Kristol.[27]

Buchanan's economic prescriptions were widely shared.
Indeed, Richard Gephardt and other leading Democrats
accepted them. However, the other crucial element in
Buchanan's appeal was a tacit racialism and a radical right
approach on social issues. Here he was able to join forces with
the elements of the conservative movement who had always
placed their primary emphasis on the social issues as the tools
for fashioning a conservative majority – Howard Phillips of the
Conservative Caucus and Paul Weyrich of the Free Congress
Foundation and Coalitions for America. Weyrich and Phillips

were present at the launch of a new organization (UBBIC) formed to unite disgruntled protectionists and business organizations, and their support in the primaries was clearly directed towards Buchanan.

Buchanan's candidacy was not, of course, seen by Bush as likely to result in the President losing the nomination. What was at issue was the damage which Buchanan's attacks could do to the party unity and in the minds of wavering voters, especially those concerned about jobs. From Buchanan's perspective the challenge was perhaps motivated as much by a desire to reestablish his own brand of right-wing politics as the predominant one within the conservative movement, especially if – as seemed increasingly likely – Bush were to lose the election.[28]

Towards the end of 1991 Bush reorganized his election team for the 1992 elections. Although Robert Mossbacher nominally headed it, Sam Skinner and Robert Teeter were seen as its most important members. Teeter took the position of campaign chairman – a position which James Baker had held in 1988. At the time columnist David Broder suggested that the Teeter-Skinner combination might presage a Midwestern focus oriented to the concerns of suburban voters rather than a strategy based on the South. Broder also wondered whether the Teeter-Skinner combination might rebuild the link between campaigning and governing which Bush's 1988 campaign had so seriously neglected.[29] As it turned out of course, Bush was not to have the opportunity of a second term to strengthen that link, and the campaign team was to be radically reshuffled in a vain attempt to avert disaster.

One casualty of the Bush reorganization (and of the effort to devise a domestic strategy which would convince voters that the administration had policies for coping with the recession) was John Sununu. Bush found that many of the people he needed for his reelection drive would not work with Sununu who had become an increasing liability, not least because of his apparent abuse of official transport for private purposes. Sununu was replaced as Chief of Staff by Sam Skinner.

In the primaries Buchanan's challenge to Bush was easily defeated. But it had unsettled the Bush camp not least because the populist rhetoric exposed the gap between Bush and the ordinary wage-earning American and laid the groundwork for a Democratic attack on the Bush administration for its failure to deal with the economic problems of the United States. Although the emergence of Governor Bill Clinton of Arkansas as the Democratic nominee initially seemed to make the Republican chances of winning the November election easier, by the time of the summer Conventions Bush was running way behind Clinton.

Candidates usually expect to use the publicity of the Convention for electoral momentum. However, the Houston conference failed to give Bush the poll boost or 'bounce' that he needed, not least because of the extent to which Buchanan and the religious right were together able to obscure the broader Republican message by their own concentration on 'family values' which were defined in terms which were extremely illiberal on such issues as abortion and homosexuality. From the perspective of the Republican strategists this was damaging to the Republican's efforts to woo suburban voters whose attitudes on such topics tended to be liberal. Vice President Quayle, who was not immediately obvious as a spokesman for liberal causes, was given the task of trying in the aftermath of the Houston Convention to soften the image created there by redefining 'family values' in a more inclusive manner.[30] However, Bush could not repudiate the extreme right position's explicitly since many of them had been written into the GOP platform. And he needed to maintain the support of the right. Indeed, as one commentator noted, the Republican Party assembled in Convention at Houston was not so much a party with splits between the right and the moderates as a gathering with internecine arguments between the different strands of the right.[31] Inevitably therefore Quayle's last-minute efforts looked like an attempt to blur the party's image for electoral reasons and could be dismissed by Democrats as both cynical and inept. But Quayle, as well as moderate figures such as Governor Weld of Massachusetts, recognized the damage that had been done at Houston and the need to try to restructure the Republican Party as a broad and inclusive grouping.

By the time of the Republican National Convention it had also become apparent that the Republican reelection team was not working well. Fredic Malek and Charles Black, senior campaign managers for Bush, had received a blistering amount of criticism from House Republicans in July not least because the poorly focused presidential campaign was beginning to damage other Republican candidates in their districts.[32] Even in the primaries it was apparent that Republicans were likely to suffer considerably as such senior figures as Guy Vander Jagt discovered.[33] To some extent the electoral mood was as much anti-incumbent as anti-Republican but the fact that such senior Republicans could be ousted created a nervous mood for the campaign.

Bush's attempt to get his campaign back on track involved moving James Baker from the State Department to instil a new sense of discipline in the team. Unfortunately for Bush this failed to work well and the same criticisms of a campaign lacking coordination were heard throughout the election and Baker himself was seen as having given up well before the end of the campaign. The relative financial weakness of the party did not help and many of the forms of state party aid which had been forthcoming in 1980, 1984 and 1988 were not given in 1992.

THE DEMOCRATS

Unlike the Republicans, the Democrats in Congress were not plagued by internal leadership battles, although their position had been undermined at the start of the Bush administration by the financial scandal surrounding Speaker Wright. However, there were deep divisions in the Democratic Party generally. The Democratic coalition created during the New Deal period had unravelled during the 1960s and 1970s to the great advantage of the Republicans at the presidential level.[34] Although there was clearly an incentive to overcome internal factionalism, to many observers the Democrats remained, even in the late 1980s, not so much a party but more an uneasy amalgam of warring factions and interest groups.

The Democrats' loss of the 1988 presidential election again exposed the divisions within the party. On the one hand there were those who believed the party had to revive its appeal to the mainstream majority and to fashion a programme which could not be accused of being ultra-liberal. Such people were increasingly associated with the Democratic Leadership Council founded in 1985 in part as a reaction to the defeat of 1984, in part as an attempt to counter the image of liberalism provided by Chairman Paul Kirk. The group attracted a good deal of support from the South and border states and it became a vehicle for the views of such Democrats as Governor Clinton of Arkansas (who became chairman of the DLC in 1990), Governor Robb of Virginia, Senator Gore of Tennessee, Congressman Gephardt and Senator Nunn of Georgia.

Until 1990 the DLC was largely a national-level organization. Over the five years of its life it had acquired a membership of some 400 elected officials and its own think-tank – the Progressive Policy Institute – to generate debate about policy. (The PPI in fact took up a number of themes which were also receiving attention in Republican ranks, notably the idea of empowerment and the 'new paradigm'.)[35] In 1990 under Clinton and Alvin From's leadership, the DLC made a concerted attempt to broaden its base. It moved to establish a grass-roots organization by establishing state-level chapters and initiated an effort to reduce its dependency on Washington fund-raising.[36] By 1992 it claimed 3,000 members and operated on a budget of some $2.5 million.[37]

Also of importance on the moderate wing of the Democratic Party was Pamela Harriman's 'Democrats for the Nineties'. Pamela Harriman's efforts for the Democratic Party earned her much appreciation and the ambassadorship to France in the 1992 Clinton administration.

Against these forces of democratic modernization were ranged the representatives of Jesse Jackson's National Rainbow Coalition (which dubbed the DLC 'Democrats for the Leisure Class') and the Committee for Democratic Values which Senator Howard Metzenbaum (supported by Ted Kennedy and Tom Harkin) had formed in 1990 to defend traditional liberalism within the Democratic Party. The extent of the intra-party divisions can be seen, for example, from Jackson's reaction to the DLC conference of May 1991 which attempted to find a new approach to the problem of quotas. Jackson called the conference 'vulgar and insulting' while Clinton urged the DLC to promote a 'scepticism towards the federal government's ability to solve many of the country's intractable problems'.[38]

Social change had also transformed the Democratic coalition. The labour movement had been weakened by economic change so that by 1991 it represented a mere 16 per cent of the non-agricultural workforce – a figure which represented less than half of its strength in the 1950s. Although American unions could still provide the Democratic Party with substantial organizational and financial support, there were tensions between organized labour and the newer breed of middle-class party activists. These tensions were not merely the tensions of style – the product of a conflict between those who were college educated and those who were not – but also of policy. These policy conflicts ranged from the different priority to be accorded to causes such as environmental protection to differences over the free-trade agreements with Mexico and the structure of American industrial relations law. Democrats in Congress, however sympathetic to labour, had to bear in mind that labour's issues and interests were increasingly out of step with the attitudes both of a large part of their own party and of a large part of the electorate.[39]

More generally there was an ideological tension within the Democratic Party between those who maintained an adherence to the liberalism associated with the Great Society programmes, the constituencies of minority groups and the poor, and those who wanted to reclaim the Democratic Party as a majoritarian party. The Democratic Leadership Council encountered fierce opposition for its efforts to revise party policy on such issues as quotas and social policy, despite the electoral antipathy to quotas and the difficulty of advancing high-spending policies in the context of deficit politics.

Democratic organization

In many ways, paradoxically, the Democratic Party as it emerged from the 1988 elections was not in too bad a shape. While the GOP had certainly continued to make gains in the South and the Rocky Mountain states, there was evidence of a shift towards the Democrats in much of the rest of the country. For example, at the presidential level in 1988 Dukakis had won or remained competitive in a large number of northern states, and at the legislative level (outside the South) Democrats had picked up a substantial number of seats. This led some observers to speculate on a possible new electoral strategy for the Democrats based on winning an electoral college majority (270 votes) from the Northeast, Midwest and Pacific South states.[40] And although the Republican Party in mid-1989 achieved very high popularity ratings in the polls, Democrats retained the edge in party affiliation. Thus Gallup in a poll reported in July 1989 found that 38 per cent of those surveyed identified themselves as Democrats, 34 per cent as Republicans and 28 per cent as independents.[41]

Against this there were serious weaknesses in the Democratic Party position according to specially conducted polls. For example, the GOP was scoring significantly better than Democrats in the 18–24 age group.[42]

Democratic Party chairman Paul Kirk had over the period 1985–89 done an excellent job in stimulating the use of new technology within the Democratic ranks. As in the Republican Party, the organizational strength of the national party had been enhanced by the use of so-called 'soft money' which had also been effective in voter registration drives. However, Kirk's retirement in 1989 presented a problem since the front-runner for the post was Ronald Brown who had been Jesse Jackson's campaign manager. Although Brown was in fact very much a Democratic insider rather than a maverick radical, some observers feared that the election of an African-American Jackson supporter to such a sensitive post would inevitably provide an impression which Republicans could exploit.

Ultimately Brown did get the post and proved highly successful at it, not least because of his own professionalism and insider political experience. But the nervousness generated by the Brown candidacy underlined the fragility of the Democratic Party's unity in the late 1980s and its vulnerability to the well-rehearsed Republican charge that Democrats no longer represented mainstream America.

During the Bush presidency some of the developments which worked against the Republicans also worked to the advantage of the Democrats. The resurgence of the pro-choice movement and hostility to state restrictions on abortion, for example, had a significant electoral impact including the election of Douglas Wilder as Governor of Virginia in 1989.

The effect of the Clinton candidacy

The race for the Democratic nomination was in many respects a disappointing one. The perception that Bush would be reelected in 1992 had caused strong Democratic candidates

such as Governor Mario Cuomo of New York and Richard
Gephardt to stand back from the race. This left a clutch of less
well known Democrats fighting for the nomination. And by
March it was evident that Clinton was the favourite in a race
where Jerry Brown remained the only strong competition.

The Clinton candidacy for the Democratic nomination was
inevitably a candidacy for a particular view of how the Democratic party should function and for a revisionist philosophy.
The Clinton campaign presented itself as a broad-based one in
contrast to the sectarianism of many previous Democratic presidential campaigns. In foreign policy, for example, Clinton
(whose expertise at this point was primarily on the domestic
front) could call on a wide range of advice and expertise,
including support from some neo-conservatives who had earlier deserted the Democrats for the Republicans because of
distrust of Democratic commitment to the fight against communism. National security and international relations experts
such as Samuel Huntington and Paul Nitze by 1992 had con-
cluded that Bush lacked the imagination to cope with the
problems of the new post-communist world order.[43]

More importantly Clinton sought to present the Democratic
Party he led as the voice of mainstream America. This he did
by two strategies. First he distanced himself from the Democratic left and especially from Jesse Jackson. (Clinton also
explicitly denounced Sister Souljah who had apparently advocated the use of violence by blacks towards whites.) Secondly
he put forward a message at the national Convention which
was calculated to appeal to the white middle class rather than
to minorities. Clinton accepted the nomination 'in the name
of all the people who do the work, pay the taxes, raise the kids
and play by the rules ... in the name of the hard-working
Americans who make up our forgotten middle class'.[44]

CONCLUSION

The character of both of America's major political parties was
modified during the Bush administration. Although most
attention since the 1960s has focused on the role of new activists in the Democratic Party, it was apparent that the tensions between issue-oriented groups and party 'regulars' had

become by the late 1980s at least as troublesome for the Republicans. The extent to which the moderate supporters of the Republican Party can effectively seize the initiative again is an open question. Certainly there was by the end of the Bush presidency some evidence of renewed organization by groups supporting free choice on the abortion issue. Moderate Republican governors also lent their support to efforts to curb the power of the right. Despite the greater emphasis on participation in the Democratic Party, the 1992 election underlined the extent to which that party could – at least for the period of the campaign – restrain their factionalism.

More remarkable in view of the trends of previous years the Democrats proved able to put together a machine superior to that of the Republicans in terms of funding and organizational efficiency. It would, however, be wrong to expect this advantage to last. Both parties have become extremely competitive and professional about fund-raising. One measure of this is the expansion of national staff at the two headquarters. Thus in 1992 the DNC, DCCC and DSCC employed together 369 staff while the Republican equivalents employed 519 full-time staff.[45] (The RNC did, however, terminate the appointment of a large number of its staff immediately after the 1992 election.) How long the Democrats will retain their unity depends on the success of the Clinton administration in delivering on his policy commitments, especially on health care and the cities. It would, however, be highly surprising if the Republican Party were to allow itself to be outflanked by the Democrats in terms of organizational expertise. But how far questions of organizational competence can be addressed before addressing the broader issues of party unity remains to be seen.

NOTES

1. For an overview of the Bush presidency which emphasises its static quality see Michael Duffy and Dan Goodgame, *Marching in Place: The Status Quo Presidency of George Bush* (New York: Simon & Schuster, 1992).
2. On this see Clyde Wilcox, *God's Warriors: The Christian Right in Twentieth Century America* (London and Baltimore, Md.: Johns Hopkins, 1992).
3. For a good recent overview of the religious right see Clyde Wilcox op. cit.

4.   The debate about the role of parties in American politics has
     generated an extensive literature. See for example David Broder, *The
     Party's Over: The Failure of Politics in America* (New York: Harper & Row,
     1972) and Larry Sabato, *The Party's Just Begun: Shaping Political Parties for
     America's Future.* (London: Little, Brown, 1988).

5.   For an overview of the role of the national party organization in this
     period see Tim Hames, *Power Without Politics: The Republican National
     Committee in American Political Life and the Debate over Party Renewal*
     (DPhil Oxon, 1990).

6.   For an early assessment see G.R. Peele, *Revival and Reaction: the Right in
     Contemporary America* (Oxford: Oxford University Press, 1984).

7.   On the campaign see Thomas Edsall, 'DNC Chairman Criticizes Dirty
     Republican Politics; Brown Calls Joint Meeting to Draft Ethics Code',
     Washington Post, 17 June 1989.

8.   Atwater's own view of the campaign can be found in David R. Runkel
     (ed.), *Campaign for President: the Managers look at 1988* (Dover, Mass.:
     Auburn House, 1989).

9.   Dan Balz, 'Yeutter Chosen to be RNC Chairman', *Washington Post,*
     8 January 1991.

10. Pinkerton was the Assistant to the President for Policy Planning.

11. Dan Balz, 'Yeutter chosen to be R.N.C. Chairman', *Washington Post.*

12. For an extremely useful interpretation of the different state traditions
     of party politics in America see David Mayhew, *Placing Parties in
     American Politics* (Princeton: Princeton University Press, 1986).

13. T.R. Reid, 'Arizona Republicans Find Religion and Politics a Volatile
     Mix', *Washington Post,* 13 August 1988.

14. *Miami Herald,* 29 November 1989, quoted in Michele McKeegan,
     Abortion Politics: Mutiny in the Ranks of the Right (New York: Free Press,
     1992).

15. Michael Isikoff, 'Christian Coalition Steps Boldly into Politics',
     Washington Post, 10 September 1992.

16. Ibid.

17. See Robert Fulton, 'Caving into the Right', *Washington Post,* 23 July
     1989.

18. For an early perspective of the problems within the Bush
     administration see C. Campbell SJ and B.A. Rockman (eds), *The Bush
     Presidency: First Appraisals* (Chatham, NJ: Chatham House Press, 1991).

19. For an insider account of the growth of conservative organization in
     the House of Representatives see Edwin J. Feulner, *Conservatives Stalk
     the House: The story of the Republican Study Committee* (Ottawa and Illinois,
     Green Hill Publishers, 1983). For an overview of factionalism in the
     Senate see C.J. Bailey, *The Republican Party in the U.S. Senate 1974–1984:
     Party change and institutional development* (Manchester: Manchester
     University Press, 1988).

20. John E. Yang, 'House GOP Challengers Fall Short: Lewis, Vander Jagt
     Reelected to Leadership Amid Bitter Divisions', *Washington Post,*
     4 December 1990.

21. Helen Dewar, 'Senator Cochran Defeats Chafee for GOP Post',
     Washington Post, 14 November 1990. On the civil rights bill see G.R. Peele,

in G. Peele, C. Bailey and B. Cain (eds), *Developments in American Politics* (London and New York: Macmillan, 1992).
22.   David Broder, *Washington Post*, 19 May 1991.
23.   *Webster* v. *Reproductive Health Services* 109 S.Ct. 3040 (1989).
24.   For an overview of the position of moderate Republicans see Nicol C. Rae, *The Decline and Fall of the Liberal Republicans: From 1952 to the Present.* (Oxford: Oxford University Press, 1989).
25.   E.J. Dionne Jr, 'Conservatives Find Reasons to Cheer Bush', *Washington Post*, 31 January 1991.
26.   P. Buchanan, *Right from the Beginning* (Boston: Little, Brown).
27.   On the neo-conservatives see G.R. Peele, *Revival and Reaction* (1984). See also P. Steinfels, *The Neo-Conservatives: The Men who are Changing America's Politics* (New York: Simon & Schuster, 1980).
28.   Charles Krauthammer, 'Why Buchanan Runs the Fight for the Right', *Washington Post*, 9 September 1992.
29.   David Broder, 'Bush's New Look Campaign', *Washington Post*, 11 December 1991.
30.   E.J. Dionne Jr, 'Quayle Tempers Campaign's "Family Values" Stance', *Washington Post*, 9 September 1992.
31.   E.J. Dionne Jr, 'Conservative v Conservative: Convention Highlights Right Wing battle for GOP's Future', *Washington Post*, 21 August 1992.
32.   Ann Devroy, 'Malek Target of Worried Republicans; Lawmakers Pounce on Campaign Chief', *Washington Post*, 30 July 1992.
33.   Vander Jagt lost his seat in Michigan 46 per cent to 41 per cent to Peter Hoekstra.
34.   See A. Ware, *The Breakdown of Democratic Party Organization 1940–1980* (Oxford: Clarendon Press, 1985).
35.   David Osborne and Ted Gaebler, *Reinventing Government* (Reading, Mass.: Addison-Wesley, 1992).
36.   David Broder, 'Moderate Democrats Trying to Grow Grass Roots', *Washington Post*, 12 December 1990.
37.   Lloyd Grove, 'Al From: The Life of the Party', *Washington Post*, 24 July 1992.
38.   *Washington Post*, 7 May 1991.
39.   Thomas Edsall, 'Democratic Coalition Strained as Labor's Clout Wanes', *Washington Post*, 16 July 1991.
40.   For an overview of the 1992 electoral outcome see Gerald Pomper (ed.) *The Election of 1992: reports and interpretations* (New Jersey: Chatham House, 1993).
41.   Maralee Schwartz, 'GOP image soars', *Washington Post*, 30 July 1989.
42.   Thomas Edsall, *Washington Post*, 17 June 1989.
43.   Stephen S. Rosenfeld, 'Return of the Neocons', *Washington Post*, 28 August 1992.
44.   Thomas Edsall, 'The Values Debate: Us v Them. At Issue is Which Party Best Represents Heavily White Middle Class', *Washington Post*, 31 July 1992.
45.   Paul Herrnson, 'American Political Parties after Three Decades of Growth', in G. Peele, C.J. Bailey and Bruce Cain (eds), *Developments in American Politics*, Vol. 2 (London: Macmillan, forthcoming, 1994).

5 Bush and the Courts
Tinsley E. Yarbrough

For better or worse, Ronald Reagan's impact on the federal judiciary and trends in constitutional law promise to be his presidency's most enduring legacy. Campaigning for a first term in 1980, Reagan refined and expanded Richard M. Nixon's 'southern strategy' – opposing court-ordered school busing, favoring tax exemptions for segregated schools, and pursuing related avenues to the souls and votes of disgruntled southern whites. In fact, Reagan opened his fall campaign in Neshoba County, Mississippi, site of the 1964 murders of three civil rights workers by Klansmen and local police, with a searing attack on federal meddling in state and local law enforcement. Nor were his appeals to the disenchanted confined to southern segregationists. For the religious right, the non-churchgoing former actor proclaimed his opposition to abortion and pornography, support for school prayer, and devotion to the nation's Judaeo-Christian heritage. For those concerned about rising crime and social programs, he scorned criminal-coddling judges and welfare 'chiselers'. For those convinced that minorities were the chief cause of the nation's social problems, he offered coded appeals, assuring one audience, for example, that he too was offended by the sight of able-bodied, foodstamp-wielding 'bucks' in supermarket check-out lines.

Liberal-activist federal judges were a major target of the candidate, his surrogates and supporters. It was thus hardly surprising that, once in office, the new president launched a campaign to remold the judiciary and American constitutional law into his own conservative image. Traditionally, the Deputy Attorney General has been the Justice Department official responsible for overseeing the filling of vacancies on the federal bench. Better to assure that his judicial nominees would reflect his views on abortion, busing, defendants' rights, school prayer and other controversial constitutional issues, Reagan shifted that task largely to the department's Office of Legal Policy, in which the issue positions of potential nominees

84

would be a central concern. The administration also established the President's Committee on Federal Judicial Selection, headed by Reagan's counsel and including key White
House and Justice officials. Operating out of the White House,
committee members reviewed prospective nominees submitted by the Office of Legal Policy as well as their own potential
choices. The ultimate degree to which the administration succeeded in securing ideologically correct nominees remains to
be seen, but it certainly had numerous opportunities to effect
enormous changes in the direction of judicial policy. During
his eight years in office, Reagan selected 378 of the 740 judges
authorized for the principal courts in the federal system –
over fifty per cent of the total.[1]

Nor were Reagan's efforts confined to the selection arena.
To a degree unprecedented in American history, he attempted
to politicize the office of the Solicitor General, the chief representative of the United States before the Supreme Court, pressing that official and his staff to pursue the administration's
conservative agenda aggressively before the high bench.
Indeed, Rex Lee, Reagan's first Solicitor General and a
staunch conservative, apparently became so alarmed at the
pace with which the administration expected him to challenge
the Court's precedents that he ultimately resigned, declaring,
'I am the Solicitor General, not the Pamphleteer General.'[2]
Administration officials also undertook a public relations campaign against the Court. When not attempting to avoid indictment on influence-peddling charges, Attorney General Edwin
Meese III, made numerous speeches accusing liberal justices of
engaging in judicial legislation and urging the Court to give
constitutional guarantees a narrow construction based on the
'original intent' of the framers. Other members of the administration, including the President, took the same tack.[3]

As the 1988 presidential campaign season began, the extent
to which George Bush would emulate Reagan's judicial
agenda was not entirely clear. After all, Bush had been raised
in a tradition of political moderation. His father, Connecticut
Senator Prescott Bush, sponsored legislation shortly before
his retirement from public office to protect voting rights,
desegregate schools and establish an equal employment commission. At Yale in 1948 George Bush had led the United
Negro College Fund drive. As a Texas Congressman, he voted

for the 1968 Fair Housing Act; as Vice President, he urged Ronald Reagan to approve voting rights legislation and sign a bill declaring a national holiday honoring Martin Luther King. Accepting his party' nomination, he had promised a 'kinder, gentler nation'.

But the 'consistency thing' has not been George Bush's strong suit. As a Congressional candidate, he had opposed the public accommodation and employment provisions of the 1964 Civil Rights Act. '[It] was passed to protect 14 per cent of the people,' he remarked after President Lyndon Johnson signed the bill into law, 'I'm also worried about the other 86 per cent.'[4] When his white constituents were outraged by his support for the 1968 fair housing law, he rushed home to assure them it would have little effect on their lives. 'Look at the 20 states with even stronger measures', he said, 'and you will find there have been no drastic changes in their living patterns.'[5] To become Reagan's running mate, he had been obliged to drop his pro-choice stance and become an ardent abortion foe – a flip-flop which perhaps helps to explain why, on beginning his unsuccessful 1992 reelection campaign, he remarked in a televised statement that he remained 'pro, er, life'. In his 1988 campaign against Massachusetts Governor Michael Dukakis, he tried to out-Reagan Reagan in appealing to conservative groups and anti-Court sentiment. Citing a historic 1943 Supreme Court decision outlawing compulsory flag salutes in the public schools,[6] Dukakis had vetoed a Massachusetts law requiring teachers to conduct such ceremonies. Bush and company scorned the Governor's lack of patriotism, and to underscore his own loyalty to 'Old Glory' Bush even visited a flag factory. Dukakis, Bush also charged in a manner reminiscent of the late Joseph McCarthy, was a 'card-carrying member' of the American Civil Liberties Union. Most effective of all were the 'Willie Horton' television advertisements condemning inmate-coddling prison furlough programs – and, indirectly, 'bleeding heart' judges, legislators and executives. While on furlough from a Massachusetts prison, Horton raped a white woman. The Republicans gave the incident prominent play, and while Bush and his campaign organization never mentioned the inmate's race, advertisements run by an 'independent' pro-Bush organization displayed Horton's black face as well as interviews with the family of his white victim.

Given the tenor of the 1988 GOP campaign and Bush's obvious belief that the continued support of southern whites, religious fundamentalists and other key elements of the Reagan coalition was critical to his chances for a second term, Bush's decision to pursue Reagan's judicial agenda, albeit with subtle variations, was entirely expected. This chapter focuses on Bush's judicial agenda – the structure and processes of judicial selection, including key appointments and the controversy they generated, and the administration's approach to abortion, flag-burning and other controversial civil liberties issues confronting the courts.

JUDICIAL SELECTION

President Bush moved quickly following his inauguration to place his own imprint on the Reagan administration's approach to judicial selection.[7] Apparently in an effort to blur the ideological focus which had added controversy to Reagan appointments, Bush's first Attorney General, Richard Thornburgh, decided to abolish the Office of Legal Policy, a key agency in the Reagan selection apparatus; transfer its non-judicial legal policy functions to a new Office of Policy Development; and return judicial selection activities to the office of the Deputy Attorney General. However, opposition to Robert B. Fiske Jr, Thornburgh's first choice for his Deputy, derailed plans to return selection oversight to its traditional home. Fiske was a prominent establishment lawyer and conservative Republican. But he had also been chairman of the American Bar Association's Committee on Federal Judiciary, which, since 1952, had reviewed and rated candidates for the federal bench. Conservatives charged that the committee employed improper ideological criteria in assessing the qualifications of Reagan judicial nominees. They especially resented the 'not-qualified' rating four members of the fifteen-member body had given Robert Bork, the distinguished but controversial Yale law professor, former Solicitor General, and appeals court judge whose restraintist constitutional philosophy had led to his rejection by the Senate. In July 1989, Fiske asked that his name be withdrawn from consideration. Amid the controversy surrounding Fiske's selection, moreover, Thornburgh had moved judicial selection activities into his office, giving a long-time associate principal responsibility in such matters.

Early in his administration, Bush also attempted to improve relations between the White House and the ABA. At least until Supreme Court nominee Robert Bork's 'paper trail' of controversial writings had doomed his confirmation, the Reagan administration had favored selecting certain judicial nominees from among law professors whose scholarship bore evidence of philosophical leanings consistent with the president's conservative agenda. In addition, Reagan nominees tended to be younger than those of his predecessors and thus more likely to enjoy a lengthy tenure. Since neither type of nominee could expect an enthusiastic ABA reception, Reagan had discontinued the traditional White House practice of sharing the names of prospective nominees with the Association's committee prior to announcement of a formal nomination.

On first taking office, Attorney General Thornburgh urged the ABA to delete political or ideological concerns from its screening process. Following extensive negotiations, he and the committee came to an agreement by which the committee explicitly disavowed review of 'political or ideological philosophy' in its evaluation of candidates.[8] The Justice Department then resumed submitting the names of likely nominees to the committee. At least during the first two years of Bush's tenure, moreover, no prospect who received a 'not-qualified' rating from a majority of the committee was submitted to the Senate, although seven nominees had been rated 'qualified' by a divided vote. A 1989 Supreme Court decision upholding the ABA's review process[9] mollified somewhat, it might be added, concerns of the administration and Senate conservatives regarding the secrecy of the committee's work and the votes of its members.

Whether in an effort to distance himself from the controversy which had swirled around certain of the Reagan nominations or for other reasons, Bush also declined to simply submit Reagan choices left unconfirmed by the Senate when Bush took office. Four of his predecessor's district court nominations, and three of Reagan's appeals court choices, were dropped from consideration by Bush.

In other respects, Bush largely adhered to the selection arrangement Reagan had created. Like members of his predecessor's administration, Bush officials insisted that prospective nominees were not being subjected to a 'litmus test' on abortion and other controversial legal issues. The President did instruct those involved with judicial selection, however, to seek out philosophically conservative candidates respectful of executive and legislative authority. Bush also extended the operation of the President's Committee on Federal Judicial Selection, through which the Reagan administration had enlarged White House influence over judicial selection. During Bush's first two years at least, the committee met weekly at the White House for sessions normally running two to three hours. In fact, White House Counsel C. Boyden Gray, who chaired the committee, appeared to play an even greater role in the selection process than his predecessor in the Reagan White House. Early in Bush's tenure Gray began consulting with and briefing the President on judicial nominations, and Bush's thoughts on such matters were transmitted to the Attorney General through Gray.

Like Reagan, Bush was obliged to yield to the dictates of 'senatorial courtesy', the custom under which presidents are expected largely to rubber-stamp the preferences of their political party's Senators in filling vacancies on the federal district courts, the jurisdiction of which is confined to individual states. Despite criticism from some Senators, the Bush Justice Department did ask Republican Senators to submit at least three names for each district court vacancy. Senators could submit a single candidate for White House consideration, however, if they were willing to submit additional names where the original choice proved unacceptable to the administration.

President Jimmy Carter had established a merit system for selecting court of appeals judges. Under his arrangement panels of lawyers and laypersons selected nominees for each vacancy, from whom the president was expected to make the formal choice. President Reagan dismantled Carter's system, and Bush chose not to revive it. Comparatively early in his tenure, however, Bush did express an interest in pursuing one element of the Carter plan – use of the system to recruit women and minorities to the federal bench. In a 30 November 1990 letter to Senate GOP leader Robert Dole, the President asked for help in finding qualified women and minority candidates.[10] In instructions to administration staffers, moreover, he

expressed an interest in highly qualified prospects without
strong party ties.

Bush would employ the modified Reagan framework for judicial selection throughout the term. The flap over Robert Fiske
slowed the recruitment process considerable early in the President's tenure. The administration submitted only two court of
appeals nominations and three district court choices to the
Senate during the first six months of 1989, and all had previously been Reagan nominees. By the end of the year, in fact,
Bush had made a total of only 22 district and appeals court
nominations. Over the first two years of his tenure, however, he
appointed 67 judges and had another 38 vacancies to fill. In
1990, moreover, Congress created an additional 85 judgeships
(74 district and eleven appeals court positions) despite the
opposition of those who pointed out that the overall federal
caseload was actually declining – from 299,164 in 1985 to
251,113 in 1990.[11] Given the new positions and the inevitability
of additional vacancies, it appeared likely that Bush would have
named over 200 judges, or nearly one-fourth of the federal judiciary, during the term. He and Reagan would thus have filled
about 75 per cent of all district and appeals court seats.

In view of Bush's mixed political record it was unclear at the
beginning of his tenure precisely what sorts of judicial nominees
he might pick. Judicial selection specialist Sheldon Goldman
suggested in an interview, in fact, that the slow pace of Bush's
initial appointments may have reflected in part the administration's own uncertainties in that regard. 'My general impression',
said Goldman, 'is that ... they are torn between different imper-
atives. The Reagan administration knew what it wanted and
went out and got it ... With Bush, it is as if he is playing Hamlet
rather than Henry V.'[12]

Gradually, though, the Bush pattern of judicial selection
began to take shape. Like his GOP predecessors, he favored
middle-aged, well-to-do white male Republicans, with degrees
from private universities. By the end of 1991, about 90 per cent
of his appointees were white and 85 per cent male; two-thirds
had a net worth exceeding $500,000. To a greater extent than
all five of his modern predecessors, moreover, Bush also drew
his nominees from the lower courts. During his first three
years in office, for example, 63 per cent of his 27 appeals court
nominations came from the district bench.[13]

In keeping with his somewhat more moderate political back-ground, Bush's nominees differed from Reagan's in a number of respects. During Bush's first two years, for example, 5.6 per cent of his appeals court nominees and 2.1 per cent of his choices for district court seats were African-American, com-pared with Reagan percentages of 1.2 and 2.0 per cent, respectively. Reagan had a somewhat weaker record than Bush for choosing women also, though both presidents' records for nominating women, African-Americans and Hispanics were poorer than President Carter's, at least through the first years of Bush's tenure.[14]

With a number of notable exceptions, Bush nominations also seemed largely to escape the controversy Reagan's choices fre-quently provoked. Reagan's district court nomination of Vaughn R. Walker, who had represented the US Olympic Com-mittee in a successful suit to prevent use of the word 'olympics' in the Gay Olympics, lapsed in the Senate at the end of Reagan's tenure. But the Bush administration resubmitted Walker's name to the Senate and secured his confirmation despite revelations he belonged to a males-only private club. Early in Bush's tenure, the administration also locked horns with Vermont GOP Senator James M. Jeffords over the dictates of senatorial courtesy. Jeffords backed Fred I. Parker, a distin-guished lawyer and long-time associate, for a district court seat, but the Justice Department insisted that the Senator submit additional candidates. Jeffords obliged but continued to insist that Parker be nominated. Following an interview, Justice officials declared that Parker was unqualified but gave no reason for their opposition. Asserting his senatorial preroga-tive, Jeffords delayed action on two Bush nominations. In addi-tion, Senate Republicans voted to back their colleague, and Joseph R. Biden Jr (D – Delaware), chairman of the Senate Judiciary Committee, informed Bush that unless the prefer-ences of home-state Senators were taken seriously, the admin-istration's nominees would face 'great' difficulty in the committee. Ultimately, Bush yielded, rubber-stamping Jefford's choice.

In the fall of 1992, civil rights groups objected to Bush's selec-tion of Alabamian Edward Carnes to replace Judge Frank M. Johnson Jr on the Court of Appeals for the Eleventh Circuit. They considered Carnes, a prosecutor who zealously pursued the death penalty for convicted felons, an unseemly replacement for Judge Johnson, revered author of numerous landmark civil rights rulings during nearly forty years as a district and appeals court judge. But with the support of Alabama's senior Democratic Senator Howell Heflin and Morris Dees, head of the Southern Poverty Law Center and a vigorous opponent of the Ku-Klux-Klan, Carnes won confirmation.[15]

But these were exceptional situations. The overwhelming majority of Bush's nominations generated no controversy, and only one met Senate defeat during the first three years of his tenure. That lone exception was Kenneth Ryskamp, Bush's 1990 choice for a seat on the Court of Appeals for the Eleventh Circuit, one of the last appeals courts not dominated, to that point, by Reagan-Bush appointees. President Reagan had appointed the nominee to a district court seat in Miami in 1986. During the trial of a damage suit against West Palm Beach police who had allowed patrol dogs to maul suspects, Ryskamp had remarked to the plaintiffs that '[i]t might not be inappropriate to carry around a few scars to remind you of your wrongdoing in the past, assuming the person has done wrong.' During confirmation proceedings for the eleventh circuit position, Senate Democrats expressed dismay at Ryskamp's comment. The nominee's affiliation with a Coral Gables country club was no help either. The club had an English-only policy because, Ryskamp explained to a Senate aide during a conversation about Cuban influence in South Florida, its members wanted a place where they did not have to hear Spanish spoken. The facility also had no African-American members and a record of alleged discrimination against Jews. Ryskamp resigned his membership, but to no avail. After Democratic Senator Bob Graham, the nominee's fellow Floridian, announced his opposition, the Judiciary Committee failed, in a tie vote, to send his name to the Senate floor, thereby effectively killing the nomination.[16]

The administration's success in getting its candidates through the Senate confirmation process did not mean, though, that the Bush choices were less conservative than President Reagan's had been. At the end of Bush's first two years as president, Reagan Attorney General Edwin Meese III exclaimed that Bush had 'done an excellent job', adding: 'The results are the same as in the Reagan administration.' George Kassouf, director of the liberal Alliance for Justice's Judicial

Selection Project, agreed, noting that Bush's nominees 'don't bring out the same kind of controversies as the Reagan nominees, but they are the same good soldiers in the conservative movement', overwhelmingly white males 'insensitive to the needs of society's disadvantaged'.[17]

The prime reason for the failure of the Bush nominations to provoke conflict seemed equally clear: unlike Robert Bork, they had generally maintained low profiles, writing and saying little which could be used against them in the confirmation process. In no instance was this absence of a controversial 'paper trail' more conspicuous, moreover, than in the President's first nomination to a seat on the nation's highest tribunal.

THE SOUTER NOMINATION

When he announced his retirement on 20 July 1990, William J. Brennan Jr had served nearly 34 years on the Supreme Court. A Democrat appointed by President Eisenhower, Brennan had not only amassed the seventh-longest tenure of any Justice, he was also considered the principal architect of the massive body of civil liberties law about which Republican presidents from Nixon to Bush had been complaining. Indeed, close students of the high bench considered it more accurate to term Chief Justice Earl Warren's tenure (1953–69), the most liberal-activist in the Court's history, the Brennan rather than the Warren era.

George Bush was not about to place someone of Brennan's judicial philosophy on the Court. He was equally determined, however, not to select a controversial nominee likely to meet Robert Bork's fate. Bush turned to David Hackett Souter, who had made President Reagan's shortlist when Bork was nominated. A Massachusetts native, Souter was raised in Weare, New Hampshire, and still lived in the same house his family had occupied in his youth. His education – undergraduate and law degrees from Harvard and a Rhodes Scholarship at Oxford – was impeccable; his career, while hardly distinguished, had been respectable and uneventful. Following law practice in Concord, Souter had served as his state's Assistant Attorney General (1968–71), Deputy Attorney General (1971–76), and Attorney General (1976–78). In 1978, he was named to a state superior court seat. Five years later, New Hampshire Governor

John N. Sununu appointed Souter to the state supreme court. By 1990 Sununu was Bush's Chief of Staff. With the former New Hampshire Governor's sponsorship, Bush appointed Souter that year to the Court of Appeals for the First Circuit. Four months later, he became the President's first Supreme Court nominee.[18]

Whatever the limitations of Souter's professional credentials, he was hardly controversial. Perhaps best of all from the administration's standpoint, he had left no 'paper trail': the nominee's only publication was a bland, non-revelatory tribute to a state justice.

Initially, in fact, the far-right core of the Bush constituency seemed more concerned than liberals with the President's choice, especially Souter's lifestyle and likely position on abortion and other volatile issues. One conservative warned Sununu, for example, that a 51 year-old bachelor who rarely dated and, until recently, had continued to live with his mother might be a homosexual! Sununu and other White House staffers assured conservatives, however, that such gossip was nonsense and also apparently convinced many that Souter would keep the conservative faith on abortion and other controversial matters. 'There were no words exchanged that would constitute any specific assurances on any specific issue', a staffer for a conservative lobbying group related in a confidential memo summarizing his conversation with the White House Chief of Staff, 'but the general thrust of the discussion definitely made me feel better.'[19]

Souter's nomination also naturally distressed liberals. His lifestyle made them doubtful whether he could relate to the problems of modern families. Since he was a Bush nominee, they feared, too, the stances he might assume in constitutional cases, despite the President's assurances that he had subjected Souter to no litmus test and had not even asked the nominee his position on abortion.[20]

Souter did a thorough job of preparing for the Senate's confirmation proceedings, however – staying out of the public eye, reviewing videotapes of previous hearings, and becoming especially familiar with the sorts of questions and responses which contributed to Robert Bork's defeat. His appearance before the Judiciary Committee during five days of hearings on his nomination was equally masterful. Unlike Bork, who had admitted his opposition to *Roe* v. *Wade*,[21] Souter repeatedly refused to comment on the abortion issue, citing the impropriety of expressing opinions on issues likely to come before him on the Court. But his reluctance was selective, and his comments on other issues generally pleased his most likely committee critics. Bork had challenged the Court's landmark 1965 ruling in *Griswold* v. *Connecticut*,[22] scorning as judicial lawmaking the majority's decision there that a state ban on the use of contraceptives violated an unstated constitutional right of marital privacy. Whether out of principle or prudence, Souter avoided that trap. Like his role model, the second Justice John Marshall Harlan, a frequent dissenter from Warren Court decisions, Souter agreed that the Constitution includes protection for marital privacy and other unenumerated rights. He also described the Warren Court's controversial 1966 decision in *Miranda* v. *Arizona*,[23] laying down standard for police interrogation of suspects, as a 'pragmatic' safeguard against coerced confessions and had kind words for other expansive civil liberties rulings as well. He even praised Justice Brennan as 'one of the most fearlessly principled guardians of the American Constitution that it has ever had and ever will have'.[24]

The nominee proved reasonably effective, too, in deflecting concerns about his record. As New Hampshire Attorney General in 1976, Souter had submitted a brief to the US Supreme Court in which he defended, unsuccessfully, the state's failure to comply with a federal law obliging employers to maintain statistics on the racial composition of their workforce. Earlier, as an Assistant State's Attorney, he had signed a brief supporting literacy tests for voters – a requirement Congress had eventually banned nationwide on the basis of evidence that such tests were often applied discriminatorily. In the most probing questions of the proceedings, Senator Edward M. Kennedy (D – Massachusetts) cited these instances as evidence of Souter's insensitivity to the problems of 'the weakest and most powerless in our society'.[25] The nominee responded that the Supreme Court itself had upheld the constitutionality of fairly administered literacy tests, that in both situations he was merely defending positions of New Hampshire's Governor, and that he considered no social problem 'more demanding of the efforts of every American ... than the removal of societal discrimination in matters of race'.[26]

Kennedy was not impressed. '[W]hen you give a response that you are just acting as the lawyer for the Governor', he lectured Souter at one point, 'we have to give some weight to the fact that you are sworn to an oath of office [to uphold] the Constitution …'[27] But the Massachusetts Senator stood alone on the committee, the only 'no' vote on the question of Souter's confirmation. On 2 October, moreover, the full Senate voted 90 to 9 to confirm, enabling the appointee to take his seat on the bench on 9 October, during the second week of the Court's 1990–91 term.

THE THOMAS NOMINATION

On 1 July 1991, slightly less than a year after President Bush's nomination of Justice Souter, a copier repairman walked into the library of a southern university. He had been listening to a radio broadcast of conservative talk-show host Rush Limbaugh, from whom he got 'all' his 'news'. 'President Bush', he chortled, 'has picked a conservative nigger Republican for the Supreme Court! Ted Kennedy and those other Washington liberals won't know what to do with that!'

The young man's crude remark was offensive but perceptive. The retirement of Thurgood Marshall – pioneering figure of the modern civil rights movement and the first black Justice – had given President Bush another judicial vacancy to fill. 'An unwritten plank in the [current Republican] party's strategy', as Andrew Hacker has observed, 'is that it can win the offices it wants without black votes. More than that, by sending a message that it neither wants nor needs ballots cast by blacks, it feels it can attract even more votes from a much larger pool of white Americans who want a party willing to represent their racial identity.'[28] Refusing to fill Marshall's place on the Court with an African-American, however, was a bolder move than the cautious Bush was likely to make, despite the urging of certain administration staffers in that direction. Given the heavy dependency of Democratic candidates on African-American votes, moreover, an African-American nominee seemed certain to win confirmation in the Democrat-controlled Senate, however slender the credentials or controversial the politics of that person. If such a choice attracted more African-Americans into Republican ranks, so much the better.

In retrospect, then, Bush's decision seemed inevitable: he would indeed pick an African-American to replace the liberal Marshall – but a conservative Republican whose views and record would please the core of the Reagan-Bush constituency. The President's choice from among the exceedingly limited pool of conservative African-American GOPers appeared equally obvious.

Clarence Thomas's triumph over his roots would inspire liberals and conservatives alike. Thomas was born poor in tiny Pin Point, Georgia, in 1948. His father deserted the family when the nominee was still a toddler. His mother picked crab for five cents a pound to support Clarence, his brother and sister. When the Pin Point shack they occupied burned, she moved the family to Savannah, where she found work as a domestic at $15 a week, while her children stayed during the day with her parents, Myers and Christine Anderson. When Thomas was seven, he and his brother moved in with their grandparents, while their sister went to live with an aunt. The dominant figure of the nominee's youth, Thomas's grandfather, a stern man who sold wood, coal and fuel oil from the back of a pick-up, provided Clarence his first home with indoor plumbing, three square meals a day, an example of discipline and hard work, lessons on black survival in the American south ('you can never look a white woman in the eye'), and an education at St Benedict's, a Roman Catholic school whose nuns would also have a tremendous impact on Thomas's life.

From St Benedict's, Thomas attended a boarding school for future priests, then enrolled at a Missouri seminary, intent on becoming the cleric his grandfather wanted him to be. To Myers Anderson's bitter disappointment, the bigotry of white seminarians destroyed Thomas's interest in the priesthood. Very soon, however, he entered Holy Cross College, then Yale Law School, from which he graduated in 1974. There followed in rapid succession stints as an assistant to Missouri Attorney General and future Senator John Danforth (R – Missouri), attorney with a chemical company and legislative assistant to Senator Danforth, Reagan appointments as Assistant Secretary of Education and chairman of the Equal Employment Opportunity Commission (EEOC), and selection by Bush, in March of 1990, to the Court of Appeals for the District of Columbia.[29]

As another African-American, retired chief judge A. Leon Higginbotham Jr of the third circuit federal appeals court would detail in a devastating published letter to Thomas,[30] the nominee had been an obvious beneficiary of the civil rights movement and affirmative action programs. Indeed, his Yale connection had led to his long association with Senator Danforth, his primary sponsor. As a member of the Reagan and Bush administrations, however, Thomas had been a vehement critic of the movement, its leaders and the legislation it had spawned. He derided those activists who 'bitch, bitch, bitch' about the administration.[31] When Justice Marshall asserted that African-Americans had little reason to celebrate the Constitution's adoption, Thomas dismissed the Justice's concerns as 'an exasperating and incomprehensible ... assault on the Bicentennial, the Founding, and the Constitution itself'.[32] Affirmative action programs, he charged, 'create a narcotic of dependency [among minorities and women], not an ethic of responsibility and independence. They are at best an irrelevance, covering up some real problems, and inevitably a stigma.'[33] In his judgement, social welfare measures had the same consequence. His sister, Emma Mae Martin, had been gainfully employed most of her life, often at more than one job. At one point, however, she had quit work and turned to welfare to care for an elderly aunt. Her lapse did not escape her brother's contempt, though Thomas's detractors wondered why he had not also attempted to help. 'She gets mad when the mailman is late with her welfare check', he told a meeting of African-American conservatives in 1980. 'That's how dependent she is.'[34] Thomas had not only attacked affirmative action and related programs. As EEOC chairman, he had eliminated the use of minority hiring goals and timetables by employers as devices for correcting racial and ethnic disparities in the workplace. He also had largely abandoned class action lawsuits which had relied on statistical evidence to prove widespread discrimination by major corporations, preferring instead to have his agency intervene merely on behalf of individuals who could prove that they personally had been the victims of discrimination. In 1990, moreover, he acknowledged that over 900 age discrimination cases had been allowed to lapse under a law requiring EEOC to investigate such complaints within two years of their filing. Critics charged that

9,000 such cases had been permitted to lapse, whether by accident or design.[35]

Thomas's EEOC record and statements obviously offended liberals. So, too, did the nominee's views on 'natural law'. In a 1987 speech to the Heritage Foundation, a conservative think-tank, Thomas had praised an article in which businessman Lewis Lehrman urged a construction of the Constitution based on natural rights principles, condemned *Roe* v. *Wade* as legitimizing a 'holocaust' fundamentally at odds with natural law, and equated the struggle to ban abortion with the anti-slavery movement.[36] Thomas termed Lehrman's essay 'a splendid example of applying natural law'.[37] The nominee had also served on a White House task force which called for *Roe*'s dismantling, and he termed the right of marital privacy recognized in the *Griswold* case a judicial 'invention'.[38]

Nor was Thomas's lifestyle likely to be any consolation to liberals. After he and his first wife divorced, he had met and married a conservative white woman. The couple attended a suburban Virginia Episcopal congregation which mixed the politics of the religious right with speaking in unknown tongues and other elements of charismatic ritual.[39]

But Thomas caused concern not only for liberals. Certain of his views, especially his suggestion that judges should construe the Constitution in the light of higher law, also alarmed conservatives who agreed with Robert Bork that the Constitution's meaning should largely turn on an analysis of its framers' intentions, rather than on judicial conceptions of justice and social utility. The Supreme Court of the late nineteenth and early twentieth centuries had used such rhetoric to protect business interests from government regulation in a line of decisions modern conservatives might applaud. Arguably, however, that same sort of thinking underlay the modern Court's recognition of abortion and other privacy rights – rulings conservatives regularly condemn.[40]

When Senate confirmation proceedings began on 10 September, Democrats on the Judiciary Committee were primed with questions. Flanked by Senator Danforth and White House handlers, however, the nominee developed a powerful portrait of his humble origins and the indignities he and his family had suffered because of their race. He also moved quickly to distance himself from his more recent past.

Not only would he not venture an opinion on the constitutionality of abortion, he asserted that he had never even taken a position on that most controversial of modern civil liberties issues (which prompted one journalist to label him a 'liar or boob'[41]). He assured the Senators, however, that he recognized a constitutional guarantee to marital privacy. He now acknowledged, too, his personal debt to the civil rights movement and its leaders, including Justice Marshall, whom he praised as 'one of the great architects of the legal battles' against racial barriers. His praise of Lewis Lehrman, he claimed, was merely a strategem for appealing to a conservative audience, not an endorsement of his subject's position. 'To the extent that he [Lehrman] uses natural law to make a constitutional adjudication ... or to provide a moral code of some sort', he assured committee members, 'I disagree with it.'[42]

Ralph G. Neas, executive director of the liberal Leadership Conference on Civil Rights, accused Thomas of 'sprinting' rather than merely 'running' from his record and ridiculed his testimony as 'the earliest confirmation conversion we've witnessed'.[43] Neas's group, along with the NAACP, NOW, the AFL-CIO and other liberal organizations, had also announced their opposition to the nomination. The ABA's judiciary committee assigned Thomas the lowest rating of any given a confirmed Supreme Court nominee, with no member rating him well-qualified, twelve considering him qualified, two terming him not-qualified, and one member not voting. Thomas's responses to the general questions of Senators regarding landmark Supreme Court decisions revealed, moreover, a limited knowledge of constitutional law – adding fuel to complaints that Thomas, the anti-quota choice of an anti-quota president, was himself a quota choice unfit for a seat on the Supreme Court.

But Thomas's race made a 'no' vote extremely difficult, especially for Senate Democrats facing reelection. When the Judiciary Committee voted on 27 September, it split seven to seven, with moderate Arizona Democrat Dennis DeConcini joining the six committee Republicans in support of confirmation. Four days before a scheduled 8 October floor vote on the nominations, however, Senator Danforth was predicting that Thomas would receive over 60 affirmative votes and clear confirmation.

HILL VERSUS THOMAS

Thomas would be confirmed, of course, but not by the margin Danforth had predicted. In its Sunday 6 October issue, *Newsday* published charges raised against the nominee by Anita Hill, an African-American conservative Republican, Yale law graduate, and law professor at the University of Oklahoma. The same day, Hill aired her allegations in an interview with National Public Radio reporter Nina Totenberg. Thomas, she claimed, had repeatedly subjected her to graphic, grossly offensive sexual remarks and detailed descriptions of scenes from pornographic movies during her years as his counsel at the Department of Education and EEOC.

The behavior Professor Hill alleged violated EEOC guidelines for compliance with federal laws forbidding sexual harassment in the workplace. Even so, President Bush claimed he was 'not the least' concerned about Hill's charges, adding that Thomas still had his 'full confidence'.[44] John Danforth and other Senate supporters condemned what they saw as a desperate, last minute 'smear' of the nominee. Judiciary Committee members, who had been aware of Hill's assertions before their vote on Thomas, had chosen not to make them public when Hill initially declined to permit her name to be associated with her allegations, and for a time after she went public the Senate leadership seemed inclined to go forward with a floor vote on the nomination. But a firestorm of public outrage quickly derailed those plans. Floor action was delayed a week so that the Judiciary Committee could hold additional hearings.

Nothing in Hill's background suggested any basis for questioning her credibility. Other women came forward with claims that Thomas had also harassed them, and witnesses testified that Professor Hill had shared with them her distress at Thomas's behavior at the time it was allegedly occurring.

But the White House, Thomas and Republicans on the Judiciary Committee developed a brilliant strategy for putting Hill, the Committee, the confirmation process and the entire Congress, rather than the nominee, on the defensive. Playing the race card and conveniently ignoring the race of his accuser, an indignant, emotional Thomas portrayed himself as the victim of a 'high-tech lynching of an uppity black'.[45] Committee Republicans sought to discredit Hill. In a generally flattering profile of Thomas, the most conservative of the nation's major weekly news magazines had reported in its 16 September issue that, while at Yale, the nominee could 'sometimes [be heard] regaling other early risers with hilarious description of the X-rated movies he like to watch for relaxation.'[46] Senator Orrin Hatch of Utah apparently had not read that profile. Hatch ridiculed Professor Hill's claim that Thomas had described such distasteful films to her and came close to asserting with coaching from the White House, that she had actually based her accounts on the records of a sexual harassment lawsuit and passages from a controversial novel. In McCarthyesque style, Wyoming Republican Alan Simpson declared that his office was being flooded with warnings that Hill was not to be trusted, but cited no specific evidence to support such concerns. Arlen Specter of Pennsylvania charged that discrepancies in Hill's testimony amounted to perjury and hinted darkly at possible criminal charges against the witness.

Nor was that all. Committee Republicans and Bush surrogates suggested that Hill was delusional. Her critics expressed astonishment, moreover, that she could have remained on Thomas's staff and on friendly terms with him if her claims were true – doubts confirming, in the eyes of Hill's supporters, the critics' ignorance of the harsh choices women face in the workplace. Finally, Thomas's supporters effectively lobbied for the position that the nominee should be judged by standards applicable to criminal defendants: unless found guilty beyond a reasonable doubt, he deserved a seat on the nation's highest tribunal.

Undoubtedly fearful of African-American voter reaction, committee Democrats were as deferential to Thomas as Republicans were contemptuous of Hill. In his opening statement, the nominee shrewdly insisted that questions about his personal life would be an improper invasion of his privacy. Such inquiries were of obvious relevance to Hill's allegations. But the Democrats meekly acquiesced. Nor did they make more than a feeble effort to counter Thomas's remarkable charge that the Senate's investigation of charges directed against an African-American by another African-American was somehow an exercise in racial bigotry.

The strategy obviously worked. By a two-to-one margin, a national survey of state and federal judges conducted the day after a Senate vote on the nomination found Professor Hill more credible than Judge Thomas.[47] A year later, 44 per cent of participants in a national poll of public opinion would assert that they believed Hill, while only 34 per cent though Thomas truthful.[48] In a survey conducted at the time of the hearings, however, 40 per cent of those polled found Thomas more credible, and 50 per cent thought he should be confirmed, while only 24 and 29 per cent, respectively, believed Hill and opposed Thomas's confirmation.[49] On 15 October, the Senate followed those returns, voting 52 to 48 to approve the nomination. It was the closest Senate vote on a successful Supreme Court candidate in this century.

THE BUSH ADMINISTRATION IN THE COURTS

Once on the Supreme Court, Justice Thomas moved quickly to fulfil the administration's hopes and his detractors' worst fears. During his first term, he did join a close vote to reverse the conviction of a defendant in a child pornography case who had been the victim of entrapment.[50] In the main, however, he assumed a stridently conservative position in civil liberties cases. However uncertain his abortion stance before confirmation, he now joined the growing Court minority urging an outright reversal of *Roe* v. *Wade*.[51] Moreover, when two prison guards beat an inmate, loosening his teeth and cracking a denture while their supervisor merely chided them 'not to have too much fun', Thomas, joined only by Justice Antonin Scalia, vigorously dissented from the majority's conclusion that such conduct could constitute cruel and unusual punishment.[52]

To date, Bush's first Supreme Court appointment has proved less predictable, albeit generally conservative in his voting. During his second term, for example, Justice Souter joined a majority in striking down graduation prayers in the public schools[53] and refusing to reconsider *Lemon* v. *Kurtzman*,[54] the controversial 1971 holding that government contacts with religion must be secular in purpose and primary effect. In another case, he joined an opinion upholding several abortion controls but refused, unlike Thomas, to support *Roe*'s complete dismantling.[55]

Except perhaps his closest intimates, of course, no one can know for certain with whom President Bush was more pleased, Thomas or Souter. The President's own ambivalence toward civil liberties issues, however, was more suggestive of Souter's jurisprudence than Thomas's.

Bush selected as his Solicitor General Kenneth W. Starr, a 1983 Reagan appointee to the Court of Appeals for the District of Columbia who had clerked for Chief Justice Warren Burger. When Starr appeared before the Senate Judiciary Committee during confirmation proceedings, Chairman Biden and other committee members – mindful no doubt of the extent to which the Reagan administration had sought to politicize the office to which Starr had been nominated – stressed the delicate position of the Solicitor General as representative of both the administration and the United States. Starr assured the committee that he would never sign an administration brief he found 'legally indefensible' and that the Solicitor General should be 'respectful' of Supreme Court precedents. But he added, 'If he is convinced that a decision returned by the Supreme Court is wrong ... then it's appropriate that the Solicitor General should argue his case.'[56]

In general, Starr has pursued the cautious, middle-ground approach his statement to the committee appeared to support. After the Supreme Court in 1989 upheld flag-burning as a protected form of protest,[57] President Bush urged adoption of a constitutional amendment to exclude flag desecration from First Amendment protection. When Congress rejected Bush's approach, adopting instead a statute similar to the state law the Court invalidated in 1989, Starr argued unsuccessfully before the Justices that they should uphold the new law and yield to Congress's judgement 'that the physical integrity of the flag of the United States, as the unique symbol of the nation, merits protection not accorded other national emblems.'[58] Starr also sought, without success, to convince the Court to uphold graduation prayers[59] and reject affirmative action considerations in the awarding of broadcast licenses.[60] He supported several school systems, moreover, in their successful attempts to secure an end to federal court supervision of their desegregation efforts, even when shifting residential patterns were causing resegregation.[61] In other cases he urged an expansion of police search and seizure authority[62] and a narrow interpretation of the entrapment doctrine.[63]

Bush's Solicitor General largely avoided, however, the direct attacks on Supreme Court precedent which characterized the Reagan administration's dealings with the courts. In abortion cases, for example, Starr urged a relaxation of the judicial standards used to evaluate abortion controls, rather than a complete repudiation of the abortion right. Arguing in support of state abortion regulations reviewed by the Justices during their 1991–92 term, Starr, urged the Court to conclude that abortion regulations should be upheld if reasonably related to the furtherance of legitimate state interests. Such a standard accords states considerably more leeway than that permitted under *Roe*, which required that abortion controls serve a 'compelling' governmental interest. As described by Starr, however, the reasonable basis standard would leave the Court free to invalidate extremely restrictive abortion controls.[64]

CONCLUSION

The state of the economy was clearly the prime issue for voters in the 1992 elections. But concerns about the Reagan-Bush impact on the federal courts and the future direction of constitutional rights undoubtedly played a role as well. An unprecedented number of women sought congressional seats, many won, and the Thomas nomination, as well as the treatment of Professor Anita Hill, was an obvious catalyst for their campaigns, the funds they were able to attract and the voter support they enjoyed. Pennsylvania Republican Arlen Specter, the only one of Professor Hill's Senate Judiciary Committee detractors to face the voters in 1992, won reelection, but only after consuming a substantial portion of crow. His female opponent was a political novice. Building on the Thomas–Hill controversy, however, she ran a strong campaign. Specter not only dropped all hint of perjury charges against Hill, he was also obliged to profess having undergone a fundamental change in his thinking regarding sexual harassment since the Thomas confirmation proceedings.

Nor were the congressional races the only 1992 campaigns influenced by the Reagan-Bush judicial agenda. Election exit polls suggested, for example, that suburban Republican voters concerned about Supreme Court restrictions on the abortion right, and appalled by the degree to which President Bush had surrendered the 1992 Republican National Convention to the religious right, gave a heavier vote to the Democratic presidential ticket than might ordinarily have been expected.

During the Senate Judiciary Committee hearings on Justice Thomas's nomination, Wyoming Republican Alan Simpson had ridiculed the concern Thomas's critics expressed over the nominee's acceptance of natural law as a basis for constitutional interpretation. 'Natural law', said Simpson, was 'but a pseudonym for ... natural opposition or natural partisanship or natural frustration' on the part of those displeased at the prospect of another conservative Justice. 'There is a natural solution for that', he added. 'Elect a natural Democrat as president of the United States.'[65] Simpson was more prophetic than he expected or hoped.

NOTES

1. For excellent studies of Reagan's judicial appointments, see the extensive research of Sheldon Goldman, including 'Reaganizing the Judiciary: The First Term Appointments', *Judicature*, 70, April–May 1987, pp. 324–339.
2. Lincoln Caplan, *The Tenth Justice* (New York: Knopf, 1987), p. 107. Caplan's work is a provocative study of the administration's efforts.
3. For a survey of the Reagan administration's first-term approach to civil liberties issues, see Tinsley E. Yarbrough (ed.), *The Reagan Administration and Human Rights* (New York: Praeger, 1985).
4. Quoted in *Washington Post National Weekly Edition*, 24–30 August, 1992.
5. Ibid.
6. *West Virginia Bd. of Education* v. *Barnette*, 319 U.S. 624 (1943).
7. Except where otherwise indicated, discussion in this section is based on Sheldon Goldman, 'The Bush Imprint on the Judiciary: Carrying on a Tradition', *Judicature*, 74, April–May 1991, pp. 294–306. Students of the courts continue to be indebted to Professor Goldman for his excellent coverage of the process and politics of federal judicial selection.
8. *National Law Journal*, 6 August 1990, p. 43.
9. *Public Citizen* v. *Department of Justice*, 109 S. Ct. 2558 (1989).
10. Joan Biskupic, 'Bush Boosts Bench Strength of Conservative Judges', *Congressional Quarterly Weekly Report*, 19 January 1991, p. 171.
11. For a summary of the judgeship bill's legislative history, see *Congressional Quarterly Almanac*, 46, 1990, pp. 520–523.
12. Ibid.

13.   *Congressional Quarterly Almanac*, 47, 1991, pp. 288–289.
14.   Biskupic, op. cit., p. 172.
15.   Richard Lacayo, 'To the Bench Via the Chair', *Time*, 14 September 1992, p. 41.
16.   Joan Biskupic, 'Ryskamp Fails to Dispel Race Bias Concerns', *Congressional Quarterly Weekly Report*, 23 March 1991, p. 748; Joan Biskupic, 'Home-State Senator's Opposition Marked End for Court Nominee', *Congressional Quarterly Weekly Report*, 13 April 1991, p. 922.
17.   Biskupic, 'Bush Boosts Bench Strength', op. cit., p. 171.
18.   The best primary source relating to the Souter appointment, of course, is US Congress, Senate Committee on the Judiciary, *Hearings on the Nomination of David H. Souter to be Associate Justice of the Supreme Court of the United States*, 101st Cong., 2d Sess., 1990, hereinafter cited as *Hearings*.
19.   'Insider Baseball: How Sununu Sold Souter', *Harper's Magazine*, November, 1990, p. 24.
20.   A transcript of President Bush's announcement is reprinted in *Congressional Quarterly Almanac*, 46, 1990, p. 509.
21.   410 U.S. 113 (1973).
22.   381 U.S. 479 (1965).
23.   384 U.S. 436 (1966).
24.   Conservative columnist William F. Buckley Jr used Souter's praise of Brennan as a basis for comparing what he termed Souter's 'cowardly' efforts to appease Senate liberals with Brennan's attempt to cultivate Senator McCarthy and other 'Commie-hunters' during his confirmation hearing. 'The Valor of Judge Souter', *National Review*, 15 October 1990.
25.   *Hearings*, p. 17.
26.   Ibid., p. 73.
27.   Ibid., p. 71.
28.   Andrew Hacker, *Two Nations* (New York: Scribner's, 1992), p. 201.
29.   This profile is drawn from a number of periodical accounts. See, for example, 'The Crowning Thomas Affair', *U.S. News & World Report*, 16 September 1991, pp. 25–30. For a succinct summary of the controversy over Thomas's appointment, see *Congressional Quarterly Almanac*, 46, 1991, pp. 274–285.
30.   A. Leon Higginbotham Jr 'An Open Letter to Justice Clarence Thomas from a Federal Judicial Colleague', *University of Pennsylvania Law Review*, 140, January 1992, pp. 1005–1028.
31.   Quoted in *Washington Post*, 2 July 1991.
32.   *San Diego Union & Tribune*, 6 October 1987, quoted in Higginbotham, op. cit., p. 1012.
33.   Quoted in *Washington Post*, 2 July 1991.
34.   Quoted in 'The Crowning Thomas Affair', op. cit., p. 26.
35.   For an excellent summary of Thomas's EEOC stewardship, see *Washington Post*, 10 September 1991.
36.   Lewis Lehrman, 'The Declaration of Independence and the Right to Life', *American Spectator*, April 1987, pp. 21–23.
37.   For an analysis of Thomas's constitutional philosophy, see Scott D. Gerber, 'The Jurisprudence of Clarence Thomas', *Journal of Law and*

Politics, 8, Fall 1991, pp. 107–141. For Thomas's own brief summaries of his thinking, see, for example, 'The Higher Law Background of the Privileges or Immunities Clause of the Fourteenth Amendment', *Harvard Journal of Law & Public Policy*, 12, Winter 1989, pp. 63–70; 'Toward a "Plain Reading" of the Constitution – The Declaration of Independence in Constitutional Interpretation', *Howard Law Journal*, 30, 1987, pp. 983–995.

38. Quoted in *Washington Post*, 10 September 1991.
39. For a profile of his second wife, Virginia Lamp Thomas, see Laura Blumfeld, 'The Nominee's Soul Mate', *Washington Post*, 10 September 1991.
40. Thomas did not begin referring to natural law in his public statements until he hired as assistants two former students of Harry Jaffa, a Clarmont College political theorist whose views on the relationship of natural law to constitutional meaning closely resembled those reflected in Thomas's speeches and writings. Jaffa has asserted that the *Griswold* decision could be defended on the basis of natural law theory. *Washington Post*, 10 September 1991.
41. Michael Kinsley, 'Liar or Boob?' *New Republic*, 21 October 1991, p. 4.
42. *Washington Post*, 11 September 1991. At this writing official transcripts of the hearings have not yet been published.
43. Ibid.
44. *Washington Post*, 8 October 1991.
45. *Washington Post*, 12 October 1991.
46. 'The Crowning Thomas Affair', op. cit., p. 29.
47. 'Hearings Turn Off Judges', *National Law Journal*, 28 October 1991, p. 1.
48. *Washington Post*, 5 October 1992.
49. *Washington Post*, 13 October 1991.
50. *Jacobson* v. *United States*, 112 S. Ct. 1535 (1992).
51. *Planned Parenthood* v. *Casey*, 112 S. ct. 2791 (1992).
52. *Hudson* v. *McMillan*, 112 S. Ct. 995, 1004 (1992).
53. *Lee* v. *Weisman*, 112 S. Ct. 2649, 2667 (1992).
54. *Lemon* v. *Kurtzman*, 403 U.S. 602 (1971).
55. *Planned Parenthood* v. *Casey*, 112 S. Ct. 1791 (1992).
56. Quoted in *Congressional Quarterly Almanac*, 45, 1989, pp. 290–291.
57. *Texas* v. *Johnson*, 109 S. Ct. 2533 (1989).
58. Quoted in *Congressional Quarterly Almanac*, 46, 1990, p. 525.
59. For a summary of his oral argument, see 60 Law Week 3351 (1991).
60. *Metro Broadcasting* v. *FCC* 110 S. Ct. 2997 (1990).
61. For a summary of his oral argument in one such case, *Bd. of Education* v. *Dowell*, 111 S. Ct. 630 (1991), see 59 Law Week 3264 (1990).
62. See, for example, the summary of his oral argument in *Florida* v. *Bostick*, 59 Law Week 3625 (1991), in which the Court ultimately upheld warrantless police encounters with seated bus travelers.
63. *Jacobson* v. *United States*, 112 S. Ct. 1535 (1992).
64. See, for example, the summary of his oral argument in *Planned Parenthood* v. *Casey*, 60 Law Week 3727 (1992).
65. *Washington Post*, 11 September 1991.

6 The Economic Policies of the Bush Administration
Stephen Woolcock

INTRODUCTION

The Bush administration inherited an economy which had seen a period of six years of credit-based growth. Although the budget deficit had fallen from 5 per cent of GDP in 1985 to 3 per cent in 1989, the expectation when President Bush assumed office was that the US economy would at best experience a period of slow growth and at worse move into a recession. The prospects for a continued decline in the budget deficit due to increased tax revenue from economic growth were therefore not too good. A renewed growth in the budget deficit was a definite risk. The challenge was to maintain economic growth, which in the short term meant managing a soft landing for the US economy, while reducing the budget and trade deficits. Throughout the Reagan years there had been constant reference to the need to reduce the budget deficit, but the economy continued to grow all the same. At the same time it was possible to argue that America could continue to finance its debt. There was also a growing belief that the dead weight of debt had, by 1989, reached the point at which it threatened the long-term prospects for the US economy.

The Bush administration's efforts to contain the growing budget deficit failed, in large part because his policies were prejudiced by his 'read my lips' pledge during the election campaign of 1988 not to introduce any new taxes. Together with Congressional resistance to significant reductions in social security and Medicare and Medicaid programmes, this meant that there was no significant reduction in the deficit when the economy was still strong in 1989. Despite offering to work with Congress President Bush lost Congressional support on the budget issue in the first round of discussion on budget reductions in 1989. He lost support for a range of reasons, including what Congress saw as an unwillingness to address the issue head on, which for Congress meant raising taxes.

The 1990 round of discussions were even more acrimonious and were also tense because of the upcoming mid-term elections. From mid-1990 the economy also lost momentum and there was less and less scope for budget reductions for fear of accentuating the recession. As a result the deficit ballooned to nearly $400 billion in 1992. Without a credible budget deficit plan the Federal Reserve Bank felt obliged to maintain tight monetary policies in order to dampen inflationary pressures. This delayed the economic recovery which only came in the autumn of 1992, too late to help President Bush's chances of re-election. Probably as damaging to the economic prospects of the US economy and the re-election hopes of Bush was, however, the loss of confidence in the ability of the government to address the central economic issues facing the US. This created a sense of drift and inaction. When the recession finally came this sense of drift was translated into dissatisfaction with the Bush presidency, which was seen as having answers for foreign policy crises but not for the difficulties facing the US economy.

In other areas of policy the Bush administration proved itself a determined opponent of more interventionist action. It resisted pressure from American industrial circles for more active policies to promote American industry, and thus the arguments in favour of a form of strategic industrial policy. It also effectively resisted Congressional pressure for more interventionist interpretations of US laws on inward investment, such as the Exon-Florio amendment to the 1988 Omnibus Trade and Competitiveness Act. Some Congressional leaders wished to see this used to prevent the large-scale acquisition of US companies by foreigners, most notably the Japanese. The Bush administration's opposition to controls on inward investment was partly because the US needed such investment to fund its budget deficit, but also because Bush genuinely favoured open trade and investment.

In international trade the Bush administration oversaw a further shift in US policy towards a greater qualification of US support for multilateral approaches and a greater tendency towards less discretion. This was an area of policy in which the scope for the exercise of discretionary power by the President was limited. Congress has, of course, always had responsibility for trade policy. The 1988 Trade Act further reduced the scope for interpretation left in the hands of the executive. Against the pressures of protectionism one could argue that the Bush administration used the unilateral provisions of Section 301, and especially Super 301 of US trade law, in a moderate fashion. But it did not prevent the drift in US trade policy away from multilateralism and towards a greater emphasis on regional or unilateral approaches.

Ultimately, however, it was the perceived inability of the Bush administration to revive the US economy during 1991 and 1992 which undermined its successes in foreign policy and thus its political support. The US economy did not have a particularly hard landing after eight years of growth. The recession which started in July 1990 and extended until the middle of 1991 was mild compared to that of the early 1980s or for that matter the recession which hit the European economies in 1990/91. The economy even showed signs of recovery just before the presidential elections in the autumn of 1992. But by that time American middle-class voters had lost confidence in the administration's ability to manage the economy. It was less the short-term difficulties, but more the lack of belief that another Bush administration could do anything to help secure a sound future for their children which led this vital group of voters to desert President Bush in large numbers.

THE BUSH BUDGETS

In early 1989 President Bush's Office of Management and the Budget (OMB), under the direction of Richard Darman, projected a budget deficit for the fiscal year 1990 of some $126 billion. This was somewhat higher than the requirements of the Gramm-Rudmann-Hollings (GRH) provisions. The GRH provisions were legislated by Congress, with the aim of achieving a balanced budget by 1993.[1] The (revised) GRH target for 1990 was $100 billion. The OMB projections were initially criticized for being over-optimistic and for being based on assumptions for rates of economic growth and inflation which were clearly on the optimistic side of the likely out-turn. The Congressional Budget Office projected, for example, a higher budget deficit of $141 billion. There was no doubt that the Bush administration's first budget of April 1989 was based on somewhat over-optimistic projections for economic growth, but the key failing was that the budget proposal did nothing to address the long-term difficulty of the budget deficit. At a time when the economy was slowing, immediate tax increases or reductions in expenditure would have been counterproductive. But had President Bush not been committed to 'no new taxes' he might have begun his presidency with a coherent plan to reduce the deficit over a number of years. Initially, Congress was arguably prepared to consider bipartisan approaches to the deficit reduction. Had such a coherent approach been adopted at the outset Bush might have spared himself the confrontations over the budget in the years that followed. These as much as anything undermined the credibility of his management of the economy. In retrospect it is easy to say that the budget issue should have been addressed earlier. The problems in reaching an agreement with Congress were, of course, formidable. But the main criticism of President Bush is that his administration made no serious attempt to address the budget issue in his first year.

The strategy for the 1989 budget proposals for Fiscal Year 1990 was to rely on fiscal drag. In other words it was argued that the increased revenue from taxes as the economy continued to grow would rise faster than inflation and thus reduce the budget deficit.[2] President Bush argued that this, along with a flexible freeze on spending (no real increases in spending), would bring about a balanced budget by 1993. The option of reducing the budget deficit by raising taxes was not acceptable to President Bush, who during the 1988 election campaign had committed himself to no new taxes. Bush's resolute opposition to higher taxes had been an important plank of his campaign both in the Republican primaries and in the presidential campaign proper. He had weakened Robert Dole's position in the Republican primaries by accusing him of 'flip-flopping' on the tax issue and had challenged the Democratic contender, Michael Dukakis, as a traditional 'tax and spend' Democrat. When questioned whether he could really deliver on his promise of a reduced budget deficit without raising taxes, Bush told his challengers to read his lips, 'no new taxes'.

In his budget speech Bush presented himself as a president wanting a more caring America and as seeking to work together with the Congress. Although the speech was initially well received, because the rhetoric contrasted with the more partisan style of President Reagan, Congress soon realized that there was little new in the approach. The Democrat controlled Congress soon came to regret its initial acceptance of the 'proffered hand' of cooperation when it became clear that the President expected Congress to decide on spending cuts to implement the 'flexible freeze' and thus pay the political price. The scene was therefore soon set for confrontation between Congress and the administration on budgetary issues which was to mark the whole of the Bush presidency. Analysts of President Bush's 1990 budget saw it as a 'slide by' budget. This meant that it avoided facing up to the real challenge of dealing with the rising budget deficit. In 1989/90 improvement growth might rightly be expected to bring about a reduction in the deficit as economic growth resulted in rising tax revenues. But most analysts argued that economic growth would soon slow or even decline at which point the deficit would increase dramatically. The National Economic Commission which had been set up to address the question of the budget deficit split between the Democratic and Republican members. As one participant put it the options open to the US were to 'go into the next century with flags flying or slouch into it'. The Bush approach did not change the approach used by President Reagan in any discernable sense so many critics of the administration felt that the US was continuing to 'slouch'.[3]

There seems to be little doubt that the Bush administration was aware of these longer-term projections of the budget deficit but chose to avoid facing up to the difficult question during 1989. The main factor in this was the inability of the President to go back on his election pledge of no new taxes so soon after being elected. The alternative course of reducing spending was blocked by Congressional opposition to major cuts and a fear that deflationary measures would precipitate a recession. In the event the economy continued to grow reasonably quickly during 1989 and the administration's projections by the OMB were not so wide of the mark. With some massaging of the figures it was possible for the administration to claim that the Gramm-Rudmann target could be achieved.[4]

From the middle of 1990 the long expected slow-down in the US economy began. The decline in output in the second half of 1990 was put down to the negative effects of the Gulf crisis on consumer confidence. The recession was called the Saddam recession by some commentators. But in reality the recession began in July 1990 before the Iraqi invasion of Kuwait. This appears to have been recognized by the administration itself, because as early as May 1990 the White House began preparing the ground for President Bush to bite the bullet and accept that tax increases would be needed to contain the growth of the budget deficit and thus provide the credibility sought by the money markets. President Bush's draft budget had been rejected by Congress with little debate and the Democratic leadership of Congress had put forward proposals for a deficit reduction of some $50 billion over five years, including tax increases. In late June President Bush officially accepted there would have to be tax increases, 'because the deficit was worse than anyone had envisaged'. This was being somewhat economical with the truth as a number of projections had pointed to the difficulties of a growing deficit if the economy did slide into a recession as it did in the summer of 1990.

The Federal Reserve Board had also made a credible budget agreement between the Bush administration and Congress a precondition of looser monetary policy. Throughout 1989 and the early part of 1990 the Bush administration had repeatedly called upon the Fed to reduce interest rates as a means of stimulating the US economy and fending off a recession. In the early months of the new administration the Chairman of the Fed, Alan Greenspan, resisted pressure from the administration because he felt that the greatest danger came from inflation. Indeed, inflationary pressure had by no means been squeezed out of the economy in 1990 and there remained fears of stagflation, i.e. stagnation associated with high levels of inflation. By tying its willingness to reduce interest rates to an agreement on the budget the Fed brought additional pressure on the administration since a recession brought about by tight monetary policy would result in a greater deficit and more difficult political choices for the administration.[5]

In the spring of 1990 Bush had appeared happy to allow the budget to run into the buffers: in other words to allow the automatic budget reduction provisions of the GRH provisions to apply. This would have resulted in sequestration of funding for defence and social programmes. But with the economy slowing the GRH provisions lost their credibility. The administration was therefore affected by the general danger signals coming from the economy. The Gulf Crisis threatened to result in higher oil prices which could have had a major adverse effect on the US economy. The number of bank failures was rising. House building starts, an important measure of the health of the real estate and consumer goods markets, dropped to an eight-year low. The dollar was falling in value and the absence of a credible agreement could have raised the risk of a crisis in confidence in exchange markets and a dollar crisis. As noted above, the Federal Reserve was holding back from interest rate cuts until a credible deficit reduction package had been agreed. It was these pressures which led President Bush to reverse his position and accept that tax increases were needed in order to reach an agreement with Congress on a credible budget package.

The decision to accept increased taxes provoked opposition from the right of the Republican party, led by proponents of further tax cuts such as Jack Kemp. With the mid-term elections in November 1990 the last thing the Republicans in Congress wanted was tax increases. In an attempt to placate the Republicans President Bush tried to get tax reductions, on capital gains taxes, but these were rejected by the Democrats. President Bush tried to appeal to the American public over the head of Congress but Congress still refused to cooperate and Bush was obliged to drop the idea of reductions in the capital gains tax. In October 1990 failure to agree on a budget created a financial crisis in the government and the President was obliged to take emergency measures to keep the government in funds. In the last few days before the mid-term elections the President finally and reluctantly signed a budget agreement which envisaged a reduction of $492 billion in the deficit over five years, made up of cuts in defence spending, cuts in Medicare and Medicaid and tax increases. But the budget 'crisis' damaged the Bush administration. To make matters worse, the recession – which increased in pace over the autumn – made the budget deal largely irrelevant, and projections gave a deficit of $300 billion for the Fiscal Year 1991.

From the middle of 1990, therefore, the economy and the linked issue of the budget began to dog President Bush. The

Gulf crisis, which began in August 1990, provided President
Bush with an opportunity to show what he could do in foreign
policy, an area in which he felt comfortable and confident, but
the Gulf crisis also resulted in a weakening of the US economy
– but not, as some had thought, either as a result of a rise in oil
prices or because of the costs of the war. In the end the United
States covered the costs of the war thanks to payments made by
its allies. The funds came mainly from Germany and Japan
which, because of their constitutional constraints, provided no
military contribution to the fighting, as well as from the Gulf
states such as Saudi Arabia. The impact of the Gulf crisis lay in
the way that it undermined consumer confidence at a time
when the US economy was already moving into a recession.

After the victory for the allies and for President Bush in the
Gulf war, the administration made a concerted effort to
present its economic policies in a convincing and credible
fashion. In March 1991 President Bush outlined his strategy of
encouraging savings; reducing the budget deficit, on which an
agreement was finally reached on a $500 billion reduction over
five years; reducing the regulatory burden on business and a
further liberalization of telecommunications; and creating new
markets for US exports by completing the Uruguay Round of
multilateral trade negotiations, completing the negotiations
on a North American Free Trade Agreement (NAFTA) with
Mexico and Canada, and ensuring other countries 'played fair'
on trade. In essence, however, the Bush administration urged
the Fed to reduce interest rates and waited for the recovery to
come. Its attempt to stimulate the economy through reductions in capital gains tax had been blocked by Congress and
other stimulative programmes would have made the budget
deficit worse and only worked with a time lag in any case.

The recession continued in the first half of 1991 with a fall of
3.7 per cent in output in the first quarter of 1991. There was a
small recovery in the third quarter of 1991 when output rose by
over 2 per cent but the longer-term prospects for the economy
did not look encouraging. After the conclusion of the budget
agreement the Federal Reserve did begin to reduce interest
rates. The Fed's discount rate was reduced in February 1991
and in May (to 5 per cent), but the economy did not respond.
Further interest rate cuts came in August and November (to
4.5 per cent) but the economy still refused to pick up. This was

in part due to the high levels of personal and corporate debt that had been built up during the 1980s. Having been forced to suffer high interest rates in the late 1980s consumers used the reduced interest rates in 1991, not as an opportunity to consume more through borrowing, but to reduce their debts. This depressed housing and general consumer product markets.

In foreign policy 1990/91 had been a year of considerable successes for President Bush. He had successfully steered the allies to victory in the Gulf War and benefited from being in charge at a time when the West 'won' the Cold War. These successes helped him achieve popularity ratings of 90 per cent in opinion polls, which appeared to put Bush in an unassailable position in mid-1991. But by October 1991 these successes appear to have been forgotten by most Americans. As one popular newspaper put it in November 1991, the average voter's sentiment was reflected in the phase, 'President Bush went to the NATO summit [which sealed the ending of the Cold War], and all I got was this lousy recession.' By November Bush's ratings had fallen to 50 per cent.[6]

When the economy failed to respond to interest rate cuts and facing an election year with the US economy still in recession the Bush administration began to get desperate. In November the President shifted his policy again. Throughout the summer of 1991 Bush had resisted pressure from conservative Republicans for tax cuts, because this would have adverse effects on the deficit and been seen as electioneering. But in November 1991, under pressure from the right wing of the Republican Party, he decided to support tax cut proposals tabled by Republicans in Congress. But the proposals were geared to help higher income Americans, who, thanks to earlier tax cuts, had already managed to increase the gap between them and the lower paid who saw their average incomes fall in real terms.[7] The tax cuts would not even have had a direct stimulative effect on the economy.

In December even the independent Federal Reserve was worried enough about the continuing inability of the economy to pick itself up to make the dramatic gesture of cutting its discount rate by a further full 1 per cent to 3.5 per cent (prime lending rates were thus reduced to 6.5 per cent), the lowest rate for 18 years. Still the economy refused to respond. Entering 1992 President Bush and his advisers knew that the prospects of Bush being re-elected in November 1992 depended on the economy, but had few options for new policies. In his final draft budget in early 1992 President Bush proposed a range of tax reductions in order to try and stimulate the economy. This effectively undermined the budget package agreed with so much difficulty in 1991. Indeed by 1992 the budget deficit had grown to some $400 billion from about $140 billion when Bush came to power.

Against this record it was not possible for Bush to be effective in any attacks on his Democratic challenger who set out reasonably detailed proposals on the budget at an early stage in his campaign. Paradoxically, after months of refusing to respond to reduced interest rates, the economy finally began to show signs of life in the autumn of 1992 just before the presidential elections. But for President Bush it was too late, the damage had already been done.

STRUCTURAL POLICIES

The Bush administration maintained a non-interventionist approach in most areas of micro-economic policy. In his adoption hearings Secretary of State for Commerce Robert Mosbacher had professed his opposition to industrial policy and maintained this stance during the Bush administration. Growing concern about the decline of American industrial competitiveness led a number of industrial groups and business spokespersons to call for more active policies. Such calls were particularly frequent in sectors considered to be 'strategic' by the companies concerned, such as electronics and semiconductors. For example, the head of Sematech, the body established by leading semiconductor producers to promote more joint research efforts, called for government backing for a more coordinated R&D. The models for such coordinated programmes were similar Japanese or European Community programmes. Throughout the Bush term of office there was an important undercurrent of opinion on the need to strengthen American industry and that the kind of arm's-length, non-interventionist policies pursued by the Bush administration were inadequate when US industries faced competition from European and Japanese companies benefiting from more active government support.

Although the support provided by such programmes as the EC's Esprit was not substantial, and American commentators tended to exaggerate the coordinated nature of European and Japanese policies in this area, the perception was that it was only the American industries that were getting no support. This undercurrent of opinion extended to include concern among industrialists and business people about the poor provision of training and education in America. Many of the issues which shaped the debate in the 1992 election, such as the need for America to rebuild its economy and the strategic importance of certain industries, were rehearsed during the years of the Bush administration. Support for more active policies could be found among business people and industrialists, a constituency which one would normally have expected to have been solidly Republican. The case for more active industrial policies had some support among members of the administration also. In April 1990 the head of the Defense Advanced Research Projects Agency (DARPA), Craig I. Fields, was removed from office for having promoted the use of defence contracts as a means of supporting specific industrial projects. The case which led to his removal involved providing support for an advanced integrated circuits producer, Gazelle Micro Circuits.[8]

In the 1990 Economic Report of the President the administration quashed any suggestion that it might be interested in pursuing a more activist approach. This report rejected calls for an industrial policy, and for trade protection, and made the case for open unrestricted access for foreign investment. The White House Chief of Staff John Sununu and Chairman of the Council of Economic Advisors, Michael Boskin, were seen as the most implacable opponents of an activist policy. The issue remained a live one, however, and one that President Bush's Democratic challengers picked up with enthusiasm in the 1992 campaign. The support given to the challenger Clinton by industrial interests, including some of the major US information technology companies, helped Clinton's credibility and was no doubt affected by the absence of any concrete signs that the Bush administration was prepared to intervene to help US industry compete.

In some areas the Bush administration did attempt active structural reforms. One of the most notable was the effort to reform US banking legislation. The US banking laws, which date back to the Glass-Steagal and Banking Laws of the 1930s, were drawn up at the time of the depression. Bank failures were seen as a significant contributing factor to the recession and the 1930s banking laws sought to limit the exposure of banks. This was done by separating banking from securities business. The other long-standing structural feature of the US banking sector was the limitation on inter-state branching. As banks had to establish subsidiaries in other states, rather than branches as would have been possible with inter-state branching, and as each subsidiary was subject to the regulations of the host state, this meant that, among other things, minimum capital requirements had to be satisfied for each state. The effect was to provide further protection against bank failure but at the price of fragmenting the US banking industry. Despite liberalization coming from the level of the states, US banks saw such restrictions as weakening their competitive position. The fragmentation of the US banking sector was highlighted by the efforts of the European Community to create a single EC financial market as part of the EC 1992 programme.

In February 1991 the Treasury Secretary Nicholas Brady presented proposals for a fundamental reform of banking and securities regulation which would have permitted inter-state banking, after a five-year transition period, and removed some of the barriers between the securities and banking sectors. This was an issue in which President Bush had a previous interest, as he had chaired an inter-agency review committee on the regulation of the banks under the second Reagan presidency, which considered many of the ideas which found their way into the Brady proposals. The objective of the Treasury was to bring about a reform of the banking regulations for long-term structural reasons. But the case for reform was also made in terms of the need to strengthen the banks' ability to lend at a time when there was a serious credit squeeze. Initially the legislation had passed through the various Congressional scrutiny committees and seemed set to pass Congress, much to the surprise of observers. But the progress of the legislation was halted by the – largely unrelated – issue of the Savings and Loan fiasco.

The Savings and Loan instructions, or 'Thrifts', have traditionally accepted deposits from a large number of small savers and provided capital for real estate investment in the United States. During the Reagan administration there was a widespread deregulation of provisions controlling the conditions under which S&Ls could lend. This resulted in the rapid growth in the supply of credit for real estate, but also led to many Savings and Loan companies becoming over-extended. Although there was a deregulation of lending activities, there was no requirement to retain minimum capital reserves, as there is in virtually all banking regulatory systems. As if this were not enough the state continued to provide guarantees for the deposits of smaller investors in the S&Ls through the Federal Deposit Insurance Corporation (FDIC). In other words the managements of the S&Ls were given more scope to lend and provided with a guarantee that any losses affecting small depositors would be guaranteed by the FDIC. When the real estate market deteriorated in 1990/91 many S&Ls collapsed and the FDIC was obliged to step in and cover the losses. When the Bush administration came to office it unveiled a rescue plan for the S&L industry with an estimated cost to the federal government of some $50 billion. By the end of 1989 the costs of the S&L rescue programme had risen to between $166 billion (administration estimate) and $275 billion (independent estimates). In April 1990 the estimates of the cost were running at $325 billion,[9] and by the early autumn of 1990 the S&L issue became a major embarrassment for the administration and for President Bush personally. The issue was presented as public resources being used to cover the losses made as a result of the unregulated greed of unscrupulous S&L managements. The costs of the bailout would have been embarrassing at the best of times but when the administration was trying to control the growth of the budget deficit by reducing entitlement benefits, it was not difficult to argue that the poor were being asked to pay for the failures of past deregulation policies. President Bush was directly affected when it became public that his son was involved with one of the S&Ls that was in difficulties.[10]

Having seen the consequences of deregulation in the S&L industry Congress retreated from reform measures in banking. From the point of view of banking reform and the objectives of the administration this linkage was unfortunate, because there was never any suggestion that the banking reforms would have resulted in the kind of calamitous deregulation that developed in the S&L case. Nevertheless the mood swung against reform and in favour of the interests seeking to block it for their own interests, such as the small banks and some of the securities houses. The final package of legislation agreed by Congress in November 1991 was only the bare bones of reform and consisted mainly of a refinancing package for the FDIC.

TRADE AND FOREIGN INVESTMENT POLICIES

When President Bush assumed office in January 1989 the GATT Uruguay Round of trade negotiations had just about reached the half way stage in its scheduled four-year cycle. In actual fact the GATT mid-term review meeting held the previous November in Montreal had failed to reach agreement and the GATT Secretary General, Arthur Dunkel, was busily trying to broker an agreement on how to proceed. One of the central issues in the negotiations, and the one that threatened agreement in the mid-term meeting, was agriculture. The US position had been to argue for the elimination of all agricultural subsidies in the face of the opposition from the European Community which was only prepared to accept reductions in subsidies as long as this did not affect the functioning of the Common Agricultural Policy (CAP).

On taking office President Bush moved the previous US Trade Representative in the last Reagan administration, Clayton Yeutter, to the Department of Agriculture. This was interpreted as a signal to the US's negotiating partners that the Bush administration was determined to get a satisfactory agreement on agriculture. The other key trade appointment was Carla Hills as US Trade Representative. In her confirmation hearings on the Hill the new USTR presented herself as a tough negotiator who was prepared to use the 'crowbar' of US trade legislation to open export markets if multilateral negotiations failed. In March 1989 agreement on the mid-term review was finally reached. This envisaged substantial, progressive reductions in support for agriculture over a specified period of time. But shortly afterwards the US, under the guidance of Yeutter, appeared to revert to the policy objective of eliminating all subsidies. This was probably a tactical shift based on past experience in trying to negotiate reductions in agricultural subsidies with the EC. It appears to have been calculated to put maximum pressure on the EC and certainly ensured that agriculture was at the centre of the Uruguay Round negotiations. But it was interpreted by the EC as unrealistic and a reversal of what the US had accepted in Montreal. The consequence was that little progress was made in the GATT negotiations during 1989 and 1990.

Throughout 1989 and 1990 the Bush administration pressed for an agreement on the Uruguay Round within the deadline agreed for the end of 1990. Progress was made on detailed aspects of what was a highly complex trade round.[11] But the deadline of the end of 1990 was missed. Under pressure from the United States and other agricultural exporters, the EC failed to come up with a reasonable negotiating position in time for the GATT ministerial meeting in Brussels in December 1990, which was supposed to have been the conclusion of the negotiations. Indeed, there was no EC negotiating position at all on agriculture until a few weeks before the meeting. The EC's position failed to meet US expectations, because the level of subsidy reduction finally offered was not considered acceptable. Perhaps more importantly the EC refused to make commitments to liberalization in each of three areas in which the US and other agricultural exporters were seeking commitments; these were: domestic subsidies, export subsidies, and import controls. Having failed to tie down the EC in previous rounds the US negotiators were determined to get specific commitments from the EC.

There was clearly a genuine desire to get a good agreement on agriculture, but it was also convenient for the Bush administration to press for maximalist solutions in areas in which other parties, notably the EC and Japan had considerable difficulties. This enabled the onus to shift onto the EC and covered the fact that in December 1990 there was little prospect of getting a deal negotiated in the GATT through Congress. Rather than risk the talks failing due to a negative vote in the US Congress, it was wiser and safer to refuse to budge on agriculture and allow the EC to take the blame for delays. President Bush was ideologically committed to free trade. As such he was probably one of a dwindling group of US political leaders who were prepared to support free trade and the maintenance of an open trading system without qualification.

Many American politicians, not to mention industrialists, trade unionists and environmentalists, were much more qualified in their support for open or free trade. As a consequence the Bush administration in the shape of its US Trade Representative, Carla Hills, and the other trade negotiators had to make sure that they did not go beyond what Congress would accept in negotiating with trading partners. The GATT negotiations were an example of the constraints under which the Bush administration worked on trade policy. It had in effect to negotiate with two parties: the US's trading partners on the one hand and Congress and all the various interest groups represented in Congress on the other hand.

With this qualification the Bush administration continued to press for an agreement in the GATT negotiations. Following the failure of the Brussels GATT Ministerial Round, the Bush administration first had to seek an extension of the so-called 'fast-track' negotiating authority from Congress. With the 1988 Omnibus Trade and Competitiveness Act Congress had granted the administration authority to negotiate for four years.[12] In order to get Congress to support an extension of this authority for a further two years, the maximum period possible without new legislation, the Bush administration had to get some assurance that the European Community was serious about wanting an agreement on agriculture. This assurance took the form of a commitment by the EC to negotiate specific reductions in each of the three categories of agricultural support. The precise level of commitment remained the substance of negotiations. Nevertheless this was enough to get the requisite support in Congress in May 1991. Negotiating authority for the North American Free Trade Agreement (NAFTA) (see below) was linked to the GATT authority.

In the early part of 1991 the Bush administration, therefore, left other Contracting Parties to the GATT to make most of the running in the negotiations. During this period some countries (Germany, Britain and the Netherlands) favoured concluding the Round by the end of the year because of a concern that it should be completed before the presidential election campaigns began. France opposed this because it wished to play for time. Previous presidential campaigns had resulted in candidates making commitments to protectionist interests in the heat of the campaign which proved troublesome afterwards.

Some important progress was made in the negotiations during the second half of 1991, and by December it was possible for the Secretary General of the GATT, Arthur Dunkel, to produce a draft final act of the Uruguay Round. This so-called Dunkel draft was not the agreed text of the Contracting Parties on all points, but an attempt at a compromise text on the authority of the GATT. The Dunkel draft was produced in December 1991 with the intention of seeking an agreement on the final details in early 1992 before the US presidential campaign got under way. But this became another missed deadline.

During the 1992 campaign trade was not a major issue. President Bush held more or less solidly to his position of free trade and support for the GATT negotiations, and Governor Clinton studiously avoided making any commitments to protectionist groups. Only Ross Perot promised protectionist policies. The politics of the campaign did, however, intrude on the negotiations in the sense that on the most politically sensitive issue, that of agriculture, neither the Bush administration nor the European Community, or more accurately the French government, could be seen to be giving ground in order to reach an agreement. In France there was the referendum on Maastricht in September 1992 and then the French general elections in March 1993 to worry about. In the US Bush could not be seen to be making concessions in order to conclude the Uruguay Round because it would have been seen as yet another example of him putting foreign policy issues before those of American farmers or businesses. This political sensitivity resulted in negotiations continuing right through the night of the election. Ultimately, however, the talks failed because of differences within the EC delegation on how to interpret the negotiating mandate given to the Commission negotiators by the member states of the EC in the Council of Ministers.

The Bush administration, therefore, performed reasonably well in the GATT negotiations. It pressed for US interests and ensured that it did not get ahead of what Congress was willing to accept. At the same time it managed to ensure that the EC took most of the blame for delays in the negotiations and at the end of the day was able to emerge as the champion of the Uruguay Round without selling any US domestic interests short. The end result, however, was that there was no agreement reached on the Uruguay Round during the Bush administration.

In 1990 the Bush administration initiated a new chapter in US trade policy by accepting the proposal made by Mexico to enter into negotiations on NAFTA to include the USA, Canada and Mexico. In 1988, during the Reagan presidency, the US and Canada had completed their bilateral negotiation on the Canada – US Free Trade Agreement (CUSFTA). This was in fact implemented during the Bush presidency because the Canadian elections delayed the implementation of the agreement until after Reagan had left office. The CUSFTA aimed at removing all tariffs on trade between the US and Canada after a short transitionary period and liberalizing services and investment. At first Canada was not keen on extending the agreement to include Mexico but had little choice but to participate once the US decided it wanted an agreement. For Mexico, as for Canada before it, probably the major motivation in the agreement was to guarantee access to the US market and to gain some control over the unilateral use of US trade legislation (see below).

From the US point of view a trade agreement with Mexico offered a means of securing enhanced access to a growing market. US industry saw the advantages in being able to move labour-intensive production south of the border and thus compete more effectively with Asian competitors. For the administration there was also a political objective in wishing to support the liberal-oriented policies of the Mexican government and to anchor such liberalization in a binding treaty. In the sense that a free trade area could also contribute to the economic development of Mexico, it would also relieve some of the pressure which arose from the existing migration of Mexicans into the United States. NAFTA also offered a means of moving ahead more rapidly than the stalled GATT talks, and offered a setting in which, as the largest player in the North American continent, the US could have a greater say in the structure of the agreement.

The NAFTA agreement was initialled by the two governments in August 1992, a significant achievement in a little over two years from the time the initial soundings were made in the spring of 1990. The agreement was in some ways more liberal than the CUSFTA. For example, it included a provision that all investment should be liberalized, except a certain number of exemptions. This is what trade negotiators refer to as a negative list approach. In the CUSFTA the only areas to be liberalized were those specifically referred to in the agreement, a positive list approach. The negative list approach is seen as being more liberal in the sense that it is not possible to exclude any sectors *ab initio.*

The NAFTA agreement was negotiated on the basis of the fast-track authority obtained from Congress in May 1990. Even before the governments could conclude the agreement it was clear that the Bush administration would have considerable difficulties getting Congress to pass the implementing legislation. The main opposition came from organized labour, which was afraid that low wages and low levels of social provision in Mexico would result in US companies migrating south of the border. The subsequent imports would then undermine the remaining US jobs through 'social dumping'. The unions had support from some Democratic members of Congress. The more serious opponents of the NAFTA, and for that matter the GATT agreement, were the environmental interest groups. These saw the lower levels of environmental protection in Mexico as a source of environmental dumping. In other words, goods made according to the lower Mexican levels of environmental standards would undercut US products and thus force the US to adopt lower levels of environmental standards if it was to remain competitive. The environmental lobbies therefore saw NAFTA and GATT as inimical to the objective of raising US environmental standards. The fact that environmental lobbies drew support from across the political spectrum made them the more formidable opponent of NAFTA. Together the labour and environmental lobbies were able to ensure that there was no progress towards implementation of the agreement during the Bush presidency. Indeed, they succeeded in ensuring that the incoming Clinton administration agreed to negotiate an additional 'tag-on' agreement on the establishment of a North American Environmental Commission to address the environmental questions raised by NAFTA. The Bush administration successfully negotiated an agreement on NAFTA but was unable to get it through Congress. In addition to the NAFTA agreement Bush also promoted the idea of a wider free trade area in the Americas with his Enterprise for the Americas Initiative (EAI).

Despite President Bush's commitment to free trade his period in office coincided with a further shift towards the use of

more unilateral trade instruments by the United States. This
was not entirely under the control of the administration. The
1988 Omnibus Trade Act followed previous legislation in reducing presidential discretion in implementing US trade law. In
particular the revised Section 301 and the Super and Special
301 provisions of the US law were designed to more or less
oblige the administration to act when it found cases of 'unfair'
trade practices. Section 301 of US trade legislation, first introduced in 1973, requires the administration to report on
instances of unfair trade practice. This must then be followed
by negotiations with the offending country. If no progress is
made in the negotiations, Section 301 enables the US to act
against exports from the country concerned in order to
enforce the provision. This has been seen as unilateralism by
the US's trading partners, because the judgement as to whether
the practice is unfair and the enforcement is made by US
authorities according to US law. Defenders of the provision
argue that it only comes into operation where GATT procedures fail or are not applicable. It is also argued that the
Section 301 actions help bring about more open markets for
everyone.

Before the 1988 trade legislation the US president had
some discretion in how to apply the Section 301 provisions,
particularly whether or not to take retaliatory action. Previous
presidents, with the possible exception of President Reagan,
had made full use of this discretion and refrained from acting
because it was generally not seen to be in the US's interests to
antagonize its trading partners. Congress criticized this weakness and argued that the interests of American industries
were being sold out to the interests of US foreign policy
objectives. The 1988 Trade Act therefore sought further to
reduce the discretion available to the President. This led to
the introduction, for two years, of the so-called Super 301 provision, which required action by the administration in cases of
unfair trade when negotiations do not progress or do not
progress quickly enough.

The Bush administration used the Super 301 provisions
with some caution. The US Trade Representative may have
threatened to use the 'crowbar' of US trade legislation to
open markets, but in practice it was used more as a threat, and
when it was used it was used in a reasonably moderate fashion

or to further US multilateral objectives. For example, one of the targets in the 1989 Super 301 action was India for its continued use of restrictive investment policies. The US, along with other OECD countries, was seeking an agreement within the Uruguay Round to prohibit the kind of trade-related investment measures used by India which were the subject of the US action.

Towards the end of the Bush administration, however, Section 301 was used more frequently and there can be little doubt that US business and Congress developed a taste for the use of such unilateral trade measures. The simple truth was that countries targeted by the threat of a 301 action generally changed their policies rather than risk the loss of access to the large US market. Such approaches were therefore seen to be more effective than multilateral GATT negotiations which took many years and only produced ambiguous results at the end. It was only the larger countries or entities such as the EC, and to a lesser extent Japan, which refused to negotiate under duress.

The other change that occurred during the Bush presidency was that US unilateralism became more aggressive. Up to the late 1980s the US had tended to use its domestic trade remedy rules to compensate the affected industries by, for example, introducing countervailing measures. In the late 1980s the objective changed from insulating American businesses from 'unfair' practices to actively seeking to change the practices or policies in the exporting country. It is this element of US trade policy which has given it the 'aggressive' unilateralist label.

In terms of bilateral trade relations the Bush administration and the Japanese government created the Structural Impediments Initiative (SII) as an alternative to the use of Super 301 against Japan when the Japanese government refused to negotiate under duress. The SII provided the cover for discussing both Japanese and American structural problems. It helped to defuse trade tensions, but Japan probably only liberalized those measures that it wanted to change anyway. Much the same could have been said of the US in the sense that the SII identified such US structural problems as the need to reduce the budget deficit, increase the savings ratio and strengthen the training and education of US workers. If one measures the SII objectives against performance neither Japan nor the US achieved the objectives set in the SII. Under sustained criticism for doing nothing to help US industry President Bush shifted his position on trade from one of standing up for free trade and ventured on a trip to Japan in order, among other things, to try and get better access for US exports. The trip in January 1992 was something of a public relations disaster and produced little in the way of results. The only image of the President that reached the American public was that of him being taken ill and collapsing during a state banquet in Tokyo and Barbara reading his speech for him.

Bilateral trade relations with Europe began with a rather tense period in which there was much talk, during 1988, of 'Fortress Europe'. The Bush administration soon established that this was an unlikely scenario for the EC's Internal Market programme, and maintained that the EC 92 programme was fundamentally liberal but that it required watching closely to ensure that no measures were introduced that would result in increased protection against US exporters. Unlike in the case of Japan, there was no structural trade deficit with Europe, and when the dollar fell against European currencies after 1985 and the US economy slowed relative to Europe in 1988/89, the US moved from a trade deficit into a healthy trade surplus with the EC by 1989/90.

INTERNATIONAL ECONOMIC COOPERATION

In the early stages of the Bush administration there was some rhetoric on the desire to cooperate with the other major economies. Indeed, in May and again in September 1989 the central banks of the G7 countries intervened in currency markets in order to stabilize (i.e. prevent a further decline in) the dollar. Apart from these actions there was the normal rhetoric on the desire to coordinate economic policies but few real results.

The G7 meetings with the Europeans and Japanese were taken up with more political issues concerning the position of the West at a time of political revolution in central and eastern Europe and then in the Soviet Union. President Bush managed to force the issue of the GATT Uruguay Round onto the agendas of the 1989 and 1990 G7 summits. But he was unable to pin the European participants down to any specific commitments they were not prepared to make in the GATT negotiations in Geneva.

The weakness of economic coordination in the G7 was illustrated by the lack of any effort to coordinate policies in the face of the approaching economic recession in 1990 and 1991. Indeed, rather than coordinate policies US and German policies were totally at odds. For example, when the US Federal Reserve Bank reduced its discount rate to 3.5 per cent in December 1991 in a dramatic effort to stimulate the US economy, the German Bundesbank moved in the opposite direction and increased its discount rate to 8 per cent in order to try and contain the inflationary pressures coming from the massive fiscal transfers to the former East German state. In both cases the policies were supported by governments that were totally preoccupied with domestic policy objectives. Clearly, in the case of the US there was a sense of frustration because it had long been arguing for Europe to reflate. But the circumstances in Germany were such that the Bundesbank had decided it had to put on the brakes.

Whatever the reasons the result of these conflicting policies was that with a 6.5 per cent interest rate differential funds flowed out of the dollar and into the deutschmark. This created an upward pressure on the DM which increased pressure within the European Exchange Rate Mechanism (ERM). Countries such as Britain, Italy and Spain which were closely tied to the DM in the ERM were obliged to hold or increase their interest rates in order to maintain the values of their currencies against the DM. But these economies, like the US economy, were more in need of reflation than deflation. As a result the markets began to doubt whether it would be possible for these countries to maintain the high levels of interest rates needed to remain within the ERM. The negative vote in the Danish referendum in June 1991 was followed by a significant flow of funds out of the dollar and into the DM in July and August. This created further pressure on the British pound sterling and Italian lira, which were forced to leave the ERM in September. Thus although the US did not cause the problems in the ERM, which stemmed from internal divergencies within the EC, low US interest rates and the resultant flow of funds into the DM accentuated pressure on the ERM. At the time neither George Bush nor his Democratic contender showed any interest apart from in the performance of the US economy.

CONCLUSION

It was the weakness of the US economy during the second half of his presidency which weakened George Bush's chances of being re-elected. The foreign policy successes of the Bush administration and its fortune to be in office when the Cold War came to an end did not, in the event, count in the face of the poor performance of the domestic economy. In one sense Bush was unlucky that the recession came when it did and lasted as long as it did. From the beginning of 1991 President Bush waited and hoped for the recovery, but the economy seemed to refuse to respond to efforts to stimulate growth through lower interest rates. In this sense Bush also paid the price for the Reagan years of credit-based growth. When the economy finally came to a halt the normal instruments, such as lower interest rates, had no immediate effect, because before they could start to spend again consumers and real estate investors first had to reduce their debt.

The double blow for Bush was that not only was the economy weak but the electorate lost confidence in his ability to resolve the longer-term structural problems which were by now generally accepted to be at least important contributing factors to the problems. The most damage to the Bush administration's economic policies was inflicted by the long battles with Congress over how to tackle the budget deficit. In this context Bush paid the price for not grasping the nettle of the budget immediately on coming to office. Rather than do so he was content to accept two 'slide by' budgets in the hope that economic growth would resolve the problem, and if that did not work the Democratic Congress could be made to pay the political price of inaction. In the end it was President Bush who paid the price as the budget deficit ballooned in 1991 and 1992 and awoke a deep concern about the future soundness of the American economy in the minds of the American electorate.

In other areas of policy, President Bush stuck to the liberal policies that had characterized previous US administrations in rejecting anything that look faintly like an industrial policy. In trade policy the Bush administration was also neither worse nor better than previous administrations. During his term of office President Bush did resist the worst protectionist pressures, but he also failed to check the trend in US trade policy away from enthusiastic support for multilateralism and towards unilateralism.

NOTES

1. This was the target for the revised Gramm-Rudmann-Hollings provisions. The original (1985) GRH provision required a balanced budget by 1991.
2. See *Financial Times*, 24 January 1989.
3. *International Herald Tribune*, 5 March 1993.
4. The Gramm-Rudmann-Hollings legislation is not based on outcome but on projected spending and revenue. In other words the administration must produce a budget which is in line with the targets for reduced budget deficits. This enabled the administration, often with the connivance of Congress, to produce a budget which in reality stood little chance of meeting the targets.
5. See statement by the Chairman of the Federal Reserve Alan Greenspan, *Financial Times*, 6 July 1993.
6. *International Herald Tribune*, 27 November 1993.
7. The gap between rich and poor increased during the 1980s. During the decade the top 1 per cent of the population increased their average annual income from $213,000 to $399,000, while the average income for the low paid fell from $7,357 in 1980 to $6,973 in 1990 (1990 prices). Put somewhat differently the top 2.5 million earners in the US, who stood to benefit from the tax proposals, earned the same as the next 100 million Americans.
8. See *Financial Times*, 24 April 1993.
9. *Financial Times*, 7 April 1990.
10. See *Financial Times*, 4 August 1990.
11. See Stephen Woolcock, *The GATT Uruguay Round: Issues for the United States and the European Community*, RIIA Discussion Paper No 30 (London: Royal Institute of International Affairs, October 1990).
12. The authority is called 'fast-track' authority because the agreement negotiated by the administration can either be accepted or rejected *in toto* by the Congress. It is not possible to accept parts of it and reject others. This approach was adopted in the 1970s because the United State's trading partners were not prepared to negotiate an agreement with the executive branch without some assurance that the Congress would adopt the agreement as negotiated.

7 Domestic Policy[1]
Dilys M. Hill

The American democratic system, although admired around the world, is not confronting the public problems that concern its citizens most. The federal government can lead an international coalition to victory in the Middle East, but appears far less decisive at home ...

The tone of domestic political discourse is as worrisome as its substance. Candidates impugn each other rather than proposing solutions. People elected to lead and govern point fingers at each other: the president blames Congress, and Congress blames the president ... Cynics about government find much to be cynical about.[2]

INTRODUCTION

Domestic policy in the Bush years shares the general air of paradox of his presidency: Bush the inheritor versus Bush his own man; Bush the insider and conciliator versus Bush the impatient critic of Congress and the 'gridlock' of divided government; Bush the 'kinder, gentler' leader versus Bush the 'stranger in his own land' visiting riot-hit Los Angeles. The paradoxical position that Bush found himself in arose essentially from the change in the American economic and political situation over his four-year term. Elected to maintain the 'feel good' status quo inherited from President Reagan, the downturn in the economy and increasing public concern over the quality of education and the availability of affordable health care brought growing demands for a more proactive policy stance. After fighting a virtually issueless – and abrasive – election campaign in 1988, Bush faced an increasing clamour over domestic issues from which his Gulf War success could not protect him.

These problems are addressed in this chapter. President Bush appeared constrained in his leadership from the start of his office: the minimalist approach to policy issues in the 1988 campaign set the stage for a minimalist domestic agenda. His Cabinet appointees and key advisers were largely conservative pragmatists like himself, who favoured laissez-faire approaches. And while President Bush had a proactive foreign policy, domestically he held a reactive stance in opposing Democratic Congressional initiatives. These aspects of his policy style were exacerbated, however, by two further impediments. On the one hand there were the constraints imposed by the budget deficit, which impeded any attempts at new initiatives. On the other hand there was the problem, widely commented on in Washington, that when the President did propose action, his attention span was too short and the follow-through indecisive.

SETTING THE SCENE

The president's first year is crucial to success. Time is on the president's side only in his first year, a 'honeymoon' period when the president can capitalise on his national mandate.[3] In this first year there is the opportunity to promote the priority issues: presidents make policy only in the sense that they choose from a limited menu and they need to promote these priorities vigorously to maintain the momentum that their electoral victory gives them. Bush had not fought on a positive platform and thus lacked a mandate for radical change. And, as Rockman stressed, he had few levers at his disposal and faced an angered Democratic majority in Congress.[4] At the same time, however, Bush had claimed that he wanted to be the 'Education' and the 'Environment' president, to promote the philosophies of the Reagan era but with a 'kinder, gentler' mien, and to extend the hand of cooperation to Congress.

The first year of Bush's presidency, however, was judged disappointing. There were few legislative initiatives, and those dealt with the immediate problems of the Savings and Loan crisis, the repeal of the catastrophic insurance programme adopted in 1988, and an attempt to contain Medicare costs.[5] Repeal of the catastrophic insurance programme highlighted the central dilemma of voter demand versus willingness to pay. While at the end of the Reagan era politicians on all sides believed the public would welcome a more active government approach to health care, drug abuse, quality education, affordable housing, child care and environmental protection, the fact remained, as Thomas Mann put it, 'a willingness to pay taxes to fund more federal services was nowhere in evidence.'[6]

Initially, this situation appeared well-suited to Bush's position as the managerial and maintenance president. The competent insider who had held many executive positions, President Bush's energy was devoted to his foreign policy agenda while domestic policy was increasingly defined more by opposing Democratic initiatives than by proposals of his own. Government by Executive Order and by veto became the hallmark of his domestic strategy.[7] At one level it could be argued that this successfully met his agenda needs. As Light has argued, given a president's resources, legislation is more expensive than vetoes in terms of the majority of congressional votes needed.[8] In Bush's case, of the 46 vetoes of his presidency, only one was overridden when, in October 1992, Congress enacted cable television reregulation (PL 102-385) over his objection. But in fact this frequent use of the veto and the bills to which he applied it revealed only too clearly his weak position in which he was forced to fall back on the weapon the Constitution gives to every president.[9]

Bush's attention to foreign affairs, and his managerial approach, left room in the system for senior aides and leading Cabinet Secretaries to wield control in the domestic arena. The assistant to the president for economic and domestic affairs (the Domestic Policy Advisor), Roger B. Porter, an ex-Harvard professor, and his Office of Policy Development, had the lead role and was responsible for the work of both the Economic Policy Council and the Domestic Policy Council. The two Councils were a continuation of the Cabinet Council system of the Reagan administration. By 1990 the Domestic Policy Council, chaired by Attorney General Richard Thornburgh, had some 15 working groups. But the most important issues were dealt with by a small group of insiders, led by the conservative and abrasive Chief of Staff John H. Sununu, and by Richard G. Darman, Director of the Office of Management and Budget, a holdover from the Reagan administration. Darman and Sununu set the broad lines of domestic policy and Roger Porter then crafted the details (for example with the Clean Air Act). Sununu and Darman were a formidable pair, outweighing the role of the third player, Secretary of the Treasury Nicholas F. Brady (originally appointed to the post by President Reagan in August 1988); Darman in fact appeared to have something of a veto power over domestic policy.[10] By contrast, Secretary of Housing and Urban Development Jack Kemp was an outsider, who, while supported by Vice President Quayle, was opposed by Darman and Sununu (see below).

These structures and processes worked well initially because the President was not pursuing an ambitious domestic agenda. After the mid-term, when Bush was expected to turn from foreign to domestic matters, conflict within the administration intensified. Sununu, who defended the moral and economic agenda of the right, and favoured business interests, engaged in a drawn-out struggle with Environmental Protection Agency William K. Reilly over implementation of the Clean Air Act. Sununu finally overreached himself, however, in trying to be Bush's top legislative strategist, political adviser and domestic policy-maker. The heart of the problem was not Sununu but the President's failure to set a direction for addressing problems.[11] Even when Sununu was replaced in December 1991 by Samuel K. Skinner, former Transportation Secretary, Republican criticism of the sense of drift continued, with calls that President Bush recall Secretary of State James Baker to take up the Chief of Staff role, a position he finally assumed on 13 August 1992.

White House Chief of Staff Skinner tried to direct policy by adding another layer of management in the White House, including Domestic Policy Counsellor Clayton K. Yeutter (appointed as the domestic policy supremo to whom Roger Porter reported) and Deputy Chief of Staff W. Henson Moore. He also created, at the insistence of Yeutter, the Policy Coordinating Group (PCG) to supplant the Domestic Policy Council, which had not met as such since the end of 1990. The PCG also replaced the Economic Policy Council which met sporadically and continued on as a permanent PCG working group headed by Treasury Secretary Brady. These structures did not conceal the battle inside the White House between right and left over policy direction, and the seeming lack of overall control compared with the Sununu regime.

ADDRESSING THE DOMESTIC AGENDA

The tortuous evolution of policy in a federal system means that domestic policy is always, as Rose has put it, in a 'seemingly interminable process of incubation' about the definition and nature of a problem and over competing solutions.[12] In this situation a conservative president could argue that since in a federal system important domestic initiatives lie with the states and localities, there is less need for a 'federal domestic agenda'. Thus for a conservative administration, doing nothing, but doing it well, is a perfectly proper position. And this argument appeared to be reinforced after the 1990 elections, when White House Chief of Staff John Sununu reportedly asserted that the President's legislative agenda was complete: Congress could convene and then agree to return home. Additionally, Bush's passive style and limited agenda were, it was argued, especially suited to the situation of divided government.[13]

That domestic policy arises in multiple decision centres in a federal system had particular resonance in the Bush years as states and localities faced the culmination of a decade of fiscal stress. In the Reagan period, although federal aid to states had dropped from 17 to 11 per cent of their own tax revenues, states were still able to help localities whose tax base was eroding. The 1990s presented a very different picture, particularly as health costs escalated. Medicaid (Title XIX of the Social Security Amendments of 1965, which was a joint federal–state programme providing health care for certain groups of low-income people) grew from less than 3 per cent of state general expenditures to 14.8 per cent in 1990.[14] The states faced increased fiscal pressure: in 1991 and 1992 states increased taxes and cut spending by more than any previous year since 1976, and voter backlash inhibited further rises. States were squeezed from both sides: the federal government mandated state expansion of Medicaid coverage, and asked states to do more in education, highways and transportation, while local governments increasingly looked to the states to make up for the loss of federal funding of water and other projects. The result was that by 1992 all three levels of government, federal, state and local, faced the prospect of not being able to maintain existing services. This was particularly pressing in health care. States took the view that this was the nation's major domestic priority but one where they would resist further efforts to shift responsibilities to them.

Thus in addressing the domestic agenda a president faces many forces already in play. The position was made more difficult in Bush's case, however, by his inheritor status, both in terms of defining his own agenda and in defending it against the right wing of his party. As Reagan's inheritor, Bush stressed a reduced federal government role, in favour of the states and localities, and the private and voluntary sectors. But pressure soon mounted from all four sectors. States and localities, as we have seen, soon fretted at the burdens they carried. Support for the private sector fitted well with the Reagan/Bush conservative philosophy but produced increasing pressure from business as the economy faltered. And volunteerism never really took off as a key element in a domestic strategy. Bush's 'points of light' acceptance speech at the 1988 Republican Convention had defined America as a nation of voluntary organizations: 'a brilliant diversity spread like the stars, like a thousand points of light in a broad and peaceful sky' in the memorable phrase coined by his speechwriter Peggy Noonan. But his programmes lacked the necessary dynamism to give substance to this approach. Although a 'Points of Light' Foundation was established in Washington DC the movement did not become, as it had been hailed, a hallmark of the Bush presidency.

The structural and financial constraints surrounding the domestic agenda are part of a longer-term problem of American government arising from intergovernmental relationships and the burden of the deficits. What was more particular to Bush was his position as a pragmatic conservative facing pressure from the right wing of his party. Warily accepted as Reagan's heir, elements on the right, never fully persuaded of his commitment to the conservative agenda, became more vocal as his term progressed. The 1980 Republican presidential contender had mocked supply-side theory as 'voodoo economics' and had appeared to support choice in the abortion debate. But Vice President Bush, the assertively loyal supporter of his president, endorsed the Republican right's position on both economics and on moral issues. Over time, these concerns became increasingly difficult to handle. The Republican right did not forgive Bush's reversal over tax rises in 1990, which reneged on his 'no new taxes' campaign

Dilys M. Hill

pledge. And the debate over moral issues finally erupted into the damaging scenes at the 1992 Republican Convention with Bush appearing to be transfixed by his own right wing rather than the opposition.

A major element in the tension within the party was the issue of abortion. Since 1980 the Republican Party platform had advocated a constitutional amendment to protect 'unborn children', opposed federal funding of abortion and favoured the appointment of federal judges who believed abortion is not a constitutional right. In 1992 the Supreme Court began hearing cases redefining the limits on abortion. In April 1992 the Bush administration renewed its call for the Supreme Court to overrule the 1973 *Roe* v. *Wade* judgment and to use a case from Pennsylvania (*Planned Parenthood of Southeastern Pennsylvania* v. *Casey*, one of a number of abortion statutes enacted in the wake of the Supreme Court's 1989 ruling in *Webster* v. *Reproductive Health Services* which gave states more leeway in adopting restrictions on abortion) to make it clear that states could restrict or even outlaw abortions. On 29 June 1992 the Justices used the Pennsylvania case to uphold a woman's right to abortion, although they also overruled a number of other cases and allowed states to impose more restrictions. Bush vetoed legislation that would have lifted the administration's ban on the federal financing of foetal tissue research and in September 1992 Bush vetoed abortion coun-selling in federally-funded family planning clinics (the so-called 'gag rule'). But Bush's position within his party remained strained, a difficulty compounded by the emergence in the spring and summer of 1992 of abortion rights' advocates in the Republican Party who wanted to pursue the issue to the floor of the Republican National Convention in Houston (and were blocked by the party managers).

Alongside moral issues the right was particularly concerned to maintain the supply-side thrust of economic policy. Bush continued the anti-regulation rhetoric of the Reagan years and appointed Vice President Quayle to the chair of the Council on Competitiveness. The Council continued the work that the Task Force on Regulatory Review (chaired by then Vice President Bush) had carried out for the Reagan administration. Reviewing regulations is the work of the Office of Information and Regulatory Affairs (OIRA) in the Office of Management and Budget; OIRA lacked a head from October 1989 onwards when the incumbent left and the administration's only nominee for the post of OIRA administrator was not confirmed by Congress. With OIRA leaderless, Dan Quayle's Council on Competitiveness stepped in to attack what it saw as over-regulation. By 1992 its main offensive, backed by the conservative right, was in the arena of environmental rights. The Council's remit was to monitor the implementation of the re-enacted Clean Air Act, which brought it into conflict with the Environmental Protection Agency and its head, William Reilly. Here again the agenda had changed its focus as economic fortunes changed: the 'Environment' president faced increasing pressure to protect jobs as recession hit, a pressure to which he increasingly yielded in his last year in office (see below).

DOMESTIC LEADERSHIP

The Bush administration was based on a risk-aversive approach in which deregulation and laissez-faire 'empowerment' prevailed over action. After the triumph in the Gulf, however, criticism grew that the expected emphasis on domestic issues had not materialized and the President was accused of vacillation and lack of leadership. The Bush administration argued, however, that not only did the President possess a coherent domestic strategy but that it had been laid out following his Inauguration in his budget address to Congress on 9 February 1989. In that address he put forward a four point plan to attend to urgent priorities, invest in the future, attack the deficit and bar new taxes. President Bush also called for a constitutional amendment to balance the budget, promoted choice (in education, housing and child care), stressed that education and a war on drugs were his top priorities, and called for a new attitude toward the environment (including the clean-up of nuclear weapon plants). But he still appeared to lack the rhetorical vigour and imagination to present his domestic priorities in a way which captured the public's attention.

These domestic themes were repeated a year later in President Bush's 1991 budget proposals. The emphasis on choice was also repeated in the 1991 focus on empowerment: parental choice of schools, tenant control and ownership of public housing, and support for Enterprise Zones. None of these proposals was new; the only really different call was for a block grant to return up to $20 billion in federal programmes to the states. Opponents still questioned the reality of such commitments given the lack of resources and the cutbacks in discretionary social programmes.

The difficulty was that the administration's approach still appeared to be one of disengagement which lacked an overall philosophy; even where promises were made, such as those on education, drugs and homelessness, these were followed by inattention, giving the impression of a lack of conviction. The 'vision thing' really was a problem. The President's image in domestic affairs was as the captor of his top aides – particularly Sununu and Darman – who dominated decisions. At the same time there was no long-term agenda or an ability to communicate the importance of issues to the public. To the President, negotiating, deal-making, were the crucial elements in domestic strategy, a position reflected in his Inaugural Day promise to 'extend the hand of cooperation' to Congress and repeated in January 1990. Though initially this must have sounded ironic in the wake of the bitter 1988 electoral campaign, the cooperative stance was pursued in the Savings and Loan rescue operation, the development of the Clean Air Act amendments and the drafting of the Americans with Disabilities Act. Indeed it was argued that the Bush administration's main domestic policy strategy was for the Deputy Secretaries of Departments to work quietly with lawmakers while the Secretary threatened veto.

President Bush's much-emphasized reactive style included some notable vetoes – on civil rights, parental leave, abortion counselling and the campaign finance reform package. The veto on civil rights was seen as part of Bush's long-term ambivalence on the issue. After insisting he wanted a bill he could sign and offering a minimalist one of his own, Bush vetoed the 1990 Civil Rights Act (on the grounds that it would promote quotas in employment practices) but later agreed to a compromise measure in 1991. At the same time, White House conservatives drafted an executive order that would have phased out federal affirmative action guidelines that had been in existence for 25 years. As a result several Congressional leaders boycotted the signing ceremony and Bush then withdrew the executive order, saying that he had never approved it.[15]

Defenders of the President's agenda pointed to the successes of the first two years of the Bush administration, with major legislation on clean air, child care, reauthorized housing programmes and civil rights for the disabled. The assertion that domestic policy *was* a coherent package was based, however, not on these achievements alone, but on the conservative principles which purportedly made up the Bush agenda. These principles were: choice and empowerment, self-help and personal responsibility, volunteerism, and the enhancement of the private sector. These principles were translated into specific proposals in the 'America 2000' education proposals, the housing and enterprise zones agenda promoted by Secretary Kemp at Housing and Urban Development, and the repeated calls for capital gains tax reduction as the centrepiece for regenerating both the economy and the inner cities.[16] The conservative principle which surrounded the domestic agenda, however, could not withstand the pressures which the Bush administration increasingly faced. By the beginning of 1992 President Bush's State of the Union address was judged to have misfired in threatening Congress with political warfare if it did not enact his budget proposals by March 20th in a 'This will not stand' echo of Desert Storm. The plans were judged not just weak on vision but weak on solutions.

To his critics on the right, however, Bush was mismanaging the agenda by diverging from the principles which Reagan had laid down as the basics of radical republicanism. By late 1991, Bush was appearing to struggle to keep the peace within the party. Some four dozen Congressmen on the right questioned Bush's handling of domestic policy and urged him to create a new post of domestic policy chief for Jack Kemp. Bush was said to have been 'taken aback' by the letter directly challenging his mastery of domestic policy.[17] In January 1992 White House Chief of Staff Samuel Skinner met with some 50 Republican House members to prevent their disappointment over economic policy from becoming rebellion. But Kemp was not favoured; when the new centralizing domestic post was created, after John Sununu's replacement by Samuel Skinner at the end of 1991, it was Clayton K. Yeutter (Bush's former Agriculture Secretary and US trade representative in the Reagan administration), not Kemp, who was named to the post. Even then, Yeutter's role was seen as that of a broker of ideas, not the architect of policy that the domestic arena seemed to need so badly.

THE PRESIDENT'S PRIORITIES – AND CHALLENGES

Bush came to the presidency stressing the priority he would give to education and to the environment. In both areas his position reflected the concern the public was expressing, and the apparent momentum for change that existed. The outcome in the two areas was, however, very different. In education, consensus over the need for improved quality was strong but progress minimal. On the environment, the President was able to claim that the 1990 Clean Air Act was a major achievement. By late 1991, however, in the face of economic downturn, major confrontation erupted between the President and Congress, and between Vice President Quayle's Council on Competitiveness and William Reilly's Environmental Protection Agency, over the way environmental regulation was being implemented.

In 1989 it looked as though education would be a lead item on the Bush agenda. This is an area in which federal funding is small (some 6 per cent of education budgets, which are primarily a state and local matter) but where Bush could give high profile leadership. In September 1989 Bush met with the nation's governors (led by Governor Bill Clinton of Arkansas) to promote education reform in the 'America 2000' proposals. The President was given credit for calling an education summit that set challenging national goals. On the other hand, he was criticized for waiting until March 1991 before the lacklustre Lauro F. Cavazos, the holdover Education Secretary from the Reagan administration, was replaced by the well-regarded Lamar Alexander to draft the education reform package.

The America 2000 proposals set six goals: to ensure that every child starts school ready to learn; to raise high school graduation rate to 90 per cent; to promote competence in core subjects; to make students first in the world in maths and science; to ensure every adult is literate; to liberate every school from drugs and violence. There was in addition a proposal for a New American Schools Development Corporation by which bipartisan business lenders would raise money to promote 'break the mould' schools in every congressional district. But the sums of money raised fell well below the targets, and the proposal met with resistance from Congress over issues of 'choice' which would have allowed funding of parental choice for private and religious, as well as public, schools.

Bush's position was that 'America 2000' was a national strategy not a federal programme: the need was for new approaches not spending more money on old ways. But even so, progress was very slow. Following the education summit in 1989, it was more than a year later before the governors adopted the six national goals and April 1991 before President Bush formally adopted them as his own.[18] The education legislation that Education Secretary Alexander promoted had at its centre the proposal to provide money to establish New American Schools, apportioned among the states according to their number of electoral votes. Money could go to any public or private group that produced an innovative school plan. But while there was strong support for choice within the public sector school system,[19] Congress opposed widening this to the private sector, and resisted voucher schemes suggested by Bush supporters. Bush recognized that since the America 2000 proposals, little had changed in the schools (as Secretary Alexander publicly admitted) and placed the blame on a Congress ruled by Democrats.

In the area of environmental issues, and the related area of energy policy, the agenda changed significantly over the four-year period. Energy appeared as a prime element on the presidential domestic agenda at the time of the Gulf War. In his January 1991 State of the Union message President Bush had promised a policy 'that calls for energy conservation and efficiency, increased development and greater use of alternative fuels'. The administration released its National Energy Strategy in February 1991 but it then languished in Congress until late in 1992, with the White House leaving the hands-on lobbying effort to Energy Department officials. Energy is a policy area where the congressional process is extremely protracted: Congress had been considering a national energy policy (since 1990 as the National Energy Security Act, intended to address the impact of oil supply uncertainties) and the related Clean Air Act re-enactment, for a decade. The debate drew in major environmental concerns; the President threatened to veto any bill that did not open the Alaska National Wildlife Refuge to oil drilling, a move rejected by both the House and the Senate. On 24 October 1992 Bush signed the Energy Policy Act (PL 102-486): the first major legislative attempt for more than a decade to reduce dependence on imported oil. The Act's main proposals were: to restructure the electric utility industry to promote more competition; to give tax relief to independent oil and gas drillers; to encourage energy conservation; to promote renewable energy; to authorize spending on Research and Development; to make it easier to license nuclear plants. It did not include the provisions for drilling in Alaska's National Wildlife Refuge that Bush had called for. And, paradoxically, in the end the Act represented a compromise that in the long term would not significantly reduce US dependence on foreign oil.

Environmental policy, for its part, was a stark example of the dilemmas of the Bush presidency. At the beginning of his term, President Bush had proclaimed himself the 'environmental president' after using the pollution in Boston harbour as a campaign issue against Democratic contender Michael Dukakis. On entering office, President Bush named the Conservation Foundation President William K. Reilly as head of the Environmental Protection agency (EPA), widely seen as making a statement about his commitment. In 1990 he announced his support for legislative efforts to elevate the EPA to Cabinet status as the Department of the Environment, a call he reiterated in March 1992.[20] And Bush continued to assert that his main environmental accomplishment was that of proposing, negotiating and signing into law the 1990 Clean Air Act. But the accusations grew after Bush's mid-term that instead of issuing the regulations necessary to implement the Act, the White House was seeking to rewrite the legislation through the regulatory process, led by Vice President Quayle's Council on Competitiveness.[21] The Council came increasingly to play a central role in the White House management of the law, having a growing influence in reviewing, halting and at times helping to rewrite new regulations, particularly those concerned with environmental safeguards. The Council forced the EPA to insert a loophole in the regulations allowing permit holders to increase pollution levels without public scrutiny. The permit rule became the battlefield for control of environmental regulations, and of conflict between Quayle and Reilly. In this conflict, Bush took the side of Quayle and the Council against Reilly and the Environmental Protection Agency.

These changes in approach arose from the pressures the President faced in trying to respond to demands that he be more active in addressing the downturn in the economy. In responding to pressures on jobs and business activity Bush appeared to be willing to attack environmental rules with a fervour not seen since the earliest days of the Reagan administration. The pattern had emerged in the summer of 1991 when the White House proposed eliminating the restrictions on development on half of the nation's wetlands; the President's view was that he had always been in favour of protecting the environment in a way that was compatible with growth.[22] In May 1992 Bush approved the Council on Competitiveness's recommendation that industry be allowed unilaterally to increase their allowed pollution emissions without public notice. In April 1992, the Secretary of Agriculture Edward Madigan had proposed the elimination of the public's right to appeal against decisions by the US Forest Service on land use and timber sales: a right the public had enjoyed for 85 years. In March 1992 Interior Secretary Manual Lujan had cancelled the public's long-established right to contest the Department's decisions to grant grazing permits, mining leases and oil exploration licences on public lands.

What was significant in all these actions was the way in which the decisions were made: by the executive branch alone, without Congressional action and often in defiance of Congressional statutes.[23] For the administration this had the advantage, at least in the short term, of allowing presidential rule through the regulatory regime rather than engaging in head-on conflict with Congress over new legislation.

By the early summer of 1992 few issues produced quite as much dissension in the White House as the environment. There was open conflict between Reilly and Quayle, strained relations with Interior Secretary Lujan, and opposition from Director of OMB Darman and Chairman of the Council of Economic Advisers Boskin. These four – Quayle, Lujan, Darman and Boskin – had pressed with increasing success to loosen environmental regulations. In addition, Bush had attracted widespread criticism abroad and at home for his stance at the UN 'Earth Summit' in Rio de Janeiro in June 1992, when he took a stand as the defender of American businesses and jobs against what he termed environmental extremists. At the same time Bush announced an increase of $150 million a year in American foreign aid for conservation of Third World forests, and changed the rules for forest management in the US to discourage clear-cutting (that is the total, rather than selective, felling of large tracts of timber).

President Bush's overall stance, however, was to scorn critics and attack allies, which was seen as a misreading of the impact of the Rio summit and a failure to make the case for his policies far enough in advance of the Conference. A final element in the administration's battle was the attack, led by Interior Secretary Lujan, on the Endangered Species Act 1973 and its protection of the habitat of the northern spotted owl in the forests of the Pacific northwest against major logging plans. Overall the result was that Bush was trying, by mid-1992, to hold on to the remnants of his earlier environmental stance, but the signal was mixed, and appeared to be undermining environmental laws.[24]

If education and the environment had been part of President Bush's original policy stance, events in 1991 forced a fresh consideration of the issue of health care reform. In November 1991 the special election for a Senate seat in Pennsylvania (occasioned by the death of Republican Senator John Heinz in a plane crash) resulted in a surprise win for Democrat Harris Wofford. Wofford, campaigning on the economy and on the need for health care reform, beat Richard Thornburgh, who had stood down as Attorney General to contest the seat.

Health care represented two major problems: many Americans had insufficient health insurance, and health costs were not only high but rising as a share of national output.[25] Bush's 1990 and 1991 State of the Union addresses had made some references to the need for reforms, but the administration's view essentially was that it was necessary to arrive at a much broader consensus on the problem and its solutions before pressing ahead with legislation. In February 1992 President Bush announced a health care plan based on tax credits or deductions to help the less well-off to buy insurance, the reform of small group insurance by pooling smaller businesses and individuals into larger groups to make it easier to buy insurance, the reform of medical malpractice laws, and the encouragement of managed care programmes in order to contain costs. The new transferable health insurance tax credits and deductions would, it was said, benefit 95 million people.[26] But universal coverage was not the main aim of the plan (which was largely the work of OMB Director Richard Darman); Bush had no specific proposals on how to find the $35 billion annual cost and no detailed bill was sent to Congress.

LEADERSHIP IN CRISIS

'The vision thing' came to haunt Bush in the spring of 1992 with the eruption of the Los Angeles riots (whose death toll exceeded that in the Los Angeles Watts riots of 1965 which had contributed to the commissioning of the Kerner Report).[27] Critics alleged that Bush had failed to give the leadership needed to meet the most important domestic crisis of his presidency. Fred Greenstein said: 'It's not just lack of vision. He [Bush] lacks any conceptualization on domestic affairs. He has no abstract way of linking his values to specific policies, of linking means and ends. So he always seems to be going in varied directions.'[28]

Some of the criticism was even harsher. President Bush, it was said, looked like a stranger in his own land when he visited the scene of the riots, his irresolution a symptom of a major flaw in his approach to policy leadership. Over the four years he appeared neither deeply interested nor involved in domestic policy issues. In urban policy, both the President and Congress had avoided taking hard political choices when faced with budget deficits and competition for scarce resources; it was much easier, it seemed, to engage in ritualistic recrimination over the cause of the riots.[29] The immediate cause was the dismissal by the trial jury of the charges against the four members of the Los Angeles Police Department accused of the beating of Roger King, whom they had arrested in March 1991 for a traffic offence, and whose actions had been recorded on an amateur video. Following the dismissal of the charges, riots erupted in the south central district of Los Angeles, an area inhabited by ethnic minorities, including Korean and Spanish speaking, as well as African, Americans.

On his first visit to Los Angeles after the riots, Bush seemed moved by what he saw and heard and, while saying that the first responsibility was to preserve domestic order, affirmed that the federal government had a fundamental role in ending poverty and despair in the cities, though this had to be done in new ways, with a fresh approach to welfare and the inner city economy and to finding ways to strengthen the American family.[30] On his return visit to Los Angeles Bush reverted to law and order and family values themes favoured by the Republican right.[31] Vice President Quayle, appealing to this constituency, spoke in even stronger terms, linking the riots to the crumbling of traditional family and personal morality, and attacking the popular television sitcom character (i.e. fictional) Murphy Brown for choosing to bear a child out of wedlock, as an example of how out of touch the 'media elite' were with ordinary family values.[32]

The administration also appeared out of touch with the public mood when the White House spokesman Marlin Fitzwater suggested that the failure of President Johnson's Great Society anti-poverty programmes of the 1960s were responsible for 'many of the root problems that have resulted in inner-city difficulties'.[33] At the same time the administration was pledging a new activism for conservative solutions which Bush had long proposed but rarely pushed. In 1992, urban policies took up only 25 pages of the 433 page presidential budget, and half of that concerned drugs and law enforcement. In essence, the argument about the failed policies of the 1960s drew attention away from Bush's most serious political weakness: the poor state of the economy and his failure to press for programmes that he himself had said were solutions. The indecision the administration showed after the Los Angeles riots played into the hands of Democrats who renewed old charges that Bush could not or would not lead on domestic policy.

On 8 May the President said that he would push aggressively for an emergency programme for poor people and cities[34] and told aides privately that Secretary of Housing and Development Jack Kemp (who had not been part of the inner circle of policymakers in the White House) understood what needed to be done.[35] Kemp's long-advocated proposals – Enterprise Zones, welfare reform and tenant buyout of public housing – were included in Bush's list of emergency proposals. This appeared to reverse Secretary Kemp's previous position; his proposals had been consistently opposed by Darman and by Treasury Secretary Nicholas Brady. Kemp had not been able to obtain support for his ideas either from White House or Cabinet officials, and his battles with Congress had had no White House reinforcements. While Bush had referred to some of the Kemp anti-poverty proposals in speeches in late 1989, he did not pursue them further. At that point the three powerful figures in the White House – Darman, Brady and Sununu – were opposed to the urban initiatives for fear that they would be taken over by the Democrats and turned into high spending bureaucratic programmes.[36]

From HUD's perspective, Darman and Brady had taken over domestic policy, both under Chief of Staff Sununu and under his replacement Samuel Skinner. But the Bush administration's core position, as that of Reagan, was to resist demands for federal provision. As Caraley has presented the plight of the cities: 'Starkly put, the Reagan/Bush administrations' ideological posture was that it no longer wanted, could not afford, and did not deem it legitimate to be the ultimate subsidizer of poor people and poor local and state jurisdictions.'[37] And from the administration's perspective, there were no votes in the inner cities. The white movement to the suburbs over the previous twenty years meant that the 'contented' people, the socially and geographically mobile, were looking not for racial justice but racial peace.[38]

The attempt by the administration to press for legislation in the wake of the riots soon met with the long-standing difficulties over taxes that had marked White House–Congressional relations. A meeting between Bush and Congressional leaders on 12 May carried strong elements of political expediency and symbolism. On 22 June Bush signed a scaled-back ($1,100 million rather than the congressional Conference figure of $2,000 million) Urban Aid Supplemental bill (PL 102-302) which retained much of the existing summer youth jobs programme but eliminated money for school and neighbourhood projects. Long-term urban policy, however, made no headway. Proposals for Enterprise Zones – but in rural as well as urban areas – gained support in Congress as part of an omnibus tax bill which included tax breaks for businesses and employees but rejected a capital gains tax reduction for which Bush had long pressed.[39] As in past disputes it was the capital gains tax provision which dominated negotiations. Any hope of new legislation ended on 4 November 1992 when Bush vetoed HR 11, the revenue Act of 1992, while stating that 'The urban aid provisions that were once the centrepiece of the bill have been submerged by billions of dollars in giveaways to special interests.' Bush went on to complain that the Enterprise Zone provisions in HR 11 accounted for less than 10 per cent of the revenue cost of the measure, 'Weed and Seed' anti-drug enforcement provisions fell far short of his plans, and the revenue provisions of the bill amounted to tax rises.[40]

Related to the indecision over urban policy as exemplified by the Los Angeles riots was the stance of the administration to anti-poverty measures and welfare reform. Though conservatives continued to argue for work-related requirements in return for welfare benefits ('workfare') and analysts across the political spectrum pointed to the growing 'problem' of an underclass,[41] little federal action was forthcoming. In 1990 Bush convened an inter-agency study group on anti-poverty measures. The group produced around a dozen major alternatives, but the Democratic Policy Council, a Cabinet-level advisory body, rejected all the recommendations as too expensive or too controversial.[42] Instead, the Council recommended that the administration should simply try to make current programmes work better; as a White House official summarized it: 'Keep playing with the same toys. But let's paint them a little shinier.'[43] Secretary of Housing and Urban Development Jack Kemp had long tried to push initiatives in this area. In November 1989 he launched an unsuccessful campaign to make HUD the focal point for an anti-poverty programme. The biennial *The President's National Urban Policy Report*, issued by HUD on 20 December 1991 (and the Department's, rather than the president's, initiative), was Kemp's attempt to set out such a programme, based on empowerment, choice, the HOPE (Homeownership and Opportunity for People Everywhere) housing provisions of the 1990 Housing Act (see below) and Enterprise Zones.

Late in his term Bush returned to the theme, stating in the 1992 State of the Union Address that it was time to replace the assumptions of the welfare state and help reform the welfare system. This again stressed the ideas of empowerment and family values, rather than specific projects. In the spring of 1992 the White House highlighted its support of federal waivers, a process which allowed Wisconsin and other states to apply for relaxation of federal rules surrounding the state provision of welfare and which placed greater emphasis on 'responsible' behaviour, including completing school, seeking work and increased benefits for those young mothers who entered into marriage.[44] This process allowed Bush to support reform that was state – rather than federal – centred, and pro-family as well. The Bush administration also pressed Congress to provide greater funding (again with the proviso that this would entail consideration of cuts elsewhere) for favoured housing programmes. The National Affordable Housing Act of 1990 (the Cranston-Gonzalez National Affordable Housing Act, S 566) was the first major initiative to provide housing assistance for the poor in more than a decade. Included in it was the Homeownership and Opportunity for People Everywhere (HOPE) project, a tenant-management and tenant-buyout programme, which Bush strongly supported. For the Democrat controlled Congress, however, this remained a small part of what was needed, particularly in the area of subsidized housing units and rent subsidies. The Bush administration had also tried to face the mounting problem of homelessness with the support of the Interagency Council on Homelessness (which had been created by the Stewart B. Mckinney Homeless Assistance Act of 1987 and which Kemp chaired) and agency investigations of the problem.[45]

Complementary to these moves on urban poverty was Bush's other strongly supported election theme – the war on drugs. This focus on drugs and crime had been a key feature of the rhetoric of the Reagan administration and was carried forward by his successor. The Bush administration spent $12.7 billion a year (twice the expenditure of its predecessor) on combating drug abuse. It was still criticized, however, as inadequate and misdirected, since although there had been some success in reducing drug dependency among white adolescents in the suburbs, addiction among hard-core drug-users increased, and high-crime inner-city neighbourhoods showed increasing unrest. In 1988 the Reagan administration had passed the Anti-Drug Abuse Act (PL100-690) which had established the Office of National Drug Control Policy (ONDCP). Bush added the country's first 'drugs czar', a position authorized by the Act, to coordinate federal action. The post was given Cabinet-level status and Bush appointed William J. Bennett (Reagan's outspoken Secretary of Education). In the spring of 1991, when Bennett left to become Chairman of the Republican National Committee (a position he held only very briefly), Bush appointed Bob Martinez, former Governor of Florida to the post. The role of the Office was overall strategy and it had no executive function.[46]

Critics still argued, however, that these moves had not resulted in better coordination among the rival elements who had jurisdiction, notably the Drugs Enforcement Agency, the Customs and Excise, local police forces and the military. The key element of the drugs policy, the 'Weed and Seed' programme (which aimed to weed out drugs use by law enforcement measures and then restore the neighbourhood by seeding with social programmes), comprised demonstration projects under the control of local federal Attorney Generals and the Justice Department rather than a universal provision. There was conflict also over aims and objectives: the Bush administration conceived the war on drugs as channelling to law enforcement agencies funds that Democrats would have preferred to spend on social programmes; as a result the extension of 'Weed and Seed' projects languished in Congress. The Republicans were accused, in effect, of redefining the problems of the inner cities as drug abuse and the breakdown of law and order rather than racial discrimination and unemployment.

The Bush administration's wider attempts at crime control also ran into difficulties. Following the Gulf War Bush urged Congress to take prompt action on pending crime legislation which eased restrictions on police forces, expanded the death penalty, included modest hand-gun controls and new measures for defendants' rights. Opposition to the bill came from both liberals and from the right; it lapsed at the end of the 102nd Congress when the Senate could not defeat a Republican-led filibuster against it.[47]

CONCLUSION

President Bush's attempt to be more proactive over education, health, environment and the troubled inner cities was still vulnerable to the charge that he lacked real commitment and active engagement. It was in the summer of 1992 when the Policy Coordinating Group under Skinner, the administration's formal policy-making unit in the White House, reactivated efforts to look at inner cities, endangered species and other issues – but by then with a second term primarily in mind.

Bush's reactive and quietist domestic agenda fitted well with his prime focus on foreign affairs. But after the end of the Gulf War President Bush had to defend a domestic record that was his own, not a continuation of the Reagan agenda. This exposed him to criticism from conservative activists, who were not happy with his programme or his progress. The result was open division within the Republican Party highlighted by the vociferous opposition of the Republican House Whip, Rep. Newt Gingrich of Georgia. The problem of 'the vision thing', remarked by Bush himself in the 1988 election campaign, continued to haunt his domestic agenda. It was difficult to counter the charges that he was essentially uninterested in domestic affairs and made little attempt to push those he did advocate to success. After the mid-term, proposals appeared to be revisions and repackaging of existing programmes which lacked new money or solid efforts to promote their implementation – a charge that Bush increasingly countered by attacking the Democratic Congress's frustration of his efforts.

In the mode of presidential domestic policy-maker Bush was the minimalist facilitator. Such criticism undervalues the conservative position of inaction as a positive stance. Doing nothing but doing it well is a purposive strategy: the question is, did he in fact do it well? The two main criticisms were that Bush was reactive and lacking in sustained commitment on the one hand, and on the other that there was no coherent strategy or focus on key issues, as there had been under Reagan. Bush's conservative pragmatism meant reaction to policy demands was both part of his managerial style and in his view an effective approach: clear each problem as it came across the desk and pass on to the next one. Similarly the charge that there was no coherent package was arguably a misrepresentation of the

situation. Bush was confronted with a divided system of government, budget deficits which precluded new initiatives and a
less-than-sympathetic media (and hampered by a fractured style
of communication). The administration argued that there had
been a coherent policy since the first State of the Union address
in 1989. It was promoting it that was the problem, with weak
public relations effort in the White House and obstruction to
legislation within Congress.

And if Bush's promotion of the right's themes of choice and
empowerment – through urban policy, education, health care
and welfare reform – meant little in the way of action, this did
not, it was said, amount to failure. In the administration's view
such empowerment and choice themes did not of themselves
call for new programmes or new funding, and failure to make
the reforms was Congress's, not the President's. It could be
further argued that Bush's position was realistic in another
sense: Congress was unable to override the President's vetoes
and Bush was able to make considerable mileage out of his
repeated emphasis that Congress blocked him but could produce little in the way of alternatives. Moreover this situation
was not new; the embattled presidency had grown since the
late 1970s, marked by conflict between the executive and legislative branches, an inherent fragmentation of domestic issues,
high media scrutiny and a lack of clear constituencies for
increasingly problematic issues.[48]

As Light has emphasized, in controlling the domestic
agenda a president has two sets of resources: internal (time,
information, expertise and energy) and external (political
support, including party support in Congress, electoral
margin, professional reputation).[49] Bush's handling of these
resources was as important as their availability. His internal
resources looked impressive in terms of the information and
expertise available to him, but the time and energy he was
willing to devote to domestic issues fell short of the demands
that the public, and the right wing of the Republican Party,
made upon him. As Mullins and Wildavsky put it, he had 'built
an advisory and management apparatus that would respond
wonderfully to the policy guidance he believes it would be
unwise for him to provide.'[50]

Bush's external resources were even more problematic. His
issueless 1988 campaign and popular vote percentage of 53 per

cent did not allow him to claim an extensive mandate. His party lost seats in Congress and he ran behind the winners in 379 of the 435 congressional districts. Bush's party support was also mixed. Although he had made appointments and expressed opinions on social and moral issues to reassure the right wing of the Republican Party, criticism grew, both inside and outside Congress. The criticism increased particularly following the budget deal with Congress in the autumn of 1990, which reneged on Bush's 'no new taxes' pledge, and after the election by the House Republican Conference on 22 March 1989 of the outspoken conservative, Rep. Newt Gingrich of Georgia, as House Minority Whip over moderate Edward R. Madigan of Illinois.

A further key to Bush's position lies in another of Light's 'external resources', public opinion. In the early days of his presidency, Bush's approval ratings had hovered in the 50+ per cent range: low for a new president. By the summer of 1989 they had risen to the impressive level of 70 per cent, and climbed even higher in the wake of the Gulf War. Ominously, however, approval fell away as the public reacted to the problems of the economy, reaching 51 per cent in November 1991 – a 16 per cent fall since mid-October. By July 1992 Bill Clinton was recording opinion poll ratings up to 30 percentage points ahead of Bush. Clearly, this resource leached away in the wake of demands for more incisive domestic leadership. Light's final external resource – professional reputation – was subject to more complex judgements. Bush's strengths as the Washington insider, with executive experience across a wide range (admittedly largely in the foreign affairs field) and eight years as Vice President, added significantly to his reputation. His pragmatism and his 'can do' style also seemed fitting. But as Hess has reminded us, the managerial presidency is not an advantage but a trap, raising public expectations about performance that cannot be met.[51]

Bush was essentially the victim of the way demands changed over the period of his presidency. On entering office he had appeared the candidate for the times: maintaining the status quo in an era of deficits when the public seemed contented with the cross-currents of divided government. He ended as the president who had failed to meet the pressures of economic recession and was criticized for his lack of leadership in a range of domestic affairs, particularly health, education and the troubled inner cities. The resources he could count on diminished and the problems grew; attempts to become chief political officer, in Hess's phrase, and thus providing moral and political leadership rather than managing policy, came too late to prevent his domestic leadership being judged wanting.[52]

NOTES

1.	I am grateful to the Fulbright Commission for the Senior Scholar in American Studies Award in 1992 which enabled this research to be completed.
2.	A.M. Rivlin, *Reviving the American Dream* (Washington DC: The Brookings Institution, 1992), p. 2.
3.	See, for example, J.P. Pfiffner *The Strategic Presidency: Hitting the Ground Running* (Chicago: Dorsey Press, 1988).
4.	Led by combative House Speaker Jim Wright (later replaced by Tom Foley) and the new Senate Democratic leader George Mitchell. B.A. Rockman, 'The Leadership Style of George Bush', C. Campbell SJ and B.A. Rockman (eds) *The Bush Presidency: First Appraisals* (Chatham, NJ: Chatham House Publishers 1991), p. 10.
5.	Catastrophic health insurance was funded through supplemental fees. Enacted in 1988, opposition rapidly grew as many of the affluent elderly who had to pay the increased fees lobbied Congress for the repeal of the programme. The programme was repealed in late 1989.
6.	T.E. Mann, 'Breaking the Political Impasse', in H.J. Aaron (ed.), *Setting National Priorities* (Washington DC: The Brookings Institution, 1990), p. 299.
7.	A. Devroy, 'For Bush, a Familiar Pattern Resumes: Agenda Focuses Overseas, Not at Home', *Washington Post*, 9 June 1991, p. A4.
8.	P.C. Light, 'Presidents as Domestic Policymakers', in T.E. Cronin (ed.) *Rethinking the Presidency* (Boston, Mass.: Little, Brown, 1982), p. 365.
9.	B. Sinclair, 'Governing Unheroically (and Sometimes Unappetizingly): Bush and the 101st Congress', in Campbell SJ and B.A. Rockman (eds), op. cit., p. 171.
10.	B. Solomon, 'Darman Sheathes His Stiletto In New White House Power Equation', *National Journal*, Vol. 24, No. 1, 4 January 1992, p. 34.
11.	B. Solomon, 'Sam Skinner's Managerial Skills Won't Assure A New Bush Message', *National Journal*, Vol. 23, No. 50, 14 December 1992, pp. 3038–3039.
12.	R. Rose, 'Organizing Issues In and Organizing Problems Out', in J.P. Pfiffner (ed.) *The Managerial Presidency* (Pacific Grove, Calif.: Brooks/Cole, 1990), p. 117.
13.	B.A. Rockman, 'How Is the President Doing?', *Atlantic Monthly*, Vol. 9, No. 3, Summer 1991, p. 56.

14. E.J. Dubin, 'Medicaid Reform: Major Trends and Issues', *Intergovernmental Perspective*, Vol. 18, No. 2, Spring 1992, p. 5.

15. W. Schneider, 'The Republicans' *Cape Fear* Scenario', *National Journal*, Vol. 23, No. 48, 30 November 1991, p. 2946.

16. Relatedly, in 1991 Bush had signed a major surface transportation bill which he claimed would mean the significant creation of new jobs. But he had fought most of the proposals that had sought to restore investment in the transportation system. In the end, rather than cast a veto during a recession and amid attacks on his lack of a domestic agenda, Bush agreed to a bill he had largely opposed.

17. A. Devroy and J.E. Yang, 'Beset by Conservatives, Bush Struggles to keep Peace in Party', *Washington Post*, 27 November 1991, p. A4.

18. *America 2000: An Education Strategy* (Washington DC: Department of Education, 1991).

19. J.E. Chubb and T.M. Moore, *Politics, Markets, and America's Schools* (Washington DC: The Brookings Institution, 1990).

20. 'Message to the Congress on Environmental Goals', *Weekly Compilation of Presidential Documents*, Vol. 28, No. 12, Tuesday 24 March 1992, p. 540.

21. D. Priest, 'Competitiveness Council Is Criticized on Hill', *Washington Post*, 12 June 1992.

22. K. Schneider, 'Environment Laws Are Eased By Bush As Election Nears', *New York Times*, 20 May 1992. Even after the November 1992 presidential election, the Council on Competitiveness was till seeking to ease the restrictions on wetlands developments. At that point the White House conceded that this would not be feasible, given the continued opposition of Reilly and the EPA.

23. A. Lewis, 'The Pillage President', *New York Times*, 28 May 1992.

24. J. Matthews, 'Industry First, Environment Last', *Washington Post*, 26 May 1992, p. A17.

25. H.J. Aaron, 'A Prescription for Health Care', in Aaron (ed.) op. cit., p. 249.

26. *The President's Comprehensive Health Reform Program*, 6 February 1992 (Washington DC: The White House, 1992), p. 27.

27. *Report of the National Advisory Commission on Civil Disorders* (the Kerner Report) (Washington DC: Government Printing Office, 1968). The Report dealt with the violent unrest across the country in the summer of 1967; nationwide the death toll reached 83.

28. As quoted in D.S. Broder, 'Historians Fault Bush's Response to Crisis', *Washington Post*, 10 May 1992.

29. R.J. Samuelson, 'A Phantom Debate?', *Washington Post*, 13 May 1992, p. A23.

30. *Weekly Compilation of Presidential Documents*, Vol. 28, No. 19, Monday, 11 May 1992 (Speech on 6 May at Los Angeles Airport, p. 784; Remarks at Mount Zion Missionary Baptist Church in Los Angeles, 7 May 1992, p. 785; Remarks to Community Leaders in Los Angeles, 8 May 1992, p. 810).

31. In election year, family values had already been highlighted. In the 1992 State of the Union Address (in what was said to be a response to urban leaders, including mayors of the major cities) President Bush

announced the creation of a National Commission on America's Urban Families, chaired by Missouri's governor John Ashcroft and co-chaired by former mayor of Dallas Annette Strauss.

32. Which received widespread – and not always complimentary – publicity; Vice President Quayle retreated.

33. J. Rovner with K. Dumas, S. Kellam and J. Zuckman, 'Rhetoric, Not Radical Change likely Result of L.A. Riots', *Congressional Quarterly Weekly Report*, Vol. 50, No. 19, 9 May 1992, p. 1247. The findings of a Gallup poll showed that the public blamed Reagan more than Johnson by better than 2 to 1. W. Schneider, 'It Takes a Crisis To Prompt A Remedy', *National Journal*, Vol. 24, No. 21, 23 May 1992, p. 1270.

34. This developed in Congress into a tax bill with many additional provisions which Bush then threatened to veto.

35. F. Barnes, 'Unkempt', *New Republic*, No. 4037, 1 June 1992, p. 11.

36. D.S. Broder, 'Urban Recipe: From Back Burner to Hot Spot', *Washington Post*, 24 May 1992.

37. D. Caraley, 'Washington Abandons the Cities', *Political Science Quarterly*, Vol. 107, No. 1, 1992, p. 16.

38. 'Race Against Time', *New Republic*, No. 4036, 25 May 1992, p. 9.

39. Bush had advocated Enterprize Zones in the 1992 State of the Union message but on 20 March 1992 had vetoed the House of Representatives tax bill (HR 4210) which had proposed ten demonstration projects in urban and rural areas but excluded capital gains tax waivers.

     Bush used his veto message to lay out the themes for his reelection bill, the 'five pillars'. These called for new trade laws and tax credits, educational reform that included school choice, health care reform, litigation reform, and no tax increases. But no legislative drive was put behind these 'five pillars'. J.A. Barnes, 'Blown Off Course', *National Journal*, Vol. 48, 31 October 1992, p. 2475.

40. 'Citing Special Interest Slant, Bush Vetoes Tax Bill', *Congressional Quarterly Weekly Report*, Vol. 50, No. 45, 14 November 1992, p. 3649.

41. See D.M. Hill, 'The American Philosophy of Welfare', *Social Policy and Administration*, Vol. 26, No. 2, June 1992, pp. 117–128. In the 1992 presidential elections Bill Clinton campaigned in support of a form of 'workfare', offering 'a hand up not a handout' to get people off welfare and into work.

42. K. Mullins and A. Wildavsky, 'The Procedural Presidency of George Bush', *Political Science Quarterly*, Vol. 107, No. 1, Spring 1992, p. 57.

43. R. Pear, 'Administration Rejects Proposal For New Anti-Poverty Programs', *New York Times*, 6 July 1990.

44. 'Statement on Welfare Reform', 10 April 1992, *Weekly Compilation of Presidential Documents, Monday April 13, 1992*, Vol. 28, No. 15, p. 625.

45. See: *Outcast on Main Street* (Washington DC: Department of Housing and Urban Development, 1992); M. Elliott and L.J. Krivo, 'Structural Determinants of Homelessness in the United States', *Social Problems*, Vol. 38, No. 1, February 1991, pp. 113–131.

46. *National Drug Control Strategy* (Washington DC: Office of National Drug Control Policy, 1991), p. 2. Martinez also defended the policy to concentrate on waging war against the international cartels rather than

on demand reduction. He was quoted as saying: 'You can't buy something for which there is no supply.' 'Supply-side drug policy' [editorial], *The Independent*, 27 February 1992.

47. J.A. Barnes, 'Blown Off Course', *National Journal*, Vol. 48, 31 October 1992, p. 2473. Congress did clear, however, and Bush signed, legislation which introduced stiffer penalties for 'carjacking'.
48. Light, op. cit., pp. 368–369.
49. Ibid., p. 354.
50. Mullins and Wildavsky, op. cit., p. 53.
51. S. Hess, *Organizing the Presidency*, revised edition (Washington DC: The Brookings Institution, 1988), p. 233.
52. Ibid., p. 6.

8 Foreign Policy
Raymond A. Moore

BUSH'S FOREIGN POLICY RÉSUMÉ

It took George Bush almost a lifetime to become the 'vicar' of
United States foreign policy but when he did on 20 January
1989, he brought with him the richest foreign policy résumé of
any US president since Dwight Eisenhower. He had served in
World War II as the youngest Naval carrier pilot, and been shot
down in combat in the Pacific. He had been an oil man in
Texas and developed a special interest in the Middle East. He
had been a Congressman and later Ambassador to the United
Nations, the Director of the Central Intelligence Agency, the
first permanent representative to China since the Korean War
and Vice President under Ronald Reagan for eight years,
where he gained the personal acquaintance of many of the
world's political leaders.

Few presidents had been better prepared by experience than
George Bush to lead the nation in the conduct of its foreign
relations especially during a period of historic transition, in
this instance the transition from the Cold War to a New World
Order. While Bush was a product of the Cold War he was no
belligerent idealogue such as the Reagan of the first term[1] nor
was he a populist idealist like Jimmy Carter.[2] Instead Bush was
the personification of the pragmatic, non-ideological prac-
titioner of the art of the possible. While he was the inheritor of
the Reagan mantle, it was more the mantle of Reagan's second
term when he struck a series of business-like bargains with
Mikhail Gorbachev rather than the crusading Reagan of the
first term, calling for the overthrow of the Evil Empire and a
trillion and a half dollar arms build-up.

BUSH'S FOREIGN POLICY TEAM

Once Bush became his own man after the election of 1988, he set out to build himself a strong team of men experienced in practical politics and international problems.

For his Secretary of State, Bush chose his close friend and political advisor, James Baker, who had served Reagan as Chief of Staff and Secretary of Treasury. Baker had earned the reputation of being a smart, capable politician who was a quick learner in the intricacies of international finance. While hardly a Kissinger or even a George Shultz when he took over the job, he quickly established himself as the man in charge with the help of his long-time assistant, Margaret Tutwiler and Lawrence Eagleburger, a State Department career officer who became his Number Two man in State and later Acting Secretary when Baker left to become Bush's Chief of Staff in a desperate effort to revive Bush's reelection campaign.

As Secretary of Defense, Bush originally wanted former Senator John Tower of Texas, but when the Senate denied him confirmation, he chose Congressman Dick Cheney who had been a Chief of Staff to Gerald Ford. Cheney knew his way around Washington and was confirmed without further controversy. He had the ability to learn quickly about arcane defense matters and soon settled into his job and became comfortable with the Pentagon's personnel and policies.

The third member of Bush's foreign policy civilian troika was retired general Brent Scowcroft who had served in the White House with Henry Kissinger. Scowcroft was a well-regarded experienced foreign policy and defense expert who brought impressive credentials to the pivotal post of National Security Advisor.

Originally, when Bush took office, Admiral William Crowe was Chairman of the Joint Chiefs; however, Crowe soon became impatient with the political colorization of National Security Council meetings and retired at the end of his term and was replaced by General Colin Powell, the first African-American head to JCS. Powell was the last NSC adviser to President Reagan and turned the job over to Scowcroft when Bush arrived at the White House. Powell in turn was serving at Faras Command in Atlanta when Secretary of Defense Cheney leapfrogged him over 50 senior generals, including the Vice-Chairman of JCS, and made him Chairman.[3]

This group, along with Robert Gates who began as Scowcroft's chief deputy and later became Director of the Central Intelligence Agency, and Vice President Quayle, comprised the core group of advisors to the President in foreign policy for the rest of his term. As the authors of *Marching in Place: The Status Quo Presidency of George Bush* point out, 'Bush revealed his priorities by naming one of the strongest foreign policy teams ever fielded in Washington: a group that cast a heavy shadow over the president's less impressive domestic advisors.'[4]

BUSH'S FOREIGN POLICY STYLE

Bush's experience, his staff and his own interests dictated that he would concentrate his energies on foreign policy if circumstances would permit him to do so. And at the beginning of his term, circumstances not only permitted him to do so, but they compelled him to do so. Only in the last year when the economy failed to recover from a long lingering recession and when the reelection campaign loomed ever closer, was he forced to turn his attention from the foreign to the domestic sphere.

The transition in foreign policy from Reagan to Bush was smooth and effortless. There was continuity in policy, if not in personnel, and since Bush was intimately familiar as Vice President with Reagan's policies and diplomatic friends abroad, he could carry on the major programs underway between the US and the USSR, and work out the details of the momentous readjustments necessitated by the triumph of the West in the Cold War.

In many ways, Bush was the beneficiary of the changes in the international system that had begun occurring during Reagan's watch. The Soviet Union was fast disappearing as a threat to the US, Gorbachev was presiding over the conversion of his country to a market economy and democratization of the political system, albeit with considerable opposition from within the battered Communist Party. Bush rode the waves of a profound transfiguration of the politics of Eastern Europe and the Soviet Union with considerable dexterity, encouraging its leaders in their reform efforts and promising political support and economic aid.

In his first two years, unlike Reagan, Bush travelled extensively with trips to the Far East, to Western and Eastern Europe, to Malta to meet with Gorbachev, to Cartagena, Colombia for a drug summit with South American presidents, to Canada and London, to Helsinki for a second meeting with Gorbachev, to Mexico and Brazil, Argentina and Chile, and the Middle East where he met with President Asad of Syria.[5]

Later as things turned sour at home he would be roundly criticized for spending more time abroad than at home and paying more attention to foreign affairs than domestic affairs. But in the beginning of his term, Bush was playing his foreign policy cards with remarkable energy and zest. He worked the phone constantly with his fellow leaders overseas, especially Prime Ministers Thatcher of Great Britain and Ozal of Turkey, Kings Hussein of Jordan, Hassan of Morocco and Fahd of Saudi Arabia, Chancellor Kohl of Germany and President Mubarak of Egypt.[6] He exuded considerable warmth in his relations with friends and allies and even with the Congress, calling for harmony and genuine bipartisanship.

To show his independence of Reagan and to stress the non-ideological nature of his administration, he replaced confrontation with compromise over Nicaragua and South Africa. Within two months he had negotiated a compromise on Contra aid with Congress and effectively removed the issue from his foreign policy agenda. With South Africa, Bush accepted Congressional sanctions, promised to enforce them more strenuously and even welcomed Nelson Mandela when he visited the country in June 1990.

FOREIGN POLICY HIGHLIGHTS

China

The first major international test President Bush was put to was in June of 1989 when Chinese soldiers were ordered to march on pro-democracy protesters, mostly students, in Tiananmen Square, Beijing. Hundreds of students were killed and thousands were taken off to jail. The President considered himself an expert on China from his diplomatic service there and orchestrated the response to the crisis. Initially, the US criticized Chinese actions, suspended military sales, cut off high level diplomacy, opposed loans to China, warned US tourists to avoid the mainland and extended the visas of 70,000 Chinese students in the US. The US also offered sanctuary to the noted dissident physicist Fang Lazhi and his wife. After the event, Bush softened the blows and reverted to a more pragmatic policy which expressed Bush's conviction that China played a vital part in overall US policy and should not be driven back into the hostile isolation of the Korean War period.

When he sent Brent Scowcroft and Lawrence Eagleburger to Beijing to normalize relations, he sent a clear statement that although the US disapproved of China's human rights policy, it still wanted to keep the door open to further cooperation in economic and political matters. This he continued to do much to the consternation of Congressional critics and human rights activists. Although China continued to seek trade and even shake up the composition of its governing council to accommodate younger and pro-free market members, it refused to accede to the administration's encouragement (and Congress' demands) that it democratize its political and cultural life.[7] When Congress suggested denying China renewal of Most Favored Nation trading status, the President strongly opposed such efforts and reiterated that he knew the Chinese best and that such tactics would prove counterproductive in the long run and even delay democratic reforms.

South America

Another area where problems arose was South America. Here Bush claimed some impressive victories. One of the biggest was the defeat of the Sandinistas in Nicaragua in free elections although President Chamarro continued to have great difficulty in establishing a stable government in that divided land. Eight other countries held democratic elections including Chile for the first time in twenty years. Unfortunately the new president soon aborted the constitution and gave himself dictatorial powers. Much the same thing happened in Brazil, although in this case the corruption of money was more important than the corruption of power.

The US also invaded Panama in Operation Just Cause and deposed Manuel Noriega, a military president who was subsequently indicted and tried in the US for corruption and drug dealing. Although the US rid Panama of a thoroughly despicable dictator, it created major dislocations in Panama due to the invasion which might have been avoided if Bush had given timely support to an earlier indigenous coup attempt by army officers. The US failed to live up to its promises to clean up the country and help it with substantial aid. Later Bush established excellent relations with Mexico and its newly elected president, Carlos Salinas de Gortari, who favored foreign investment and a free market. The President eventually signed a Free Market Agreement with Mexico, which when combined with the one with Canada promised a North American free market.

The Soviet Union

The year 1989 also brought profound changes in Europe and the Soviet Union. Soviet President Mikhail Gorbachev and his Foreign Minister Eduard Shevardnadze made it clear to Bush and Baker that they were willing and eager to make far-reaching arms control agreements with their one-time adversaries. In the winter of 1989–90 they allowed the unravelling of the Soviet Empire without major violence and opened a new day for political freedom in Eastern Europe. The Berlin Wall fell and the door was open for the reunification of Germany. Eventually Gorbachev's external policies of loosening controls over Warsaw Pact countries crept inward and allowed the non-Russian states to seek independence, a development which ultimately led to the dissolution of the Soviet Union itself. These truly momentous events which signalled the end of the Cold War and the triumph of the West were watched with approval by the Bush administration. Opportunities for a world free of fear of a nuclear war, free of a continued Communist threat, of the arrival of a democratic and free market Eastern Europe and Soviet Union, were quickly recognized. Gorbachev, Shevardnadze, Baker and Bush made progress toward a Conventional Forces Treaty in Europe agreement and a Strategic Arms Reduction Treaty. They worked closely together on German unification and Middle East issues. As Berman and Jentleson have observed, 'Perhaps the highest compliment is that US–Soviet diplomatic relations were normalized. Not all conflicts were settled, and not all interests have converged, but the process of diplomacy among leaders of these two former adversaries was regularized.'[8]

Bush embraced Gorbachev warmly during 1989 and 1990, only to see him gradually lose control over the country to his former protégé, now rival, Boris Yeltsin. As the bottom fell out of the Soviet economy, Bush was suddenly confronted with not just a new and willing diplomatic partner, but a new Russia and a collection of newly independent states, all in varying degrees of economic, social and political disarray, and all clamoring for US aid and support. These problems confronted Bush and Baker for the remainder of their term of office and were left for President Clinton when he took office in January 1993.

Germany

The unification of Germany under Chancellor Helmut Kohl's leadership received the strong support of the United States. As John Newhouse has observed, 'As Bush and Baker saw matters, a unified Germany would be a source of stability during a period of change, provided that the enlarged nation continued to be a member of NATO.'[9] Both interceded with Gorbachev to support unification and accept the new Germany as part of NATO. This historic development created problems as well as opportunities. Paris and London became worried about Germany becoming the new colossus of Europe. Germany, itself, tried to rebuild East Germany and the new Russia and protect her economy against inflation and recession.

All of these actions created problems for the Bush administration and they tried to wrestle with them as the US economy turned sour. German interest rates remained high, and unreasonably high price supports for agricultural products in European Community countries contributed to increased tensions between the US and Europe. These surfaced at a G7 annual summit meeting in Houston in 1990 and in the subsequent breakdown of negotiations over tariff reductions in London. Carla Hills, the administration's chief trade negotiator, eventually recommended that sharp tariff increases be placed on European wines, liquors and cheeses. From the euphoria of reunification to the trade and financial tensions of 1992 proved to be a short and rocky road in US–German relations under the Bush presidency.

Japan

With the collapse of the Soviet Union and the unification of Germany came a new and different situation in world politics that saw the emergence of an economic 'big three' consisting of the US, Germany and Japan. As the threat of nuclear war receded, the main arena shifted to trade and finance. US–Japanese relations took on added significance and Bush and Baker found themselves deeply involved in maintaining a stable relationship with a former enemy which grew to be an economic superpower with the encouragement of the US. This became increasingly difficult as the US became the world's number one debtor nation and Japan became the world's number one creditor nation. US trade with Japan became increasingly unbalanced and Japan's reluctance to relax her trade barriers to US imports added fuel to the fire. Japan-bashing in the US and US-bashing in Japan became favorite in-country sports.

Although Bush and Baker were in large measure detached from economic policy, Carla Hills spent a great deal of her time in office in hard bargaining with the Japanese over the terms of trade. The resulting failures for most part made for hardening of feelings, not between the US and Japanese governments, but between American and Japanese citizens. When President Bush visited Tokyo in January of 1992, he literally went begging for jobs and trade concessions to close the unfavorable balance of trade. He had little success in spite of taking the presidents of the big three automobile companies with him. The US misfortunes in its own economy, its declining position in world trade and its weakening influence in world politics, all added up to making the Japanese worry about the strength and stability of its military protector and best customer. As the Bush-Baker term ran down in 1992, the Japanese encountered their own problems with an economic recession and shrinking overseas assets. Both countries were concerned with world-wide recessions and growing trade rivalries between Europe, Asia and the US.

The Persian Gulf War

The defining moment of George Bush's presidency came when he led a United Nations coalition in war against Saddam Hussein's Iraq. The moment came after the Reagan-Bush administrations had supported Iraq in the Iraq–Iran war which ended in 1988. After the war, Bush continued to support Saddam in the hope that he could be a moderating force in the Middle East and a long-range counter force to Iran. In 1989 both the Central Intelligence Agency and the Defense Intelligence Agency agreed that Iraq was not likely to destroy the area because it was still recovering from the after-effects of the war with Iran. From 1988 until almost the invasion of Kuwait on 1 August 1990, the administration continued to aid Iraq with export–import bank guarantees, trade encouraged by the Commerce and State departments and opposition to Congressionally imposed sanctions as late as two days before the invasion.[10]

When, however, in the spring of 1990 Saddam Hussein began making speeches attacking Israel and Kuwait's treatment of Iraq and then deploying eight divisions along the borders of Kuwait in July, the US took note. But it was not convinced that Iraq was intending more than bluffing Kuwait on debt settlement or at most gaining control of the Rumaila oilfield and two islands in the Persian Gulf. US Ambassador April Glaspie told Saddam on 25 July that the US was deeply concerned about Iraq's recent actions and would defend its vital interests, but it still wanted friendly relations with Iraq and had 'no opinion in Arab–Arab conflicts, like your border disagreement with Kuwait.'[11] Saddam's reassurances that Iraq had only peaceful intentions and that future negotiations would defuse the current crisis further convinced most of the US intelligence community that it was irrational for Iraq to invade Kuwait when it could gain most of what it wanted from negotiations backed by King Fahd of Saudi Arabia, King Hussein of Jordan and President Mubarak of Egypt.

When, in spite of US wishful thinking to the contrary, Iraq actually invaded, conquered and occupied Kuwait, President Bush was quick to condemn the actions and supported fully the United Nations in resolutions calling for Iraq's withdrawal –

and later for collective action to oust Iraq from its occupation of Kuwait.

As the President explained in his press conference of 30 November 1990:

> We're in the Gulf because the world must not and cannot reward aggression. And we're there because our vital interests are at stake. And we're in the Gulf because of the brutality of Saddam Hussein ... Our objectives remain what they were since the outset. We seek Iraq's immediate and unconditional withdrawal from Kuwait. We seek the restoration of Kuwait's legitimate government. We seek release of all hostages and the free functioning of all embassies. And we seek the stability and security of this critical region of the world.[12]

Bush's fervent diplomacy with NATO allies, with the Soviets, the Chinese, the Israelis, assorted Middle Eastern countries and United Nations' member states, proved successful, not only in the passage of strong UN resolutions but of organizing, deploying and utilizing a United Nations military force commanded by US General Norman Schwarzkopf. Bush resisted pressure in Congress and from his own advisers to wait for an embargo to force Iraq into compliance with UN resolutions. He felt he could not wait for eighteen months, that time was not on his side and the UN coalition was bound to break up before that date. When on 12 January 1991 Congress grudgingly passed a joint resolution authorizing the President to use US military force pursuant to UN Resolution 677, Bush had the political backing he needed to pursue a military option if Saddam refused to comply with UN resolutions. When Saddam failed to comply, Bush and the UN opted for war 16 January 1991 and turned Operation Desert Shield into Operation Desert Storm. It proved resoundingly successful, with a ground offensive lasting only 100 hours.[13] Saddam's forces were soundly defeated and driven from Kuwait. The UN's resolutions were upheld and the Coalition managed to hold together and work successfully until the cease fire of 27 February 1991 was in place. British, French, Saudi and US forces played important roles in the Coalition victory and, considering the number of players, the complexity of the issues involved and the difficulty of the terrain, it is remarkable that the fighting went as smoothly as it did. As I have observed elsewhere, 'It provided a textbook case study of a UN collective security action and of US leadership in coordinating and directing an international coalition.'[14]

As a result of Bush's leadership and the US-led Coalition's quick victory, the US came out of the war as a big winner, militarily and politically. This was especially so in the UN where it had previously lost influence and in the Middle East where the Soviet Union lost power and status. In the war's aftermath, the US was restored to its status as number one superpower and was placed in the enviable position to lead efforts to build a New World Order which included a general peace settlement in the Middle East and a revitalized United Nations capable of taking action to preserve the peace when regional disputes broke out.

It was a 'lovely little war' from which Bush had emerged a victorious world statesman with remarkably high approval ratings both at home and abroad. If he had been able to replace the Old World Order of the Cold War with a New World Order free of nuclear terror, a cooperative Soviet Union and an effective international organization, then perhaps his place in history would have been secured.[15]

Unfortunately for President Bush, the victory was shortlived. His ceasefire after a hundred hours made for convenient and attractive public relations, but it did not allow the UN forces time to carry out a decisive blow against Iraq's war machine. Nor did it accomplish the ousting of Saddam Hussein and he remained in power mocking and threatening until the end of Bush's single term of office.

In the Middle East, Bush and Baker had better luck and when Israeli elections brought Rabin to power and removed Shamir, the outlook for a peace settlement appeared brighter than it had for years. With the Soviets removed as a regional power and ally of Syria, the Syrians, who had supported the UN effort against Iraq, entered serious conversations with the Israelis. Baker's efforts seemed to be bearing fruit when he was called upon to rescue Bush's ill-fated effort for reelection. The negotiations sputtered on for the rest of Bush's term with the parties involved waiting to see if President Clinton's administration would take a hands-on policy toward the troubled Middle Eastern peace process.

Yugoslavia and Somalia

Toward the end of George Bush's presidency he was confronted by two peripheral issues. One was the civil war in Yugoslavia, occasioned by the breakup of that country into several independent states. The other was the outbreak of mass starvation in the African country of Somalia where populations were again caught in war between clans.

They were peripheral because the administration felt it could not intervene directly with military force. In the Yugoslav case, the European Community could not agree on a policy of intervention and the United Nations was left with a situation where it could only try to facilitate a diplomatic solution, and air-lift food and medical supplies to the beleaguered citizens of Bosnia who were being 'ethnically cleansed' by the rival Serbs. Bush supported the UN efforts and tried to put pressure on the parties to effect a cease fire, but in spite of threats to use military force to stop the siege of Sarajevo and allow humanitarian aid to its citizens, the fighting among the Croatians, Bosnians and Serbs continued throughout 1992. Over two million refugees from the fighting created a major headache for diplomats and humanitarian aid groups as well. The danger remained as Bush left office that the Serbs would expand the fighting into Kosovo and provoke the Albanians, the Greeks and the Turks to intervene in the dispute.

In Somalia, the specter of mass starvation had long hung over that unsettled country. People caught between warring clans who would not allow outside agencies to bring in food and supplies had been suffering for years, but in 1992 the situation deteriorated markedly. The United Nations, particularly UNICEF, and Non-Governmental Organizations such as Oxfam, Irish Concern and church groups, tried to help as best they could: yet until the clans reached a peaceful agreement there was little hope that the crisis would pass. The Bush administration supported aid efforts and in December 1992, US and allied forces landed in Mogadishu, the capital, to suppress clan violence and distribute food. Over 30,000 troops were dispersed throughout the country. Efforts to bring about a permanent political settlement and prepare the country for UN supervision lingered on for the next president to cope with as Bush left office.

The threat of a trade war

Just as the election of 1992 was taking place, the threat of a trade war erupted when the US Trade Representative Carla Hills announced that the US was going to impose a 200 per cent increase in tariffs on European, mostly French, wines and other assorted products. The administration did this reluctantly after waiting in vain for five years for Europe to cut tariffs on soybeans and oilseeds which were twice called for by international arbitrators. If the European Community did not respond, then the US said it would consider raising the ante from $300 million to over a billion dollars.

The Europeans, led by the French, threatened to retaliate and commence a genuine trade war which might undermine further the world economy and disrupt ongoing GATT talks on trade expansion which were close to fruition and promised to add $100 billion to world trade if completed. All parties to the dispute, except the French, desperately searched for a solution and it seemed likely that the Germans would persuade the French Socialist government under Mitterrand to forego domestic political considerations and diplomatic isolation and compromise on farm subsidies enough to avoid an escalating trade crisis. Bush, displaying considerable patience in the face of blatant provocation by the EC and its French president Jacques Delors, 'acted with restraint and skill in managing this dispute in the midst of the US election campaign.'[16] An agreement was reached on 30 November 1992, but subsequent French objections during the GATT negotiations in Geneva put in question whether the European Community can negotiate on behalf of its members.

ACCOMPLISHMENTS

Without much question the major accomplishments of the Bush presidency were in the field of foreign policy. Not only did his experience prepare him for the job, but his interest and gifts were in the field as well. He talked knowledgeably about world affairs and enjoyed the travels, the contacts and conversations with foreign leaders. In January 1991 *Time* magazine printed a double image of George Bush on its cover and dubbed him 'Men of the Year'. It lauded one image for his 'commanding vision of a new world order' and criticized the other for showing 'little vision for his own country'. This was a perceptive appraisal of Bush as president and even Bush himself seemed to understand this when he campaigned for reelection as the man who ended the Cold War, rid the world of fear of nuclear war, reunited Germany, made Europe whole and free, and helped create a New World Order by leading United Nations' forces in upholding international law and punishing an aggressor nation in Operation Desert Storm. Even allowing for a generous amount of self-aggrandizement in an election year, there is enough fractional insight in this appraisal to take it seriously. While it is hardly accurate to credit Bush for the 1989 upheaval in the Soviet Union and Eastern Europe, he nonetheless gave sympathetic support to Gorbachev as he manfully tried to modernize the Soviet Union and liberate the satellite states. Later, he helped Yeltsin as he struggled to keep Russia afloat.

Bush's watchful waiting on these events as well as those in China may not have pleased his critics who wanted a more activist policy, but he did not rock the boat during turbulent times and did keep a steady hand on the wheel.

Bush also played his hand skillfully in the German unification process. His strong support of Kohl and his intervention with Gorbachev made the unification process go smoothly and rapidly. His conclusion of various disarmament agreements, including the START treaty with the Soviet Union and later Russia, his free trade agreements with Canada and Mexico and his convening of a Middle East Peace Conference at the conclusion of the Gulf War, must all be counted as major accomplishments.

Bush was at his best in organizing the political and military coalition against Saddam Hussein, as even a severe critic of the Gulf War conceded:

If Bush hid his hand at home, his diplomacy was masterly. He revitalized a dispirited and moribund United Nations, brought the Arabs and Israelis into tacit alliance, and walked hand in glove with the Soviets and Chinese to counter Saddam. The oil-rich Gulf states, the Germans, and the Japanese picked up most of the tab. The Syrians were brought back into the fold of accepted behavior. The Turks, the Egyptians, and the fractious French worked easily in tandem. No one but Bush could have built such an alliance, or held it together so tenaciously. His personal rapport with world leaders was unparalleled.[17]

The authors of the best book thus far on the Bush presidency, *Marching in Place*, subtitled their critical study, *The Status Quo Presidency of George Bush*. They assessed his Gulf War performance in the following glowing words:

> In the Gulf crisis, George Bush found something to believe in. He saw almost immediately that Iraq's invasion of Kuwait threatened vital US interests and must be reversed – probably by force. And perhaps for the first time in his long political career he never wavered ... His vigorous personal diplomacy welded together an international coalition embracing such unlikely partners as Syria, Israel, and the Soviet Union ...
>   Through it all Bush radiated an eerie calm and sense of command. Gone was the shrill, arm-waving creature who repeatedly reversed himself on taxes, civil rights, and abortion. The qualities Bush displayed throughout the Gulf crisis – stubborn resolve and adherence to principle, resourcefulness and foresight – were particularly striking in contrast to his feckless performance at home ... In the Gulf crisis Bush performed with uncommon conviction and ingenuity, but he served as he did at home: as a warrior for the status quo.[18]

The conclusion that Bush was an agent of the status quo in the Gulf War has some credence, but also some dubious inferences. While it is true that Iraq was forced to leave Kuwait, its Royal family was restored to power and Saddam Hussein remained in place in Baghdad, it is hardly true that the status quo remained in the UN or in the Middle East. The UN got a new lease on life from the Gulf War with a decent chance that it might evolve into a reliable and workable instrument of peaceful change. The Syrians were politically housebroken and became part of the peace process. The Soviets were removed as a major player in the region; nevertheless the possibility emerged of US–Russian cooperation to cope with regional quarrels and the emerging interdependency agenda. While a New World Order still remained a chimera, taken together these changes in the status quo could augur well for the future landscape of world politics.

Bush also deserves credit for thwarting a coup attempt against Corazon Aquino in the Philippines and working out an agreement with the new President Fidel Ramos to continue US–Philippine military cooperation in spite of the closing of Clark Air Base and the naval base at Subic Bay. He rid Panama of Noriega, supported Gorbachev in the unsuccessful coup attempt against him by unreconstructed hardliners, and watched a decline in terrorist activities. The last was probably due in part to Syrian occupation of Lebanon, Hafez Asad's decision to oppose his old rival Saddam and Iran's nursing its wound after the Iran–Iraq War – all of which George Bush had his hand in. Late in his term, Bush became very active, dispatching troops to Somalia, threatening to enforce 'no-fly zones' in Iraq and Bosnia and negotiating a new Strategic Arms Reduction Treaty, known as Start II, with Boris Yeltsin and the Russians. The Treaty would eliminate three-fourths of the 20,000 nuclear warheads by 2003, including total elimination of multi-warhead land-based missiles. It is the most extensive disarmament treaty yet signed and was completed in six months. By virtue of intensive negotiations by Lawrence Eagleburger and last minute concessions by both sides, George Bush was able to leave office with a major triumph.

SHORTFALLS IN POLICY

Measured against Bush's sizeable achievements in foreign policy were some notable shortfalls. If it is true that Bush assembled a first-rate foreign policy team of experienced pragmatists, it may also be true that Bush and his team were short of ideological commitment to the ideals of democracy and human rights. As A.M. Rosenthal of *The New York Times* has noted: 'President Bush showed no recovery from the professional distortion of so many American foreign policy bureaucrats. Like them, he suffers from the inability to grasp that dictators are inherently dangerous because no amount of appeasement can remove their survival instinct to solve problems by oppression at home and war abroad.'[19] He further notes that Bush did not understand, 'that American power and American democratic idealism have to be combined to create American effectiveness and that one without the other is crippled.'[20]

This is a criticism many commentators levelled against Bush for failing to sustain strong opposition to the Chinese after the Tiananmen Square massacre. The same criticism also obtained in restoring the Royal family to power in Kuwait without the promise of democratic reforms and in winking at Gorbachev's early suppression of independence movements in the Baltic states. He was also under fire for failing to give early and quick support to the democratic forces in Eastern Europe and those in Russia led by Yeltsin. Even former president Richard Nixon chastised Bush and his advisers for their failure to seize a historic opportunity to shape the future of Russia and the newly independent countries formed from the dissolution of the Soviet Union. Indeed Duffy and Goodgame go so far as to assert that 'without the Gulf War, George Bush as president would be easier to dismiss. He might have been seen as an irresolute, do-nothing president whose answer to economic decline was to cut taxes further for the rich, who applauded from the sidelines as freedom swept across Europe and who invaded Panama mainly to prove his manhood.'[21]

Regarding the Gulf War, Bush is vulnerable to the charge that he allowed Saddam Hussein to be armed and aided by the United States and its allies for several years prior to Iraq's attack on Kuwait. Such have been the charges from the press, from Congress and from the fallout of the Banco Nazionale del Lavaro bank scandal in Atlanta, that the affair was dubbed 'Iraqgate'. The judge in the trial against the bank manager of Lavaro accused the US government of obstructing the investigations and the Justice Department, the Central Intelligence Agency and the Federal Bureau of Investigation all got into the act of accusing each other of suppressing and distorting evidence about the bank's sizable loans to Iraq. According to William Safire, 'Iraqgate is the first global scandal. The leaders of three major nations are implicated in a criminal conspiracy: first to misuse taxpayer funds and public agencies in the clandestine buildup of a terrorist dictator; then to abuse the intelligence and banking services of these nations to conceal the dirty deed; finally to try to thwart the inexorable course of justice.'[22]

When Bush decided to end his appeasement of Saddam Hussein, he reversed a deeply flawed policy based on the false premise that the Iraqi dictator could be cajoled into becoming a stabilizing force for peace in the Middle East.[23] In addition, Bush's premature cessation of hostilities on 27 February 1991 allowed elements of Iraq's army and Republican Guard to escape across the Euphrates River into Basra. On top of this, Schwarzkopf's failure to ground Iraqi attack helicopters and the administration's failure to help Shiite and Kurdish resistors after calling for their uprising subtract from the fruits of victory.

Undeniably the biggest failure was Bush's inability to get rid of Saddam himself. In spite of covert and overt attempts to remove him, he remained in power. In Schwarzkopf's view, Iraq was defenseless if the UN forces had wanted to invade Baghdad and depose Saddam, but it must be said that the UN political coalition would have been severely strained in such an undertaking which would have also involved long-term occupation of the country. Nonetheless the fact that Saddam remained in power proved a running sore for the administration and the UN inasmuch as he continued periodically to defy UN inspection teams and surreptitiously rebuild his arsenal.

The Bush administration is also guilty of failing to follow through with its promises to clean up and reform Panama after Noriega's overthrow. It may have been premature in its diplomatic recognition of the Ukraine without forcing it to adhere to the Nuclear Non-Proliferation Treaty.[24] On such issues as the world environment, global warming, acid rain and the Clean Water Act of 1990, Bush played a better game than he talked when he was under pressure from affected business interests. On birth control and abortion policy toward the Third World and payment of the US debts to the United Nations, the Bush administration's record is downright dismal. It must be said that Bush's shortcomings as a domestic president, his belated and ineffectual attack on the economic recession, his inability to get along with Congress and his inadequate response to the budget deficit all combined to weaken the country within and without and led to a general downsizing of US power and influence from the military and diplomatic heights generated by the Cold War. As Bush prepared to leave office the United States was too often perceived by Japan and the European Community as a country with profound internal problems which weakened its capability to exercise world leadership, correct its budget and trade deficits and compete successfully in a world market.

Lastly, just before Bush left office he exercised his pardon power and exonerated former Secretary of Defense Casper Weinberger and five other officials involved in the Iran-Contra scandal, thereby ending the inquiry for all practical purposes and protecting himself against further investigation. The independent Counsel, Lawrence Walsh, who had conducted the investigations for six years accused the President of undermining the principle that no man is above the law. At the same time, a separate inquiry was under way into the role that Bush, James Baker and State Department aides played in allowing unauthorized entry into Bill Clinton's passport files during the election.

ASSESSMENT

For a one-term president, George Bush presided over more momentous changes in the complexion of world politics than most two-term presidents. While George Kennan was no doubt right when he wrote that 'no country, no party, no person won the cold war',[25] Richard Pipes had a point when he replied that 'if President Bush takes the blame for America's plight in the global economic recession, why deny him recognition for a happy event [the end of the Cold War] that occurred on his watch.'[26] The fact is that Reagan presided over the growth of the deficit and the breakup of Communism and the Soviet Empire and George Bush was on the receiving end of both. If Korea was Truman's war and Hoover was saddled with the Great Depression, then Bush is entitled to a place in history as the president who guided the Ship of State through some perilous waters and helped some of his fellow · chiefs of state to find new routes to the safer harbors of freedom, democracy and market economics. Granted the results

were not all good as the rise of ethnic, religious and national-
istic rivalries in the former Soviet states and Eastern Europe
attest, but when seen in broad perspective, Bush was the
world's leading statesman when great events took place that
changed the world dramatically.

Bush may have had a 'minimalist strategy'[27] at home and 'no
clear agenda beyond muddling through',[28] but at least in foreign policy he had a feel for the game acquired from long
exposures to lands, leaders and problems outside Texas, Maine
and Washington. He enjoyed foreign policy and his days at the
CIA were his most exciting.[29]

Stephen Graubard in *Mr. Bush's War: Adventures in the Politics
of Illusion*, writes that 'For President Bush, like his predecessor,
knew little of the world and was so abysmally ignorant of its
complexities as to genuinely mistake a temporary political gain
for himself and his party for a national and international gain,
and to herald it as such.'[30] Bush may have been 'reactive', not
'proactive', practised status quo policies rather than crusading
ones and been stronger on politics than economics, but it is
most unfair to characterize him as inexperienced and ignorant
of world affairs. Compared to Reagan, Ford and Johnson he
was experienced, prudent and competent. Compared to
Nixon, Truman and Eisenhower he lacked depth, vision and
initiative. Yet overall, Bush was at his best in foreign policy. He
was trained and prepared for public service and if his service
on the home front was far from outstanding, his conduct of
foreign policy from 1989 to 1993 was more than adequate.
Lester Thurow rightly suggests that, 'America's success in the
War in the Gulf proves that it is, and will be, a military superpower in the century to come. But its success in the Gulf in no
way guarantees that it will be an economic superpower in the
twenty-first century.'[31]

Bush's inadequacies in domestic economic and fiscal policies,
in dealing with the world's interdependency agenda and in
moving the country forward to meet the demands of competing in the world market of the twenty-first century will make it
more difficult for his successor to keep America an economic
superpower. Yet on the other hand, Bush's arms control agreements, his financing of the Gulf War with 'other people's
money', his liquidation of the Cold War and his removal of the
threat of nuclear war and international terrorism will make it

easier for President Bill Clinton to reduce the military budget, downsize the armed forces, redirect the energies and resources of the country to rebuilding the infrastructure, increase investment, upgrade research and development and adopt new technologies for a new century. In the end, if Bush had performed as well on the home front as he did on the foreign front, he would not have joined Carter, Ford, Hoover and Taft as America's only one-term presidents of the twentieth century.

NOTES

1. Dilys M. Hill, Raymond A. Moore and Phil Williams (eds), *The Reagan Presidency: An Incomplete Revolution?* (London: Macmillan, 1990), Chapter 9, 'The Reagan Presidency and Foreign Policy', pp. 179–198.
2. M. Glenn Abernathy, Dilys M. Hill and Phil Williams (eds), *The Carter Years: The President and Policy Making* (London: Frances Pinter/New York: St Martin's Press, 1984), Chapter 4, 'The Carter Presidency and Foreign Policy', pp. 54–83.
3. Bob Woodward, *The Commanders*, (New York: Simon & Schuster, 1991), pp. 81–82.
4. Michael Duffy and Dan Goodgame, *Marching In Place: The Status Quo Presidency of George Bush* (New York: Simon & Schuster, 1992), p. 136.
5. Larry Berman and Bruce W. Jentleson, 'Bush and the Post-Cold-War World: New Challenges for American Leadership', Table 4.1, *Bush and Foreign Travel: The First Two Years*, pp. 100–101, in C. Campbell SJ and B.A. Rockman (eds), *The Bush Presidency: First Appraisals* (Chatham, New Jersey: Chatham House 1991).
6. Op. cit. p. 99.
7. 'Chinese Shake Up Top Party Group: Free Market Gains', *The New York Times* 20 October 1992, p. 1.
8. Berman and Jentleson, op. cit., p. 112.
9. John Newhouse, 'The Diplomatic Round: Shunning the Losers', *The New Yorker*, 26 October 1992, p. 44.
10. 'The Road to War', *Newsweek*, 28 January 1991, p. 56.
11. 'The Glaspie Transcript: Saddam Meets the U.S. Ambassador', 25 July 1991, in *The Gulf Reader* (New York: Times Books, Random House, 1991), pp. 122–133. See also Pierre Salinger and Eric Laurent, *Secret Dossier: The Hidden Agenda Behind the Gulf War* (New York: Penguin Books, 1991), pp. 45–63.
12. *The New York Times*, 1 December 1991, p. 4.
13. See Steve Garber and Phil Williams's chapter in this volume on the military side of the conflict.
14. Raymond A. Moore, 'The Case for the War', in Marcia Lynn Whicker, James P. Pfiffner and Raymond A. Moore (eds), *The Presidency and the Persian Gulf War* (New York: Praeger, 1993), p. 185.

15. Since the war, there has been an avalanche of books on the subject. Among the many published are the following: Jean Edward Smith, *George Bush's War*; Stephen R. Graubard, *Mr. Bush's War: Adventures in the Politics of Illusion*; Norman Schwarzkopf, *It Doesn't Take a Hero*; Ramsey Clark, *The Fire This Time: U.S. War Crimes in Gulf*; Roger Hilsman, *George Bush vs. Saddam Hussein: Military Success: Political Failure*; Richard P. Hallion, *Storm Over Iraq: Air Power and the Gulf War*; Hedrick Smith (ed.), *The Media and the Gulf War*; Robert W. Tucker and David C. Hendrickson, *The Imperial Temptation: The New World Order and America's Purpose*; Judith Miller and Laurie Mylroie, *Saddam and the Crisis In the Gulf*.

16. Jim Hoagland, 'Kohl Should Put Squeeze on French in Dispute with U.S.', *The State*, Columbia, SC, 10 November 1992, p. 11-A and *The New York Times*, 11 November 1992, p. 1.

17. Jean Edward Smith, *George Bush's War* (New York: Henry Holt, 1992), p. 8.

18. Duffy and Goodgame, op. cit., pp. 134–135.

19. A.M. Rosenthal, 'Clinton and the Mideast', *The New York Times* 11 April 1992, p. A-11.

20. Ibid.

21. Duffy and Goodgame, op. cit., p. 133.

22. William Safire, '1st Global Political Scandal', *The New York Times*, 12 November 1992, p. A-13. *New York Times* columnists William Safire, Anthony Lewis and Leslie Gelb relentlessly pursued the matter of the arms buildup in Iraq and the bank scandal in Atlanta as did Congressman Henry Gonzales and John Conyers. See *New York Times* reportage on 19, 26, 30 October and 2 November 1992.

23. For a spirited defense of Bush's pre-war strategy see Brent Scowcroft's op. ed. article in *The New York Times* of 15 October 1992.

24. See William C. Parter, 'Ukraine's Nuclear Trigger', *The New York Times*, 10 November 1992, p. A-11.

25. George F. Kennan, 'The GOP Won the Cold War? Ridiculous', *The New York Times*, 28 October 1992, p. A-15.

26. Richard Pipes, 'Credit Where It's Due For Cold War's End', *The New York Times*, 6 November 1992, p. A-14.

27. Duffy and Goodgame op. cit., p. 12.

28. 'America Changes the Guard', *Newsweek*, November/December 1992, p. 22.

29. Ibid.

30. Stephen R. Graubard, *Mr. Bush's War: Adventures in the Politics Illusion* (New York: Hill & Wang, 1992), Preface, xii.

31. Lester Thurow, *Head to Head: The Coming Battle Among Japan, Europe and America* (New York: William Morrow, 1992), p. 21.

9 Defense Policy

Steve Garber and Phil Williams

INTRODUCTION

A popular view of the Bush administration is that although it failed miserably in many aspects of domestic affairs, especially economic policy, it was much more successful in its foreign and defense policies. The President's own interest in security, together with events such as the interventions in Panama and Kuwait, give credence to this conclusion. When examined closely, however, the record of the Bush administration in defense policy is more complex than this suggests. There were considerable achievements, but the administration's defense policy was criticized – for different reasons – by both conservatives and liberals.

This is hardly surprising: the administration was confronted with the most fundamental changes in the security environment since the onset of the Cold War in the late 1940s. Although Bush came to the presidency with considerable experience in foreign policy, by the end of 1991 the world in which he had gained most of his experience had largely disappeared. The fall of the Berlin Wall, the disintegration of the Soviet empire, the unification of Germany and the subsequent collapse of the Soviet Union removed the threat against which the United States had mobilized for over forty years. Judgements and assumptions about military planning which had long been taken for granted were suddenly obsolete. Consequently, the Bush administration had the enormous task of adjusting the American military establishment to the end of the Cold War.

At the end of the Bush presidency this task was well under way – but much remained to be done. There were several reasons why the administration had not gone further. The first was the deliberate choice of a hedging strategy. Given the lingering uncertainties over the future of Russia, continued threats to regional security and stability, and the re-emergence of nationalist and ethnic conflicts in Europe, the administration had initiated a program of significant but limited change designed to guard against a reversal of the positive trends, *and* avoid actions liable to degrade American security in the post Cold War era.

The second was the Bush administration's conception of the US role in the post Cold War world, a role that was defined as facilitator and honest broker rather than architect for a new security structure.[1] Accordingly, the administration tried to adjust existing institutions and mechanisms for new tasks rather than to create what was sometimes described as a new security architecture. Inevitably this led to allegations that the Bush administration was unimaginative, too cautious, overly passive, unwilling to discard Cold War stereotypes and reluctant to dismantle existing structures. The administration responded by enunciating the notion of a New World Order which was designed to provide an intellectual and conceptual framework for managing international security problems after the Cold War. Ultimately, however, the New World Order proved to be an elusive concept, more rhetoric than substance, and more useful in legitimizing the struggle against Saddam Hussein than in establishing mechanisms and modalities for global security. The Bush administration did little to transform a hazy vision into a realistic design. This hesitancy resulted in part from an underlying ambivalence on the part of an administration reluctant to concede the reins of international leadership yet sensitive to the limits of American power.

One consequence of both the ambivalence and the hedging strategy was that the Bush administration's defense policy had something of an ad hoc quality: as well as bringing to fruition major arms reductions with Moscow through the START One and START Two Treaties and playing a crucial role in dismantling the military confrontation in Europe, Bush intervened in Panama, the Gulf and Somalia, increased the role of the military in the drug war, amended President Reagan's Strategic Defense Initiative in ways which made it more modest yet still very expensive, and continued the process of downsizing the United States military that had actually begun in the mid-1980s. The President did all this while facing a Congress in which charges that military cuts did not go far enough went hand in hand with efforts to ensure that the military 'pork barrel' remained intact. Congressmen wanted cuts in defense spending but not in their districts. The Bush administration's defense policy, therefore, had to reconcile the changes in the international environment with domestic interests and institutions which were reluctant to change.

The starting point for the administration, of course, was the legacy of its predecessor. The next section looks briefly at this legacy. After this the chapter discusses the Bush administration's personnel and decision-making style in defense policy. Attention is then given to the evolution of the defense posture, to the pattern of defense spending in the Bush years, and to the plans that were set in motion for adjusting the United States military establishment to the end of the Cold War through the development of the Base Force and cancellations or reductions in specific weapons programs. The Bush administration's arm control policies and its overseas commitments are also explored, while the following section looks at the use of force by the administration. The conclusion examines the legacy of the Bush administration in defense policy and offers an overall assessment of its performance in this area.

THE REAGAN LEGACY

Conservative critics of the Bush administration alleged that it was simply a caretaker government, reaping the benefits of Reagan's military policy: the United States won the Cold War on the watch of George Bush but the victory was really a triumph for the policies of Ronald Reagan, especially his emphasis on 'negotiation from strength'. Although there is some truth in this, the Reagan record and legacy was more mixed than is sometimes suggested. Not only did Reagan continue a military build-up that had been initiated by Jimmy Carter, but he also brought this build-up to an end. The increases in the military budget in the first half of the 1980s were not sustained into the second half of the decade. In fact, budgetary authorizations declined fairly steadily during most of Reagan's second term. In real terms (that is, after inflation has been taken into account) defense authorizations fell by 4.4 per cent in Fiscal Year (FY) 1986, by 3.8 per cent in FY 1987, by 2.1 per cent in FY 1988, and by 1.4 per cent in FY 1989.[2] This decline stemmed from a combination of political pressure, economic constraint and the changing atmosphere in superpower relations.

It contributed to 'a sense of confusion and indecision over fundamental aspects of US defense policy' and 'an emerging agenda of critical choices that had to be made sooner rather than later'.[3] Among the issues still unresolved at the end of the Reagan presidency was the fate of the strategic nuclear force modernization program. The M-X and Midgetman missiles and the B-2 bomber were highly controversial weapon systems, while the President's Strategic Defense Initiative was even more problematic. As the US–Soviet tensions of the first half of the 1980s were dissipated by the Reagan-Gorbachev détente the question marks about the costs and benefits of these programs became even more insistent.

Yet this new détente also promised to ease the dilemmas posed by the juxtaposition of a budgetary crunch and nuclear modernization programs. The Intermediate Nuclear Forces Treaty, which abolished missiles with a range between 500 kilometers and 5,500 kilometers, and the continued negotiations on strategic arms control opened up new possibilities for nuclear force reductions. In spite of the legacy of confusion, therefore, the Reagan inheritance held out considerable promise. An improving relationship with the Soviet Union, a commitment to a continued dialogue with Gorbachev, and a sense of pragmatism that belied the ideological belligerence of the first four years, provided a basis on which the Bush administration could deal with some of the unresolved issues.

THE BUSH ADMINISTRATION: KEY PERSONNEL

Although the Bush administration was more pragmatic than its predecessor, initially it was rather skeptical about the new détente with Moscow. In the 1988 election campaign Bush talked about a 'competitive strategy' towards the Soviet Union and subsequently initiated a major review of foreign and security policy. Encompassing much of the bureaucracy, this 'strategic review' appeared to stifle initiative during the first months of the new administration.

The slow start in defense policy also stemmed from an unexpected political controversy. The President's first nominee for

Secretary of Defense, former Senator John Tower, encountered significant opposition, especially from Sam Nunn, Chairman of the Senate Committee on Armed Services. Revelations about Tower's personal behavior, combined with concerns that he was too conservative to manage a period of transition in US defense policy, helped fuel the opposition. After six weeks of intense debate the Senate, on 9 March 1989, rejected Tower's nomination by a vote of 53 to 47, a vote that went largely along party lines. Tower's replacement, Richard (Dick) Cheney, was confirmed on 17 March by 92 votes to zero.

Along with National Security Adviser Brent Scowcroft and Secretary of State James Baker, Cheney formed a national security team that harked back to the Ford administration – where all three had held office – and was regarded as experienced and pragmatic. The team was completed in the summer of 1989 when General Colin Powell was nominated as Chairman of the Joint Chiefs of Staff to succeed Admiral William Crowe.

The Bush security policy team established close personal relations with each other. For the most part, differences over policy were aired privately rather than publicly. Although debate was often vigorous, the differences were mainly about tactics and timing rather than fundamentals. Consequently, divergences among top officials did not become disruptive in the way they had during the Carter and Reagan presidencies. One result, however, was that the decision-making process sometimes appeared closed and rather insulated from external sources of advice that could have led to better informed policies.

If the insulation issue was to become something of a problem during the Gulf Crisis, it was not evident during the early months of the administration. Although the overall impression was one of considerable unity, there were divergent assessments of the Soviet Union with Cheney rather more skeptical than other members of the team about the nature of the changes in the Soviet Union and reluctant to place too much reliance on Gorbachev. With Baker's visit to Moscow in May 1989, however, a more favorable assessment began to prevail. And against a background of complaints over a lack of vision, President Bush at NATO's fortieth anniversary summit in May 1989 proposed a major new initiative in conventional arms control. The more moderate threat assessment was also evident in the Defense Department's annual publication on

Soviet military power which in September 1989 contained the sub-title 'Prospects for Change' and acknowledged that the likelihood of a US–Soviet confrontation was far lower than at any time in the postwar period. The downward revision of the Soviet threat also provided new opportunities to accommodate fiscal pressures.

DEFENSE BUDGETS AND PROGRAMS

In spite of his concern with establishing a distinctive imprint on defense policy, President Bush continued along the path of defense budget reductions outlined by the Reagan administration. In real terms (i.e. after allowing for inflation), and excluding the costs of Desert Storm and Desert Shield, DOD budget authority declined by 2.9 per cent in FY 1990, 9.6 per cent in FY 1991, 2.8 per cent in FY 1992, and 9.0 per cent in FY 1993.[4] Congress contributed to these cuts and, at times, made the administration move faster than Bush and Cheney preferred. Yet the Congressional role went beyond pressure for budget cuts: Congress established priorities different from those of the administration, defended programs that the Secretary of Defense regarded as expendable, and refused to provide the level of funding that the administration wanted for other programs.

The complexities of the Congressional role became evident when, in his first budget proposal, Cheney attempted to cut weapons systems which were unnecessary or not cost effective. His two main targets were the Navy's F-14D fighters built by the Grumman Corporation and the V-22 Osprey troop carrier, a cross between a plane and a helicopter being produced for the Marine Corps. The House of Representatives voted to fund both programs whereas the Senate gave more support to Cheney. Working with the Conference Committee Cheney agreed to allow Grumman a 'soft landing' by accepting funding for twelve more planes so long as the production line was closed thereafter. Enough money was added to the budget, however, to continue development of the Osprey – which would continue to be an issue throughout the Bush presidency.

Critics of Cheney's budget proposal complained that the administration was cutting conventional forces in favor of strategic programs. Consequently, efforts to save the F-14 and the Osprey were accompanied by assaults on strategic systems, including the administration's request for 132 B-2 bombers. The House of Representatives in particular was concerned about the $70 billion price tag for the B-2 program. The administration itself had contributed to this concern. 'The severity of the budget crunch facing the Pentagon, as demonstrated by Defense Secretary Dick Cheney's proposals to kill programs, was a factor in arousing concern about the B-2's cost.'[5] With support for the administration from the Senate, however, the House-Senate Conference approved $4.3 billion for the B-2. Although this included money to procure two of the planes, Congress also demanded a report assessing the implications of buying less than the 132 currently planned.

Another controversial issue was the Strategic Defense Initiative. The Bush administration did not have the same kind of commitment to SDI as its predecessor. Vice President Dan Quayle was one of the most outspoken proponents of SDI, but National Security Adviser Brent Scowcroft, a much more authoritative figure on security matters, was skeptical of the program, arguing that if the ultimate purpose was to protect retaliatory forces, other options such as enhanced mobility were more cost effective. Rather than abandoning the program though, the administration began to revise its objectives and place more emphasis on the 'Brilliant Pebbles' concept which envisaged a multitude of small interceptor missiles in orbit. Bush asked for $4.9 billion to move ahead with the research and development. Although this was almost a billion less than Reagan had planned, the House of Representatives voted to trim it to $3.1 billion, while a more sympathetic Senate voted for $4.54 billion. The two chambers eventually compromised on $3.8 billion. This was significantly less than the administration had requested and reduced the SDI budget below the amount budgeted for the current year – the first time Congress had acted in this way.

Controversy also surrounded the modernization of strategic retaliatory forces. The House in particular was unsympathetic to the Bush administration's efforts to deploy both the M-X missile and the Midgetman. It capped the deployment of the rail-based M-X at 50 while deleting funding for the Midgetman. Because of a more sympathetic Senate, however, the Conference Committee agreed to provide just over a billion dollars for both missiles.

In terms of readjusting the defense budget and program, therefore, 1989 marked a year of cautious tinkering. The reduction in the budget was spread widely; although a decision was made to retire an aircraft carrier, the *Coral Sea* – thereby preventing the Navy from attaining its goal of fifteen carriers – for the most part the administration postponed hard choices. Congress ultimately acquiesced in this approach and made only very modest changes.

If the predominant mood was one of retrenchment, the administration also gave the military new tasks. President Reagan in 1986 had issued a National Security Decision Directive which characterized illegal drugs as a 'threat to the national security of the United States'. The Bush administration took this further and in 1989 the Department of Defense was made the lead agency for detection and monitoring of the aerial and maritime transit of illegal drugs into the United States. It was also given the responsibility of integrating command, control communications and technical intelligence assets into an effective communications network to support drug enforcement activities. Finally, the National Guard's role in state drug interdiction and enforcement operations was expanded.[6] Initially reluctant to take on this role, the armed services looked at it rather differently after the events of late 1989. Yet throughout the Bush presidency military involvement in the drug war remained a controversial issued dogged by continued question marks about the appropriateness and effectiveness of military activities.

By the end of 1989, it was clear that more drastic changes would be brought about in the defense budget and its programs. The fall of the Berlin Wall effectively ended the Cold War. This provided new opportunities for cuts in the military budget. With President Bush supporting the deficit reduction efforts of OMB Director Richard Darman, the stage was set for more far-reaching changes. As early as November 1989 there were reports that Secretary of Defense Cheney had told the military services to cut $180–195 billion from their budgets over the next four years and that he was considering far-reaching options for reducing the United States military presence in Western Europe and for power projection elsewhere.[7]

It was also announced that the FY 1991 defense budget would be cut by 2 per cent after inflation was taken into account.[8]

The rationale for reductions was strengthened in December 1989 when President Bush met with Mikhail Gorbachev in Malta and agreed to intensify efforts to reach accords on nuclear and conventional force reductions. This was followed up by Bush in his State of the Union Address in January 1990 in which he proposed that United States and Soviet forces in the central region in Europe be restricted to 195,000 personnel each – well below the 275,000 limit he had proposed at the NATO Summit in May 1989. The cuts, however, would be asymmetrical, with the United States having to withdraw about 80,000, and the Soviet Union about 370,000.

Although the Bush proposal presaged a new flexibility in United States defense policy, this was not evident in the administration's budget request for FY 1991. In spite of the upheaval in Eastern Europe, the administration 'recommended only modest troop reductions and weapons cuts' and sought 'major spending increases for numerous strategic weapons systems'.[9] Its request for $295 billion represented a 2.6 per cent decrease in spending when inflation was taken into account, but there were many on Capitol Hill who felt that this did not go nearly far enough in adjusting to the new security environment.

Not surprisingly, therefore, defense policy continued to be a source of contention. The most salient political issue in the first half of 1990 – although not the most important – and one which continued to reverberate thereafter, was base closures. With 86 domestic bases already in the process of being shut down as a result of a 1988 package, proposals for further closures could hardly fail to be controversial. It was made more so by a proposal which seemed to have a partisan overtone. Cheney announced on 29 January that he intended to close 47 bases – 35 in the United States and twelve overseas. Since 29 of the 35 domestic bases slated for closure were in Democratic congressional districts it appeared that the 'hit list' was predominantly political.[10] 'The proposed base reductions immediately became the most contested issue in President Bush's budget request, even though no fiscal 1991 funds were involved.'[11] To defuse the issue Congress established an eight-member bipartisan commission to produce a specific list of base closures which could not be amended by Congress and which had to be accepted or rejected by the President as a single package.

One of the other major bones of contention in the first half of 1990 was how much the budget should be cut. Although Cheney appeared inflexible, arguing that the changes in the Soviet Union and Eastern Europe were not irreversible, this was a stalling tactic to allow the Pentagon itself to devise a coherent long-range response to the changes in the threat. While arguing with Congress, Cheney was also making the services themselves devise plans for reductions and restructuring. Planning documents were submitted to Cheney by the service chiefs on 1 May and it was reported on 12 May that General Powell, Chairman of the Joint Chiefs of Staff, had acknowledged that it would be possible to make more far-reaching cuts than those which had been publicly discussed by the administration.[12]

There were in fact other signs of flexibility in Cheney's position. As early as April 1990 he had reduced from 132 to 75 the number of B-2s requested by the administration. In the event, Congress provided $2.35 billion for procurement of the B-2 but did not clarify whether this could be used to acquire new planes or only for cost overruns. In effect, Congress 'resolutely sidestepped the issue'.[13] Elsewhere Congress took a firmer stance and provided only $2.89 billion for strategic defense – $1.7 billion less than Bush had requested. Overall Congress authorized $18 billion less than the administration had requested. Had it not been for the Iraqi invasion of Kuwait on 2 August 1990 – an event which cast some doubt on optimistic prognoses for the post Cold War era – the cuts might have been even greater. Ironically, the invasion occurred on the day that the administration revealed its plans for a far-reaching downsizing in the American military establishment – which was in large part an attempt to respond to criticisms that there was no coherent strategy to meet the challenges of the 1990s. The proposals for restructuring were overshadowed somewhat by the crisis in the Gulf. In the autumn of 1990, however, Congress and the administration worked out a comprehensive budget deal which committed the administration to continued reductions in the defense budgets as part of the efforts to control the overall deficit. Funds cut from defense could go to deficit reduction but not to domestic programs without violating the limits on domestic spending.

Partly because of this deal and partly because of events in the Gulf – where both personnel and weapons systems performed very effectively – the 1991 debate over the defense budget was less acrimonious. The key development in defusing controversy over defence, however, was the administration's plan to move towards what was called the Base Force – which would involve a 25 per cent reduction in the United States armed forces by the end of FY 1995.[14]

The Base Force involved substantial cuts for all three services. The proposal to reduce the United States Army by roughly one third, going from 28 divisions (eighteen active) to eighteen divisions (twelve active). The plan for the Air Force was that it would go from 36 to 26 Fighter Wing Equivalents with active forces going from 24 to fifteen Fighter Wing Equivalents, and the active aircraft inventory falling to 5,300 by 1995. The projected cuts for the Navy were also substantial: the Navy was to be reduced to twelve aircraft carriers and from 546 ships to 451 ships with corresponding personnel reductions. Unlike the other services the structure of the Marine Corps was to remain intact. The three Marine Expeditionary Forces (MEFs) would continue to include three divisions and three air wings, but with significant manning reductions within the existing structure.

The Base Force was not simply about reductions. It also involved both conceptual and organizational restructuring in an attempt to identify specific military requirements for the post Cold War era. The rationale was that the United States had to have an appropriate combination of forces to fulfil four tasks: deterrence, forward presence, crisis response and reconstitution. While continued reliance would be placed on forces for deterrence, and United States forces would remain forward deployed in Europe and Asia to minimize the prospects for miscalculation, the United States had to have a capacity to respond decisively to crises and to reconstitute its forces should a more serious long-term threat re-emerge. To meet these needs four major force packages were identified: Strategic Forces, Pacific Forces, Atlantic Forces (which would also deal with contingencies in South West Asia) and Contingency Forces. These force components would be supported by capabilities in transportation, space, research and development, and reconstitution. The Base Force represented an effort by the Bush administration to rationalize the United States force structure for a world in which the threat of Soviet aggression had disappeared but in which instability and regional threats were still present. Accordingly the Base Force was designed to ensure that the United States retained a capability to fight two regional wars simultaneously.

In 1991 the Bush administration also attempted to revitalize the program for strategic defense. The President proposed refocusing SDI into a system devised for Global Protection Against Limited Strikes (GPALS). The rationale was that the threat of a calculated first strike from the Soviet Union had disappeared, but that other potential threats remained – it was necessary to protect against accidental launches, unauthorized strikes and deliberate attacks by small nuclear powers which might be impervious to deterrence. The cost was estimated at between 40 and 100 billion dollars for 1,000 space-based interceptors and 750 ground-base interceptors at six sites. To proceed towards this goal the administration requested $5.2 billion for a system which envisaged an initial ground-based defense in South Dakota by 1996. Congress approved $4.15 billion, of which $390 million could be used for continued work on 'Brilliant Pebbles', while also passing a directive that Bush should negotiate with Gorbachev to amend the ABM Treaty.

If there was a compromise on SDI, in 1991 Congress grasped the nettle on the B-2 bomber even though stealth technology had performed so well in the Gulf. In spite of authorizing $1.6 billion for continued research and development and $1.8 billion for parts and supplies, Congress mandated that no planes beyond the fifteen already authorized could be procured unless the Pentagon certified that operational problems had been solved and both the House and Senate voted an additional $1 billion for an additional plane. The other controversial strategic programs, the M-X and Midgetman, became less of an issue after President Bush announced cutbacks in United States strategic forces in a major unilateral initiative on 27 September 1991.

The issue of base closures, by contrast, remained controversial and very painful for Congressmen with bases in their districts. Nevertheless, the procedure worked out in 1990 for base closures facilitated progress in 1991. On 15 April Cheney sent a list of closures – which targeted 31 major bases – to the eight-member Congressional Committee set up to scrutinize the administration's recommendations (see above). After deleting four bases from the original list, the Committee sent the list to the President who also approved it. A last-ditch effort by some members to block the closures was defeated by 364 to 60 votes on 30 July thereby allowing them to proceed.

Another politically sensitive issue was manpower – and the balance between reserve and active forces. Congress refused to accede to the administration's request to cut the National Guard and reserves by 107,000, preferring to cut by only 38,000. It did agree to cut active duty personnel by over 106,000. Even more important was the Congressional action to repeal the law which prohibited women from flying combat missions. This was based largely on the performance of many of the 35,000 women who had been stationed in the Gulf during the war, and ran against the advice of the Chiefs of Staff of the Air Force and Navy.

In other areas, Congress was reluctant to make too many changes in the proposals of an administration which had enunciated a persuasive program for a phased military retrenchment. The demise of the Soviet Union at the end of 1991, however, precipitated a vigorous debate over the pace and extent of reductions.

Throughout 1992 both Secretary of Defense Cheney and General Colin Powell had to justify a strategy without a threat. The case was argued largely in terms of the need to maintain the combat effectiveness of United States' forces against unexpected contingencies. Concerns about the impact on employment and the economy of rapid downsizing made the administration's case more persuasive, especially in an election year. In his 1992 Annual Report the Secretary of Defense noted that 'in many cases the industrial base will not be able to respond in a timely fashion if it is allowed to wither away.'[15] To prevent this, Cheney argued, greater sensitivity to the possible need for reconstitution was required.

While the emphasis on the need to protect the defense industrial base was compelling, critics argued that, in other respects, the administration was simply offering a scaled-down version of the Cold War force posture. The President in his State of the Union Address in January 1992 tried to respond to these concerns by proposing to cut an additional $50 billion from the defense budget over the next five years (i.e. taking the baseline established in January 1991). This included a cut of $10 billion for FY 1993. The changes included a plan to purchase only 20 B-2 bombers and not the 75 announced by Cheney the previous year. The administration requested $2.69 billion for the final four planes rather than the $3.5 billion for seven planes as had been planned.

Although he welcomed these changes, Les Aspin, Chairman of the House Armed Services Committee, argued that they did not go far enough in taking account of the demise of the Soviet Union. He characterized the administration's request as 'a one-revolution budget in a two-revolution world'.[16] While Cheney reiterated the need to hedge against uncertainty, Aspin continued to argue that the Pentagon was presenting a slimmed down Cold War budget rather than one based on a 'bottom up' review.[17] Aspin outlined several options for discussion, including an alternative to the Base Force requiring more substantial budget cuts. Although this plan emphasized US sealift requirements, in other respects the cuts envisaged were much larger: under Aspin's proposal the Army would go down to nine active and six reserve divisions, the Air Force down to ten rather than fifteen active and eight rather than eleven reserve wings, and the Navy to 340 ships. While this contributed significantly to the quality of the defense debate in 1992, Congress did not opt for the more drastic cuts, and appropriated only $7 billion less than the administration had requested.

Surprisingly, the administration received the funding it had requested to bring the fleet of B-2 bombers to twenty. Although Congress was less forthcoming on strategic defence – providing only $3.8 billion of the $5.4 billion requested – it took several initiatives of its own. These included a ban on all nuclear test explosions after 30 September 1996. Of more immediate import, Congress acknowledged the difficulties caused to local communities and defense firms by the downturns in military spending and appropriated an addition $1.5 billion to facilitate the process of conversion from military to civilian industry.

This additional funding together with the more general quiescence in the Bush administration's proposals for FY 1993 reflected election year concerns that dramatic cuts in the defense budget 'would cost defense jobs during a recession.'[18]

There was also an implication that the Base Force concept represented a major – if still incomplete – shift towards a viable post Cold War strategic posture and defense budget.

UNITED STATES COMMITMENTS IN ASIA AND EUROPE

A key element in the Base Force concept was the maintenance of a forward military presence – at lower levels than during the Cold War – in both Europe and Asia. The pattern in both regions was one in which the administration emphasized continuity rather than change, and articulated new roles and missions to replace those which had dominated policy during the Cold War.

In relation to Europe, the Bush administration played a key role in reforming NATO for the post Soviet world. Yet this was not easy. NATO had long faced an overt and direct threat and with the end of the Cold War appeared to lose its role and rationale as well as its enemy. Largely as a result of the initiatives of the Bush administration, the Alliance gradually moved away from an emphasis on force modernization and implemented reforms designed to adjust to post Cold War Europe. Changes were made in force structure, strategy, the relationship with the newly independent states of Eastern Europe, and the balance of effort between Western Europe and the United States.

NATO moved from a heavy dependence on nuclear weapons and high levels of preparedness at the conventional level to a more relaxed posture in which nuclear weapons were very much in the background and greater emphasis was placed on flexibility and crisis management. In addition, a multinational corps system replaced the system of national corps. The changes in posture were accompanied by a new strategic concept which was made public on 7 November 1991 at the NATO Heads of Government meeting in Rome. The Rome Declaration noted that security policy was predicated on three elements: 'dialogue, cooperation and the maintenance of a collective defense capability'.[19] The military dimension of the alliance would remain, but would serve a much broader concept of security than in the past, and one which recognized that the threat was instability rather than overt military aggression against Western Europe.

A third area of change was the relationship with the states of Central and Eastern Europe – especially Poland, Hungary, and Czechoslovakia – and the former Soviet Union. A North Atlantic Cooperation Council was established which provided a mechanism for regular meetings between NATO members and the states of Eastern Europe and eventually the former Soviet Union. The agenda for these meetings included defense planning, democratic concepts of civil/military relations, civil/military coordination of air traffic management, and the conversion of defense industries to civilian production. If the NACC became a useful forum for consultation, however, it did not satisfy those in the new democracies who saw an extended NATO as the preferred security framework for Central Europe.

The final, and most vexed, area of change was the shift in the balance of effort and responsibility in NATO from the United States to Western Europe. The Bush administration exhibited considerable ambivalence on this, wanting to share more of the burdens but reluctant to relinquish United States leadership in the Alliance – except in relation to the Yugoslav crisis which was presented as primarily a European responsibility. During 1991 the administration was not only cool towards efforts by the Western European Union to play a more prominent role on security issues but also critical of the Franco-German initiative to form a Eurocorps, arguing that NATO should remain the primary vehicle for maintaining European security. By the end of 1992, however, steps had been taken to ensure greater cooperation between the Western European Union and NATO – and the United States had gone at least some way to ensuring that it was not faced by a concerted European position on security matters – a concern that can be traced back at least as far as the early 1970s and the Nixon administration.

In a sense this was part of a tacit bargain between Western Europe and the United States in which Washington agreed to maintain an American military presence in Europe. The Bush administration wanted this both as a component of the overall strategy of forward presence and as a means of maintaining American influence in Europe. Bush acknowledged, however, that there were opportunities for reductions in the presence and projected that United States force levels could be reduced to 150,000 personnel by 1995. To many critics, however, even

150,000 seemed too high when there was no compelling rationale for these forces. It was far from certain that the presence would translate easily into influence, while the administration's argument that US troops in Europe contributed to stability rang rather hollow in the light of the turmoil in Yugoslavia – and the inability of the Europeans or NATO to do anything about it.

Ironically, although the presence in Europe had been the major overseas commitment of the United States throughout the Cold War, the Bush administration enunciated a more sophisticated rationale for maintaining a presence in Asia than it did for its European stance. In response to a Congressional mandate DOD produced a report, *A Strategic Framework for the Asian Pacific Rim: Looking Towards the 21st Century*, in which it enunciated the rationale for the forward presence in Asia. The main argument was that even though the Cold War was over the United States still played the role of 'regional balancer, honest broker, and ultimate security guarantor' and would continue to be 'the region's irreplaceable balancing wheel'.[20] Conversely, disengagement would be destabilizing. As Under Secretary of Defense for Policy, Paul Wolfowitz noted, 'A reduced US commitment to the region, whether perceived or real, would create a security vacuum that other countries would be tempted, or might feel compelled to fill. Our policies, political, economic and security, must be designed to prevent such a vacuum from occurring and to support our unique and central stabilizing role.'[21]

At the same time, the Bush administration acknowledged that 'measured reductions' in ground and air forces in South Korea, Japan and the Philippines were possible without undermining regional security. In the event, in 1991 the eruption of Mount Pinatubo led to the closing of Clark Air Force Base. Negotiations over continued use of the naval base at Subic Bay resulted in disagreement over the cost of the lease, and with popular sentiment in favor of a US withdrawal President Aquino requested that United States forces leave the Philippines. In spite of this, the United States continues to maintain a military presence in Southeast Asia and has strengthened its relations with Singapore. Moreover, the plan for phased troop reductions from South Korea was temporarily halted in 1992 because of North Korea's nuclear program. By the end of the Bush administration, therefore, the United States' military presence in Asia was still significant with 39,000 military personnel in South Korea and 47,000 in Japan.

If the Bush administration held the line against pressure for military disengagement from forward positions, it also succeeded in enunciating a persuasive rationale for a phased military retrenchment in Asia that would maintain the United States' role in the region while allowing for greater burden-sharing by both Japan and South Korea. As regards Europe, the record was more mixed. The administration provided a rationale for a continued, although smaller, military presence and helped devise a new strategy for NATO in which crisis management, peacekeeping and peacemaking loomed much larger. Yet events in Yugoslavia revealed the limited applicability of this new strategy. In both Western Europe and the United States there was great, and understandable, reluctance to become involved. A modest contingent of NATO forces contributed to UN peacekeeping efforts in 1992, but for the most part the Bush administration was content to pass on the problem of the war in Bosnia to its successor. In other areas, however, President Bush was far less reticent about the resort to military force.

THE USE OF FORCE: PANAMA, THE GULF WAR AND SOMALIA

During its four years in office the Bush administration used military force on three major occasions. The first use of force was in Panama, the second in the Gulf and the third was the humanitarian intervention in Somalia in the closing weeks of the Bush administration.

The United States intervention in Panama to oust General Noriega was indicative of the increased priority given to the war on drugs in the first year of the Bush administration. It came against a background in which the administration applied legal, economic and diplomatic sanctions to Panama in an attempt to oust General Manuel Noriega. Noriega's involvement in drug trafficking had transformed him from an ally into a political liability. The situation was especially embarrassing for President

Bush who, as the Director of Central Intelligence, had met with Noriega on several occasions. The CIA tried to foment unrest but an internal coup attempt against Noriega on 3 October 1989 by members of the Panamanian Defense Forces was crushed.

In mid-December 1989, political tension between Panama and the US increased when Noriega proclaimed himself head of the Panamanian government and intensified his denunciations of the United States. On 16 December a US Marine was killed by members of the PDF. Operation Just Cause was launched in the early morning of 20 December. The American force of over 10,000 troops stationed in Panama as part of US Southern Command was more than doubled to approximately 22,000. The objectives of the operation were to capture Noriega and bring him to justice in the United States, to protect the 35,000 Americans in Panama, to secure the Canal, and to restore Panama's democratically elected government.

Within a few days the PDF – which was estimated to number 3,500 soldiers, 11,000 police and national guardsmen, and some paramilitary 'dignity brigades' – was defeated by well-trained US forces equipped with advanced night-vision capabilities and the F-117 stealth fighter. Although the opposition had not been formidable, the difference between Just Cause and the US invasion of Grenada in 1983 was striking. After Grenada, the US military had been severely criticized for failures in planning, communications, coordination and logistics. Just Cause, by contrast, was based on extensive contingency planning and implemented very effectively. Even so there were concerns about the possibility of urban guerrilla warfare and complaints that United States' political objectives were poorly defined. The chaos that reigned for the first week or so of the American occupation and the initial failure to find Noriega intensified the criticisms. Noriega eventually reappeared at the Vatican embassy in Panama, claiming political asylum. On 3 January 1990 he surrendered to US forces and was flown to Miami to face federal drug charges.

Criticism of the intervention was largely along partisan lines, with Speaker of the House Tom Foley arguing that it was unnecessary to send 24,000 troops to arrest someone. Les Aspin and Patricia Schroeder also voiced criticisms of the administration.[22] Sam Nunn, on the other hand, supported the intervention but was critical of some of the mistakes he felt had been made. There were also concerns over the number of civilian casualties: one estimate in mid-January was that while 314 Panamanian troops, 23 US troops and three US civilians had been killed, 220 Panamanian civilians had also lost their lives.[23] The debate was truncated by the fairly rapid withdrawal of the additional forces deployed in Panama, but some critics continued to argue that the intervention had achieved very little. It restored democracy to Panama, but had little impact on the flow of drugs to the United States or on Panama's role in the international drug trafficking business. There was also a lingering suspicion that Bush had acted so decisively in order to dispel the 'wimp factor' and to augment his image as a strong president.

A more serious challenge to United States' interests emerged within six months of the invasion of Panama when there was still considerable optimism about the prospects for peace and order in the post Cold War world. The Iraqi invasion of Kuwait on 2 August 1990 sparked off a major international crisis that was to lead to the Bush administration's greatest triumph yet would also raise serious questions about the efficacy of its policy both before and after the confrontation. Critics argued that the administration had helped to arm Saddam Hussein and had resisted Congressional efforts to impose sanctions in response to the regime's appalling human rights record. Others even suggested that Iraq had been given tacit permission to invade Kuwait. Ambassador Glaspie in a meeting with Saddam Hussein on 25 July had suggested that the United States regarded the problem with Kuwait as an Arab problem in which United States' interests were not directly involved. At this juncture, however, the United States thought that Iraq was simply trying to coerce Kuwait; an invasion was not expected. With the invasion of 2 August, that assessment changed.

The administration toughened its stance, partly because of what it saw as an impending threat against Saudi Arabia, and partly because the President viewed the crisis as the first test of the post Cold War international order. Iraqi actions were so blatant in their contravention of the norms of sovereignty and non-intervention, that, as far as President Bush was concerned, they could not be allowed to go unchallenged. There was also a growing acknowledgement that Saddam Hussein's ambitions to emerge as a pan-Arab leader combined with the build-up of Iraqi power was a long-term threat to regional security in the Gulf. Another consideration that encouraged a vigorous response by the Bush administration was a traditional concern with credibility – a concern that was not only transferred from the rivalry with the Soviet Union to the confrontation with Iraq but was also linked to the domestic standing of the President and his concern to avoid any appearance of weakness. The President himself was also influenced in his stance by a meeting with British Prime Minister Margaret Thatcher in Aspen.

The result was that in the initial meetings of the President and his advisers concerning the Iraqi invasion, there was agreement that the United States had to respond.[24] In a National Security Council meeting on 3 August, National Security Adviser Brent Scowcroft framed the issue in a way which suggested that the United States could not allow the invasion to become an established fact. The President himself sometimes engaged in decision-making by public pronouncement – as when he emphasized in remarks to the media that the invasion could not be allowed to stand. If this reflected the concern with displaying a strong image to the American public, it also reflected the President's conviction that the crisis was also a struggle between good and evil. One consequence of this may have been that the President decided very early on in the crisis that he would use force if necessary. Yet this was not simply a matter of personal decision. President Bush adhered to the precepts established by the Carter administration – that the Gulf was a region where United States vital interests were involved – and reaffirmed by the Reagan administration in the 1987 decision to re-flag Kuwaiti oil tankers. The Carter Doctrine contained an implicit presumption that Washington would not permit a significant portion of the world's oil supplies to fall under the control of a single power. From this perspective Iraq's bid for regional hegemony in the Gulf was unacceptable.

On 5 August 1990 Secretary of Defense Cheney was sent to Saudi Arabia to underscore the American commitment. Two days later the United Nations voted for a sweeping trade embargo against Iraq. Yet this did not prevent Saddam from declaring the annexation of Kuwait and detaining all foreign nationals. For its part the United States decided to blockade all Iraqi exports and to deploy 45,000 marines to the Gulf as part of a massive military operation which became known as Desert Shield. On 23 August Bush announced the mobilization of 40,000 reservists. On 26 August the United Nations approved the use of force to enforce the naval blockade of Iraq. By the first half of September over 100,000 US troops were in the Gulf and it was estimated that the cost of the operation would be somewhere in the region of $15 billion – a cost that the United States increasingly demanded should be shouldered by its allics.

The big change, however, came in late October 1990 when the decision was taken to deploy two heavy armored divisions (which included 700 tanks) from Europe to Saudi Arabia. When this was announced on 7 November – after the mid-term Congressional elections – Pentagon officials explicitly acknowledged that it provided the administration with an offensive option and represented a new phase in American military operations in the Gulf.

This change was accompanied by intense negotiations to obtain the support of other members of the United Nations Security Council for a resolution authorizing the use of force to eject Iraq from Kuwait. Although the Soviet Union and other governments felt that insufficient time had been allowed for economic sanctions, agreement was finally reached on a resolution which authorized the use of force to eject Iraqi forces from Kuwait after 15 January.

This constant increase in pressure did not make Saddam Hussein back down. Part of the reason was that threats were not applied consistently by an administration which wanted to coerce Saddam Hussein yet was also concerned with maintaining domestic support by making clear that it wanted to avoid war if possible. Many Congressional critics, including Senate Armed Services Committee Chairman, Sam Nunn, preferred continued reliance on economic sanctions rather than the use of force. With public opinion also divided there was considerable agonizing on Capitol Hill. By delaying a vote until a few days before the United Nations Resolution ran out, however, the President placed Congress in a position where a negative vote would undermine the international coalition and repudiate the UN resolution authorizing the use of force. Even so the

Senate vote of 12 January was very close with 52 votes authorizing the use of force against Iraq and 47 against. The outcome in the House was a rather more comfortable victory for the president with 250 votes in favor and 183 against.

Part of the reluctance to use force stemmed from concern about the probable level of United States casualties. The Iraqi army was the fourth largest in the world, was battle-hardened from the struggle against Iran, possessed significant chemical warfare capabilities, and had established what appeared to be formidable defensive positions. In the event, the war went much better for the United States than even the most optimistic commentators had predicted. On 16 January the United States and its coalition partners initiated a sustained aerial bombardment that severely degraded Iraqi power. The targets included command and control assets, Iraqi military units and facilities that were part of the Iraqi nuclear program. There were several occasions, however, on which significant civilian casualties were inflicted.

The air campaign contributed enormously to the overall success of the United States' strategy. For the most part, American high-technology weapons were very effective – especially the Tomahawk cruise missiles and the F-117 Stealth fighter bomber. The Patriot anti-missile missile, which was an upgraded anti-aircraft missile, did not perform as well as was claimed at the time, but proved to be politically and symbolically important. By supplying Patriot to Israel for use in defense against Iraqi SCUD missiles, the administration was able to forestall Israeli entry into hostilities – an action that could have split the coalition.

As well as a triumph for high technology and the United States Air Force, the military campaign was also a triumph for the Commander, General Norman Schwarzkopf. Schwarzkopf's final ground offensive involved a major flanking movement, the speed and intensity of which had a devastating impact on Iraqi resistance. The superior firepower of the M-1 tank, and the dominance of the air, led to a rapid victory. Within 100 hours of its start the ground war was over. What Saddam Hussein had predicted as the mother of all battles became a rout.

Even this military victory was not without its critics. Much of European public opinion was appalled at what it saw as a slaughter of Iraqi forces and felt that the campaign could have been brought to an end sooner. Many critics in the United States, however, felt that the coalition should have marched on Baghdad and removed Saddam. There were suggestions that Schwarzkopf himself had not wanted to stop. For Bush, however, maintaining the wartime coalition for the subsequent peace was an important consideration – and extending United States objectives beyond the liberation of Kuwait would have undermined United States credibility in the Arab world. Nevertheless, there were obvious costs to this restraint. The survival of the Republican guard – which was Saddam Hussein's main power base – the subsequent violence against the Kurds, the continued efforts by Iraq to obstruct United Nations' inspection of its nuclear facilities, and loopholes in the continued economic embargo meant that military victory did not translate into an equally impressive political victory. Saddam Hussein continued to be an irritant to the Bush administration.

The victory in the Gulf, therefore, was more qualified than the initial rhetoric suggested. And if the war was a triumphant exercise in American diplomatic leadership and military strength, the dependence on allies for financial support highlighted American economic weaknesses. The euphoria and the patriotism which greeted the end of the war was accompanied by a strong sense of relief, and the United States did not seem particularly anxious to carry on being the world's policeman. Although there was subsequently considerable discussion about intervention in the conflict in Yugoslavia, concerns that it was a potential quagmire combined with a sense that American interests were not at stake ensured that there was no large-scale intervention.

Yet in the last two months of the Bush administration there was another military intervention. Bush as a lame duck president was able to act more decisively than during the election campaign, and in response to continued media coverage of the famine and political anarchy in Somalia, presented a plan to the United Nations for United States' forces to be deployed, on a short-term basis, to restore order and ensure the resumption of food aid. The CIA had made clear to the President that the prospects for the restoration of a stable government were bleak since the state in Somalia had effectively collapsed. There were also concerns that intervention might be much easier than disengagement. In spite of this, Operation Restore

Hope went ahead. The President deployed 28,000 American marines to Somalia. In the spring of 1993 these forces were replaced by a United Nations contingent.

In terms of his willingness to use military force, Bush was probably the most activist president since the Vietnam war. He was also very successful as a war president. Indeed, the victory in the Gulf seemed to provide redemption for failure in Vietnam. The services themselves had restored morale and overcome many of the problems of the late 1960s and early 1970s, while the military build-up that had started under Carter and continued under Reagan provided highly professional, well-equipped forces. For all this, there appeared to be something anachronistic about the readiness of the administration to use force, especially in view of the continued economic problems faced by the United States. If Bush played the role of commander in chief very effectively, he was also active as chief negotiator for the United States and was persistent in his pursuit of arms control agreements with the Soviet Union and subsequently with Russia.

ARMS CONTROL

During the Bush presidency, arms control negotiations were almost invariably running behind political change and, in the view of some observers, were irrelevant to the security problems of the post Cold War world. The administration, however, saw arms control as a way of dismantling Cold War military structures and bringing them into line with new political realities. Arms control also provided a way of reducing the nuclear risks associated with and resulting from the breakup of the Soviet Union.

The earliest arms control achievements of the Bush administration were in the field of conventional weaponry. The Bush initiative at NATO's Fortieth Anniversary Summit gave a considerable boost to the Conventional Forces Europe (CFE) negotiations. After further movement during 1989 the talks stalled in the spring of 1990 as Moscow held up progress in order to settle the issue of German unification in the 'two plus four' framework. As a result of the changes in NATO announced in the London Declaration in July 1990, however,

Gorbachev accepted continued German membership in NATO and was willing to move ahead on conventional arms control.

The CFE agreement was signed in November 1990 at the Paris meeting of the Conference on Security and Cooperation in Europe. The Treaty, which covered the area from the Atlantic to the Urals, limited tanks to 20,000 apiece for NATO and the Warsaw Treaty Organization (WTO) – a figure which meant marginal cuts for NATO and very substantial cuts for the WTO states. Armored Combat Vehicles were to be limited to 30,000 per alliance, artillery pieces to 20,000, helicopters to 2,000, and combat aircraft to 6,800. These ceilings required asymmetrical cuts by the Soviet Union and its allies and led to a situation of conventional military parity, something NATO had never been able to achieve through its own efforts. Equally important, the agreement included a substantial and intrusive verification regime which increased transparency and confidence. The CFE agreement highlighted the continuing trend towards demilitarization in Europe and was a major symbol of the end of the Cold War.

If 1990 was the year of conventional arms control, 1991 was the year in which Bush and Gorbachev signed a Strategic Arms Reduction Treaty (START) which marked the culmination of a protracted negotiation process that had started in the early 1980s. The Treaty established equal ceilings on the number of strategic weapons which could be deployed by the United States and the Soviet Union and imposed equality in terms of throw-weight – an area where the Soviet Union had traditionally had an advantage. Each side was limited to 1,600 strategic nuclear delivery vehicles, (ICBMs, SLBMs and heavy bombers), 6,000 total accountable warheads, 4,900 warheads on ICBMs or SLBMs and 1,100 warheads on mobile ICBMs. In addition, the Treaty imposed a limit of 1,540 warheads on 154 heavy ICBMs, a limit which required a 50 per cent cut in the Soviet heavy missiles force. It also established highly intrusive verification procedures.

As the Soviet Union began to collapse after the failed coup of August 1991, the Bush administration saw the Treaty as insufficient to deal with the problem of 'internal proliferation'. In an effort to reduce the nuclear danger, President Bush on 27 September announced a series of unilateral measures including the removal of strategic bombers from day-to-day alert status, the return of their weapons to storage areas, and the immediate stand-down of the ICBMs earmarked for deactivation under the START Agreement. Bush also announced a halt to the development of the rail garrison basing mode for the M-X missile as well as the mobile portions of Midgetman, the elimination of 1,740 nuclear artillery shells and 1,250 short-range land-based missiles, and the withdrawal of nuclear weapons, including nuclear armed cruise missiles, from surface ships and attack submarines. Bush also reiterated his desire for an agreement with Moscow to eliminate all nuclear missiles with multiple warheads.

Although these unilateral steps did not depend on reciprocity, Gorbachev responded positively by announcing that he would eliminate all nuclear artillery shells and tactical nuclear warheads. Although the disintegration of the Soviet state temporarily halted progress, the Bush administration quickly opened a serious dialogue on arms control with the new leader of Russia, Boris Yeltsin. In spite of the old problem of reconciling sacrifices between two states with very different force structures, on 17 June 1992 Bush and Yeltsin issued a Joint Understanding on Reductions in Strategic Offensive Arms. The framework they outlined was to be translated into a formal treaty as soon as possible. In early December President Bush initiated another round of personal negotiations with Yeltsin. The result was that the two leaders met in January 1993 and signed a START Two Treaty which stipulated that by 2003 Russia will have reduced its forces to 3,000 warheads and the United States to 3,500. Under the provisions of the treaty all MIRVed ICBMs are to be eliminated while SLBM warheads are to be reduced to 1,750 or less. There were question marks about the implementation of the Treaty. Not only would this depend on Yeltsin's authority but also on the willingness of Ukraine, Kazakhstan and Belarus to relinquish the nuclear weapons under their control.

Such concerns notwithstanding, the arms reduction achievements of the Bush administration were considerable. Although START Two could be dismissed as outmoded or inadequate, the Treaty provided a framework for an orderly reduction of nuclear weapons. It was also testimony to the perseverance of an administration that was highly sensitive to the dangers inherent in an unregulated dismantling of Cold War military structures, especially the Soviet nuclear arsenal. If the Bush administration achieved most of its arms control objectives, what can be said about its overall performance in defense policy?

ASSESSMENT AND CONCLUSION

In assessing the Bush administration's performance in defense policy, it is essential to keep in mind the sheer size of the tasks if faced. Managing defense policy in a period of rapid and enormous geopolitical transition presented challenges that were more complex than those faced by any administration since that of Harry Truman. Lacking a familiar framework, yet acutely sensitive to the possibility that the end of the Cold War did not mean an absence of future security challenges for the United States, the administration ultimately recognized the futility of attempting to maintain the status quo. Although it could have reached this point more rapidly than it did, part of its antipathy to rapid policy changes stemmed from a concern that American military strength not be reduced too precipitously. Indeed, by moving to the Base Force, pursuing arms control agreements, and maintaining its commitments overseas at lower levels the administration charted out a compromise course that reflected the cautious pragmatism of the President himself.

This compromise satisfied neither the left nor the right. Yet liberal critics who complained about incrementalism in defense policy not only ignored the difficulties of bringing about change in a very conservative and bureaucratic defense establishment, but also underplayed the very real changes the Bush administration made. On the other side, conservative critics who believed that the Bush administration was throwing away the military strength established by the Reagan administration, not only failed to acknowledge that the downward trend in defense authorizations had been underway since the mid-1980s but also downplayed the very real changes in the security environment that permitted a substantial reduction in American military strength.

More moderate critics argued that the administration did not go far enough in reconfiguring forces for the new challenges they would have to face in the mid and late 1990s, especially if the United States became involved in peace-making in Yugoslavia or other areas of turmoil and instability. Although this has more credence than some of the other criticisms, it ignores the time required adequately to restructure and reconfigure armed forces for new missions. The Bush administration certainly started this process and devised a military posture and strategy which involved substantial retrenchment and reduction while hedging against the emergence of new threats. This was a rational approach to what was intrinsically a highly political activity. Yet there was a clear limit to its vision: the administration saw the Base Force as the end point rather than as a transitional stage to a smaller military. This was both a major achievement and a major shortcoming of the Bush defense policy.

NOTES

1. The point here is extended from the excellent analysis of the US role in Europe presented by Michael Brenner, 'Finding America's Place', *Foreign Policy*, No. 79, Summer 1990, pp. 25–43.
2. See Dick Cheney, Secretary of Defense, *Annual Report to the President and Congress 1993* (Washington: Government Printing Office, 1993) p. 25.
3. Steve Smith, 'US Defence: the Reagan legacy and the Bush predicament', in Michael Pugh and Phil Williams (eds) *Superpower Politics* (Manchester: Manchester University Press, 1990), p. 60.
4. Cheney, op. cit., p. 25.
5. See *Congressional Quarterly Almanac 1989* (Washington: Congressional Quarterly, 1990), p. 414.
6. The White House, Office of National Drug Control Policy, *National Drug Control Strategy: Budget Summary*, (Washington, DC: Government Printing Office, January 1990), pp. 140–141.
7. See, for example, Fred Kaplan, 'Cheney orders Pentagon Cuts', *Boston Globe*, 18 November 1989, p. 1.
8. Ibid.
9. Molly Moore, 'Troops, Arms Cut Modestly; Strategic Spending Up', *Washington Post*, 30 January 1990, p. 1.
10. See *Congressional Quarterly Almanac 1990* (Washington: Congressional Quarterly, Inc., 1991), pp. 693–694.
11. Ibid., p. 694.
12. See Patrick E. Tyler, 'Military Chiefs Detail Plans to Cut Troops, Weapons', *Washington Post*, 12 May 1990.
13. *Congressional Quarterly Almanac 1990*, op. cit., p. 687.

14. Fuller details of the Base Force can be found in the statements by Cheney and General Powell before the Senate Committee on Armed Services, 31 January 1992. See *Department of Defense Authorization for Appropriations for Fiscal Year 1993 and the Future Year's Defense Program. Hearings before the Committee on Armed Services*, United States Senate, 102nd Congress, Second Session (Washington: Government Printing Office, 1992), pp. 11–32 and pp. 52–86.

15. Quoted in 'Cheney: Industrial base impact to be considered at every milestone', *Aerospace Daily*, 26 February 1992.

16. Quoted in 'Aspin, Cheney Spar Face-to-Face But Stay Far Apart on Budget', *Congressional Quarterly Weekly Report*, 8 February 1992, p. 322.

17. Ibid.

18. See 'Pentagon Gets Most of Its Wish List', *Congressional Quarterly Almanac 1992* (Washington: Congressional Quarterly, 1993), p. 483.

19. *Rome Declaration on Peace and Cooperation*, Rome Summit, 8 November 1991.

20. Prepared Statement of Paul Wolfowitz, Under Secretary of Defense for Policy in *The President's Report on the US Military Presence in East Asia: Hearings before the Committee on Armed Services*, United States Senate, 101st Congress, Second Session, 19 April 1990 (Washington: Government Printing Office, 1990), p. 17.

21. See Wolfowitz's presentation to the Committee in ibid., p. 7.

22. Martin Tolchin, 'Legislators Express Concern on the Operation's Future', *The New York Times*, 22 December 1989, p. 20.

23. David Pitt, 'The Invasion's Civilian Toll: still no official count', *The New York Times*, 10 January 1990, p. 13.

24. Bob Woodward, *The Commanders* (New York: Simon & Schuster, 1991), p. 227.

10 Conclusion
Dilys M. Hill and Phil Williams

The verdict of the American electorate on President Bush was passed in November 1992: George Bush joined Jimmy Carter and Gerald Ford as the only incumbent presidents since 1945 who failed to get reelected. Moreover, much press commentary suggested that the Bush presidency, rather like that of Gerald Ford, was transitional: if Ford provided a postscript to the Nixon presidency, the four years of the Bush presidency were essentially an epilogue to the Reagan era. Unlike Ford, however, Bush became president with an election victory of his own. Moreover, Bush cannot be dismissed as another Jimmy Carter. Unlike Carter, who was the quintessential outsider and never came to terms with the peculiarities and demands of politics in Washington,[1] George Bush was an insider. He had considerable experience in government, and had served a long apprenticeship for the presidency. Consequently, Bush did not have to engage in the kind of 'on-the-job training' that characterized Carter.[2]

Yet for all this, the Bush presidency gradually appeared to unravel. By 1992 there seemed to be a leadership vacuum as the administration confronted 'institutionalized gridlock', something that was particularly criticized by Ross Perot, who provided a strong independent challenge to Bush's reelection. Moreover, President Bush himself often appeared to be out of touch with the problems of the American people, especially in the aftermath of the Los Angeles riots. It became even more evident during one of the televised debates when he was asked a question about how the state of the economy had affected him – and failed to understand the question let alone provide an answer.

Although it is possible to distinguish between the achievements of the administration and the final campaign to perpetuate it for another four years, the verdict of the electorate on Bush can be understood as both a reflection of a mishandled campaign and a commentary on the substance of domestic policies for four years. Indeed, Bush's failure to get reelected has many dimensions, some of which are related to his personality, some to the failures – and the achievements – of his administration, some to the 'mood' of the times, and some to the cyclical movements of the economy. If there was sometimes a failure of political imagination on the part of the Bush administration, it also has to be acknowledged that Bush confronted a number of obstacles which greatly contributed to his eventual political demise. Indeed, in considering the reasons for the single-term presidency, it is essential to consider not only the Bush administration's own shortcomings but circumstances over which it had little or no control.

Whatever the extenuating circumstances, however, the poor quality of the campaign for the President's reelection should not be underestimated. The administration went from complacency to panic, to disarray, and finally to a negative campaign that not only managed to appear both desperate and unseemly but also provoked Barbara Bush to express her distaste for some of the mudslinging that the President was engaged in. The predominant approach at the outset was complacency. The candidates for the Democratic nomination were known for a while as the 'seven dwarfs' and it did not appear as if any one of them could seriously challenge an incumbent who had led the nation to perhaps its most successful military venture since 1945. The problems faced by candidate Clinton in the early part of 1992 seemed to confirm the desultory nature of the challenge posed by the Democrats.

It was partly because of the weakness of the Democrats and the expectation that their campaign would be as inept as that of 1988 that it appeared for a while that the main challenge to Bush was from the conservative wing of his own party. A few months later, however, the picture was very different: not only had Clinton become a much more serious contender but Ross Perot had emerged as an independent counter-attraction for many conservative voters. The response of many conservative Republicans to this dual challenge and to what they saw as the 'waffling' of the President was to reaffirm their message.

The tension between Bush and the conservative wing of the Republican Party was nothing new, but had a particularly disruptive effect on the 1992 Republican campaign. Relationships with his right wing had always been problematic and it was only his loyal service to Reagan which had made Bush palatable to many conservative Republicans in 1988. The appointment of Quayle as Vice President, which was designed to placate and neutralize the right, succeeded only in establishing a rallying point within the administration for conservative Republicans. Moreover, the President's own leadership was increasingly attacked by the right wing which was very bitter at what it saw as the greatest mistake of his presidency – the budget agreement of 1990. For conservative Republicans the pledge not to raise taxes was sacrosanct.

The attacks were intensified in response to the slow start of the President in his efforts to get reelected. Republican supporters and donors complained – not without reason – that the President looked as though he had no agenda, no message and was not giving domestic leadership. The challenge for the Republican nomination mounted by Pat Buchanan was both a symptom of this underlying dissatisfaction and a rallying point for its expression. The President's initial response was one of conciliation: every time Buchanan did well in the primaries, Bush made a concession to the right – firing the head of the National Endowment for the Arts, promising to veto any new abortion-rights bill and campaigning on 'family values'. The day before the Georgia primary Bush told *The Atlanta Constitution* that his support for a tax increase in 1990 was 'a mistake'. Yet these gestures by Bush seemed to be motivated by expediency rather than conviction, and did not satisfy the right. Consequently, although Buchanan withdrew from the race, he played a significant role at the Republican Convention and, along with Quayle and the conservatives, dominated the proceedings and shaped an agenda focused on 'value' issues such as the sanctity of the family and the 'right to life'.

In terms of the Bush reelection campaign, this had two unfortunate consequences. The first was that Bush was not entirely comfortable with the salience of these issues or the militancy with which they were pushed. In 1988 he had displayed a willingness to engage in negative campaigning in order to be elected. As president, however, he had emphasized conciliation and consensus – neither of which were easy to reconcile with either the conservative agenda or the personalized attacks on political opponents that the Republican campaign managers seemed to want. Indeed, the tension between his own predilections and the requirements of political expediency may have contributed significantly to the lacklustre quality of the President's own campaigning during the last few months before the election. While Bush gave speeches on conservative themes, these were much more muted than those given by the Vice President, a contrast which only served to highlight the diffidence of the President.

The second – and even more serious – consequence of the conservative Republican dominance was that it led to an emphasis on themes which had little impact on an electorate concerned about the economy. Even if Bush had been more committed to, and enthusiastic about, the Republican platform it is not clear that this would have generated greater public support. As it was, the genuflections to the right had little impact on the mass of voters who were not angry about deviations from conservative principles but about the state of the economy. Looking for leadership on this issue they were unable to find it in President Bush.

The poor quality of the Bush campaign for reelection and the problematic relations between the President and the conservative wing of the Republican Party can only go so far in explaining what went wrong with the Bush presidency. The shortcomings of the Bush administration were rooted in part in the President's own style and personality. The poor campaign was itself a reflection of the inability of the administration, and especially its leader, to provide the kind of decisive leadership that many Americans wanted. The pragmatism that had promised so much at the outset seemed to leave a vacuum of leadership. The President's decision-making style placed more emphasis on obtaining agreement round the table rather than on achieving a decisive outcome. The lack of a strong sense of vision also translated into an inability to explain what the President wanted, what he was doing, and why he was doing it. Although senior aides in the administration argued that the White House public relations operation was defective, that Bush actually had a domestic agenda and that the problem was simply getting the message across to the public, this is not entirely convincing. While Bush's disavowal of Reagan-type 'handlers' in the White House may have impaired the communication of his message and blurred his 'style' – speech writers in the Bush White House were low in the pecking order and did not have close and continuous contact with the President – the problem cannot be written off as a public relations failure.

Even allowing for the fact that Bush was very difficult to write speeches for and that he had a diffident style, the President's failure to use the power to persuade was more to do with the lack of a message than the shortcomings of the messenger or the messenger's speech-writer. Without the 'vision thing' that he had derided and a clear-cut programme that he wanted to implement, the President's message was inevitably somewhat blurred. There were occasions, of course, when Bush did seem to have clear objectives, but even these were not always particularly effective. His use of grim solemnity in the 1992 budget speech failed to produce the effect intended by his 'this will not stand' Desert Storm analogy. In terms of substance, the President did little more than reiterate or reformulate previous proposals, from capital gains tax cuts to research and development tax credits to fewer regulations to line-item veto.

The leadership gap became even more pronounced after the Los Angeles riots which made many Republicans acknowledge the need for an active approach to urban problems. The LA riots provided an opportunity for Bush to assert his leadership as he had done in Operation Desert Storm, but he failed to do this, vacillating between a hard line on law and order and compassion for the inner cities. Not surprisingly, his standing in the polls fell: by mid-May it was down to 28 per cent and seemed to be part of the bleak mood of the country. In the spring and early summer of 1992 Bush appeared to be groping for a more suitable stance than the status quo, but appeared to be able to do little about the economy. In the NYT/CBS News poll of 17–20 June only 34 per cent approved of the way Bush was doing his job, down from 39 per cent in early May. Seventy-eight per cent of those polled disapproved of the way he was handling the economy.

The domestic agenda was a powerful drag on the President's popularity. Public opinion polls showed that people were uncertain what the President meant by his statements on domestic affairs. They were not clear about how he had tried to lead the nation since 1989 or about how he would achieve his goals if reelected. Bush listed his domestic accomplishments as an education programme that set goals for schools, child care, air pollution, rights of disabled, and his appointments to the federal bench. Yet none of these seemed particularly imaginative, promised to deal with long-term economic problems, or was sufficient to dispel the crisis of leadership.[3]

Given the failure of Bush to develop a domestic vision or programme this was not surprising. As Bert Rockman noted, 'Bush committed the cardinal sin of politics by implying that the status quo often is better than existing alternatives.'[4] Moreover, there was a sense in which the failure of leadership was cumulative and reinforcing. While the perception of a president as effective reinforces his power, a perception of him as ineffective is difficult to dispel and undermines his ability to provide leadership. The pragmatism that had initially seemed to be a welcome contrast with Reagan became a liability as Bush suffered from a lack of identification as a principled leader, especially when compared with his predecessor.[5] He also suffered from the fact that, at the popular level at least, Reagan had managed to obscure the extent of the United States' economic problems. His legacy to Bush was a major imbalance between demands on government and resources to meet those demands. The great communicator had also been the great illusionist.[6] Nevertheless, the Bush stance was that of consolidation and adjustment, not major policy initiatives or reversals. Consequently, it was only a matter of time before the illusions, especially about the economy, were dispelled and a mood of pessimism became deeply entrenched. Moreover, efforts to deal with this mood seemed to have little impact. The President's visit to Japan in January 1992 – a visit in which he was accompanied by the chief executive officers from the major car manufacturers and put pressure on the Japanese to take steps to open their markets to US automobiles – seemed clumsy and inept. One result of all this was that when President, in the last months before the election, claimed – with some justification – that the economy was improving, this had little impact on the level of public support.

If Bush failed to provide leadership in responding to domestic problems, in foreign policy he did rather better in spite of the fact that he headed a conservative administration in a revolutionary age. In some respects this is hardly surprising, nor is it as novel as was sometimes suggested during the Bush era. The complexities of the modern presidency may have given rise to a situation where all incumbents, even those who are inexperienced in foreign policy, find that this is the one area which allows decisiveness and substantial achievement. Even if the foreign affairs presidency is generally more attractive than the domestic affairs presidency, however, this was particularly pronounced in the Bush administration. Not only were the President's experience and interests in foreign policy but the monumental nature of the changes that were taking place in Eastern Europe and the Soviet Union demanded constant attention. Although Bush was sometimes accused of being reactive in his response to these developments, he presided over the demise of the Soviet Union in a way which helped to maintain confidence and stability amidst the great upheavals. He also orchestrated a major diplomatic and military triumph in the Gulf. Yet Bush did not obtain the political rewards that might have been expected from either the successes of United States military actions or from the extraordinary global changes. The last of the Cold War presidents, he obtained little political credit for the end of the Cold War.

Part of the reason for this is that Bush was essentially a foreign policy president in a domestic policy era. He had to confront a public mood which seemed increasingly introspective. Perhaps even more important, though, is that Bush was the victim of success in foreign policy: not only did the changes Bush presided over seem to provide an opportunity for a reallocation of attention and resources from foreign policy to domestic policy, but at the very point where Bush must have thought that the success in the Gulf would ensure his popularity, historical reputation and easy reelection, he was beset by domestic setbacks. First, there was the recession which grew in intensity in 1991 and which had not gone away by the beginning of 1992. Second, there was the challenge from the conservative right in the primaries. Third were the Los Angeles riots. As 1992 wore on, the mood of the electorate became not just that of apathetic disillusion but anger at the failure of Washington to provide leadership and solutions to problems. Although Bush tried to direct the anti-incumbent mood at Capitol Hill he could hardly fail to be its most prominent target.

Ironically, the very success that had been achieved in the Gulf and the strong decisive leadership Bush had provided contributed significantly to the resentment directed against the White House. As Sidney Blumenthal noted:

> By mobilizing national energies for war, while maintaining passivity on the domestic front Bush prepared his own disintegration ... Bush's reluctance to use the federal instrument at home after deploying the military abroad was the very soul of contradiction – at least, in the American tradition. Foreign policy did not, as he assumed, offset domestic; instead, the contrast of command and fecklessness rapidly diminished him. War inflated the illusion of omnipotence – and then punctured it.[7]

Having seen the kind of leadership Bush could provide, the electorate expected him to display the same kind of commitment to dealing with the economic and social threats and challenges faced by the United States. When he did not do so the disillusionment was extensive and was manifested, in part at least, in support for Ross Perot.

It is ironic that Bush did not reap lasting political benefits from foreign policy success. Yet the President may have contributed to this not only because of the marked contrast between his activism on foreign policy and his passivity on domestic issues but also by his decision to expend the leadership resources produced by the successful ending of the Gulf War on efforts to win a Middle East peace settlement. This not only turned out to be protracted, elusive and messy, but if anything, highlighted the roving role played by Secretary of State Baker rather than that of President Bush himself. It also strengthened the perception that the administration was continuing to subordinate domestic needs and concerns to its preoccupation with foreign policy.

While Blumenthal is right that the contrast between foreign policy leadership and domestic passivity hurt Bush, even without the added expectations which arose in the aftermath of the Gulf War there would have been a natural tendency to look primarily to the presidency for solutions to the problems faced by the United States. After all, there is no alternative source of leadership: 'In a political system where the weight of inertia and complexity is considerable, the capacity to launch something new is scarce. The president stands out among American political actors for an ability to initiate action.'[8] Conversely, when the president fails to initiate the kind of action that is expected or desired, there is an inevitable sense of disappointment and frustration.

This may not be unique to Bush. The cycle of initial hope followed by disappointment and disillusionment increasingly seems to be a function of contemporary American political life and the development of what Barbara Hinckley termed 'the symbolic presidency'.[9] On the basis of an extensive analysis of inaugural and policy speeches, Hinckley has argued that the picture of American government which is portrayed by presidents themselves focuses on presidential dominance: 'Presidents act alone, with few reminders of Congress, the executive bureaucracy or the divergent interests of interest groups.'[10] This picture is strikingly consistent across presidents who almost invariably present themselves as 'without peers. Apart from the flag and the seal of office, presidents show themselves without companions or background detail.'[11] Perhaps even more significant in the context of the present discussion, each new president tends to claim a new beginning and offer new promise. In Hinckley's words, 'The past is symbolically abolished with each inauguration' which also holds out great promise for the future.[12]

Rather than engage in real innovation, however, presidents tend to recycle familiar forms and old symbols. Even so the media tends to reinforce the symbolism factor. 'During the first months of George Bush's presidency, the press criticized the lack of "vision" in his speeches, the absence of a clear sense of direction in his leadership, and his low public profile.'[13] The implication of this, as Hinckley acknowledges, is that the expectations that have created the symbolic presidency are too powerful now to be turned aside.[14] Unfortunately for presidents the expectations that they themselves have helped to create mean that presidential failure is virtually preordained.

The problems caused by the 'symbolic presidency' are compounded by the contradictory expectations of the electorate. Opinion polls indicate that people want a just, decent, humane, trustworthy man in the White House. Yet the public just as strongly demands the qualities of toughness and decisiveness.[15] Reconciling these divergent expectations will often prove impossible. As one analyst has commented, in spite of the emphasis upon the three branches of government 'we place capacious hopes upon and thus elevate the presidential branch'.[16] It is not entirely surprising therefore that some political scientists have discerned what they believe to be a recurring pattern in which a president's popularity and public support decline steadily after the first few months in office. The trend may be interrupted by rallying points, such as those occasioned by military intervention overseas, and to a lesser extent major speeches, but the basic trend of decline is immutable.[17] Pocketbook issues provide the downside, foreign policy events the rallying points.

When Bush is criticized for his lack of leadership, therefore, this has to be balanced by a recognition that the expectations placed on the president are unrealistic. Moreover, as Bert Rockman has noted, the opportunities presidents have to exercise leadership are influenced by the problems surrounding them and the political and social conditions shaping their possible responses.[18] In this respect, Bush faced problems over which he had very little control yet which contributed to his political demise.

The first problem was that Bush came to office after a period in which the United States had become 'a choiceless society, substituting denial and rhetoric for meaningful action'.[19] The result was a spiral of debt and deficits accompanied by significant decline in areas of public provision and policy such as health and education. Moreover, these problems tended to be interlinked in ways which made them even more intractable. The budget deficit, in particular led to what has been termed the fiscalization of all policy discussion and the politics of constraint.[20] The Balanced Budget and Emergency Deficit Control Act of 1985 – more popularly known as Gramm-Rudmann-Hollings – originally required a balanced budget by Fiscal Year 1991; in 1987 Congress acknowledged this was impossible and extended the deadline to 1993. This meant, however, that almost everything Bush tried to do would be considered in relation to its impact on the deficit.[21] It also meant that one of the tools for dealing with recession – increased domestic spending – was not as readily available to the administration in 1991 and 1992 as it had been to previous presidents.

Both the choiceless society and the budget deficit were major problems in their own right. Yet they were also a function of divided government which can lead to conflict, paralysis, a failure to deal with fundamental challenges and the indefinite postponement of hard decisions. Neither the President nor Congress has an 'interest in or feels the necessity of forcing the public to reconcile its incompatible preferences' of low taxes and high benefits.[22] Moreover 'in divided government, it is not merely the separated institutions of government that must overcome their built-in rivalries but the opposing parties themselves. And that is bound to be a difficult, arduous process, characterized by conflict, delay, and indecision, and leading frequently to deadlock, inadequate and ineffective policies, or no policies at all.'[23] In this situation, if a president sends major initiatives or proposals to Congress, there is an inbuilt propensity for rejection. For Congress to do otherwise is tacitly to acknowledge that the president is a good leader, something that would only strengthen him and his party for the next election.[24] By the same token, the president will have little sympathy for Congressional initiatives.

There are two consequences of this, one at the level of presidential effectiveness, the other at the level of political campaigning. The first, as James Sundquist has noted, is that in divided government, presidential leadership becomes all but impossible.[25] It is the system that is at fault, and not the individual president.[26] Yet it is the president's reputation which suffers, since 'The classic test of greatness in the White House has been the chief executive's capacity to lead Congress.'[27] The second consequence is that such a system leads to presidential efforts to blame Congress for the failure to resolve national problems. From this perspective the efforts by Bush to use Congress as a scapegoat during 1992 were a function more of the systemic problems of divided government than of the specific issues in dispute or even the political opportunism of the administration.

Although Bush was not the first president to face divided government, he did so at a time when there was considerable uncertainty about the most appropriate policies for the United States to adopt to deal with its problems. What Mann has described as 'a lack of consensus among policy specialists on how best to deal with the country's most serious problems proved to be another force inhibiting action.'[28] There was real uncertainty about the best ways to enhance the United States' economic competitiveness, to improve the quality of public education, or to deal with the problems of racial tension, crime and drugs that had become such pervasive features of life in American cities.

The same was true in foreign policy. The choices during the Cold War had revolved around the appropriate balance between deterrence strategies on the one side and dialogue on the other. Yet, new problems which had emerged such as the war in Yugoslavia were much more intractable and therefore more demanding. The era of easy options and simple remedies in both domestic and foreign policy was over by the late 1980s. Moreover, if the difficulties of devising effective strategies for tackling social policy were widely recognized in the policy community, the uncertainty among analysts was mirrored by uncertainty among politicians.[29] The implication of this is that the failure of the Bush administration to develop a coherent strategy for dealing with the domestic economic and social problems facing the United States was part of a more fundamental crisis of confidence about the ability of government to make a difference. The failure of policy and strategy was rooted in a more profound failure of analysis.

This is not to imply that the problems are insoluble. Nor is it to condone the lack of imagination of the Bush administration in responding to them. It is simply to argue that many of the problems faced by the United States in the early 1990s are structural in nature, the result of secular trends which have been allowed to develop unchallenged. As such they are not readily amenable to short-run solutions. The difficulty for presidents is that they have to display results in the short term – which is in effect three years, given the demands of the reelection campaign – or their term is over.

In this connection, another disruptive factor is the relationship between the presidency on the one side and the press and television on the other. Some commentators have even argued that the press in effect constitutes the opposition government and that the United States is moving from party democracy to media democracy.[30] Although Bush was reputed to be on much more open terms with journalists than was Reagan, this did little to diminish the aggressively critical stance toward the presidency which has been evident since the perceived betrayals of Vietnam and Watergate. Nor is this the only problem. Perhaps even more debilitating for the presidency is the tendency of press coverage of federal government to centre on controversy. Publicizing personality feuds and policy debates within the administration tends to make interesting news but greatly complicates the president's task of coordinating his top officials.[31] Highly publicized quarrels can make the president look like a poor manager even if they are not his fault.

At the same time, efforts by the White House to manage the news and use the press and television for its own purposes exacerbate the problem. 'Presidents have helped erect barriers to their own leadership by overemphasizing media events, which frequently only reinforce the cynicism of journalists and citizens alike.'[32] Presidents enter the White House promising openness and accessibility to the media. After a relatively brief honeymoon, they come to regard the media as a constant source of criticism and annoyance whereas the media tends to see the White House as withholding information and attempting to cover up its own shortcomings or wrong-doings.[33]

The implication of all this is that, although the failures of the Bush administration were partly self-inflicted, they also reflected problems that go well beyond a particular presidency. Many of the difficulties faced by Bush had little to do with the shortcomings of the President himself or his advisers; rather, they were symptoms of more deep-rooted problems at least some of which have become endemic. The presidency is suffering above all from a gap between expectations and capability that may reflect a more fundamental crisis of identity and purpose, the root of which is that Americans understand the need for power but distrust its exercise. Indeed, there are so many contradictions in the presidency, which is 'At once all powerful yet curiously impotent, majestic if suspect, and meritocratic while astoundingly incompetent', that the expectations which surround the inauguration of a new president are bound to be disappointed, the symbolism to be tarnished.[34] Perhaps the most appropriate, if slightly generous, epitaph for President Bush therefore (and one which after only six months into the Clinton administration looked as if it might also be applicable to Bush's successor) is that he failed to live up to expectations which were impossible to meet.

NOTES

1. M. Glenn Abernathy, Dilys M. Hill and Phil Williams (eds), *The Carter Years: The President and Policy Making* (London: Frances Pinter/New York: St Martin's Press, 1984).
2. This characterization of the Carter administration was presented by Roger Hilsman.
3. Andrew Rosenthal with Joel Brinkley, 'Old Compass in New World: A President Sticks to Course', *New York Times*, 25 June 1992, A1.
4. Bert Rockman, 'That Elusive Quality Called "Presidential Leadership"', *Cosmos*, Vol. 2, No. 1, 1992, p. 72.
5. Ibid., p. 75.
6. Dilys M. Hill, Raymond A. Moore and Phil Williams (eds), *The Reagan Presidency: An Unfinished Revolution?* (London: Macmillan/New York: St Martin's Press, 1990).
7. Sidney Blumenthal, 'All the President's Wars', *The New Yorker*, 28 December 1992/4 January 4 1993, pp. 68 and 70.
8. Bruce Miroff, 'Monopolizing the Public Space: The President as a Problem for Democratic Politics', in Thomas C. Cronin (ed.), *Rethinking the Presidency* (Boston, Mass.: Little, Brown, 1982), p. 219.
9. Barbara Hinckley, *The Symbolic Presidency: How Presidents Portray Themselves* (New York/London: Routledge, 1990), p. 50.
10. Ibid., p. 56.
11. Ibid., p. 133.
12. Ibid.
13. Ibid., p. 142.
14. Ibid.
15. Thomas C. Cronin, 'The Paradoxes of the Presidency', in R.E. DiClerico (ed.), *Analyzing the Presidency*, 2nd edition (Guildford, Conn.: Dushkin Publishing Group, 1990), p. 53.
16. Ibid., p. 55.
17. See the analysis of this debate in Charles C. Euchner, 'Public Support and Opinion', in *The Presidents and the Public* (Washington DC: Congressional Quarterly, Inc., 1990), pp. 75–90.
18. Rockman, op. cit., p. 75.
19. Peter G. Peterson with James K. Sebenius, 'The Primacy of the Domestic Agenda', in Graham Allison and Gregory F. Treverton (eds) *Rethinking America's Security* (New York: Norton, 1992), p. 59.
20. Thomas E. Mann, 'Breaking the Political Impasse', in Henry J. Aaron (ed.), *Setting National Priorities* (Washington DC: The Brookings Institution, 1990), p. 298.
21. Ibid.
22. Ibid., p. 304.
23. James L. Sundquist, 'Needed: A Political Theory for the New Era of Coalition Government in the United States', in DiClerico (ed.), op. cit., p. 90.
24. Ibid.
25. Sundquist, op. cit., p. 91.
26. Ibid., p. 93.

27. James McGregor Burns, *Roosevelt: The Lion and the Fox* (New York: Harcourt, Brace, 1956), p. 186.
28. Mann, 'Breaking the Political Impasse', op. cit., p. 300.
29. Ibid., p. 301.
30. Dom Bonafede, 'The Presidents and the Public', in *The Presidents and the Public* (Washington DC: Congressional Quarterly, Inc, 1990), p. 7.
31. Robert M. Entman, 'The Imperial Media', in DiClerico (ed.), op. cit., p. 159.
32. Ibid., p. 163.
33. Bonafede, op. cit.
34. Alan Wolfe, 'Presidential Power and the Crisis of Modernization', in Cronin (ed.), op. cit., p. 139.

Index